THE
COMPLETE
IDIOT'S
GUIDE TO

D1431988

Mindfulness

*by Anne Ihnen, MA, LMHC,
and Carolyn Flynn*

ALPHA

A member of Penguin Group (USA) Inc.

To my dearest dear ones, Dave and Brian.
—Anne Ihnen
To Emerald and Lucas, my stone and my light.
—Carolyn Flynn

ALPHA BOOKS

Published by the Penguin Group

Penguin Group (USA) Inc., 375 Hudson Street, New York, New York 10014, USA

Penguin Group (Canada), 90 Eglinton Avenue East, Suite 700, Toronto, Ontario M4P 2Y3, Canada (a division of Pearson Penguin Canada Inc.)

Penguin Books Ltd., 80 Strand, London WC2R 0RL, England

Penguin Ireland, 25 St. Stephen's Green, Dublin 2, Ireland (a division of Penguin Books Ltd.)

Penguin Group (Australia), 250 Camberwell Road, Camberwell, Victoria 3124, Australia (a division of Pearson Australia Group Pty. Ltd.)

Penguin Books India Pvt. Ltd., 11 Community Centre, Panchsheel Park, New Delhi—110 017, India

Penguin Group (NZ), 67 Apollo Drive, Rosedale, North Shore, Auckland 1311, New Zealand (a division of Pearson New Zealand Ltd.)

Penguin Books (South Africa) (Pty.) Ltd., 24 Sturdee Avenue, Rosebank, Johannesburg 2196, South Africa

Penguin Books Ltd., Registered Offices: 80 Strand, London WC2R 0RL, England

International Standard Book Number: 978-159257-767-5
Library of Congress Catalog Card Number: 2008920826

10   09   08   8   7   6   5   4   3   2   1

Interpretation of the printing code: The rightmost number of the first series of numbers is the year of the book's printing; the rightmost number of the second series of numbers is the number of the book's printing. For example, a printing code of 08-1 shows that the first printing occurred in 2008.

Printed in the United States of America

Note: This publication contains the opinions and ideas of its authors. It is intended to provide helpful and informative material on the subject matter covered. It is sold with the understanding that the authors, book producer, and publisher are not engaged in rendering professional services in the book. If the reader requires personal assistance or advice, a competent professional should be consulted.

The authors, book producer, and publisher specifically disclaim any responsibility for any liability, loss, or risk, personal or otherwise, which is incurred as a consequence, directly or indirectly, of the use and application of any of the contents of this book.

Most Alpha books are available at special quantity discounts for bulk purchases for sales promotions, premiums, fund-raising, or educational use. Special books, or book excerpts, can also be created to fit specific needs.

For details, write: Special Markets, Alpha Books, 375 Hudson Street, New York, NY 10014.

Publisher: *Marie Butler-Knight*
Editorial Director: *Mike Sanders*
Senior Managing Editor: *Billy Fields*
Executive Editor: *Randy Ladenheim-Gil*
Book Producer: *Lee Ann Chearney/Amaranth Illuminare*
Development Editor: *Lynn Northrup*
Senior Production Editor: *Janette Lynn*

Copy Editor: *Jan Zoya*
Cover Designer: *Becky Harmon*
Book Designer: *Trina Wurst*
Indexer: *Heather McNeil*
Layout: *Ayanna Lacey*
Proofreader: *Jovana San Nicolas-Shirley*

Contents at a Glance

Contents

Introduction

One fall morning, Carolyn was up before dawn to prepare for a weekend retreat in Santa Fe. In the quiet, as she watched the sun nudge its way above the turquoise ridge of the Sandia Mountains, what she was most aware of was the disquiet in her mind. It had been a VERY HARD WEEK—a tough book deadline and a demanding business client she referred to as "That Which Sucks Out My Life Force Energy." At that moment, what she wanted most was to flee her own life.

In the tranquil pink dawn light, she stayed with this disquiet, letting all the "what if" change-her-life scenarios spin out until … it was quiet. It became absolutely clear: she did not need to do any of those things; she did not even need to go to the retreat to find peace. She realized that what she really, really wanted was mindfulness. And she had it right then, in that moment.

Carolyn did continue to Santa Fe, but she carried this mindfulness with her throughout the day, and she realized: *This is always available to me.* During the retreat, suddenly her vision became clear and sharp, with all colors and shapes in the room vivid and well defined. She had a taste of living with clarity. She had come back to her body, in gratitude and compassion—to her home. She had come back to dwell in kindness with her own mind. She had come back to taste her own life, just as it was.

Anne began meditating as a graduate student in psychology. She was learning about person-centered therapy, which focuses on the present-moment experience, and she thought meditation would help her develop her skills. This began an amazing journey for her into her inner landscape. She found that meditation not only helped her work as a therapist, it also helped her begin to heal the wounds she took on during the first 45 years of her life. She discovered how disconnected she had become from herself; it was as if she'd been asleep all her life. And as she continued to practice, to wake up, she discovered the richness and joy that's always been there, just waiting for her to reclaim it.

Anne's meditation practice has helped her calm the anxiety that has troubled her since she was a teenager and has led her to create deeper, more authentic relationships with the people in her life. She is less reactive to what's happening around her and more able to weather the storms that life tosses her way. In 2003, she lost two of her immediate family members, and her meditation practice was invaluable to her as she grieved and began healing from these losses.

Mindfulness practice is like that—an ally and supporter. It helps you live with clarity, compassion, and lovingkindness in your relationship to your life.

You may have picked up this book because your life is stressful or because you're in pain. Your life may be in crisis right now due to an illness, or you may have lost a relationship. You may have tried all the usual ways—surgery, drugs, therapists, retreats, workshops, other people's advice. All of those can be useful and effective, but mindfulness gives you practical tools to end the internal struggle, the striving, and the suffering. It's a simple technique that gives you a new way to *see* and *be* in your life.

How to Use This Book

This book is divided into six parts, each bringing mindfulness into your life in a way that can become simply the way you live:

Part 1, "What Does It Mean to Be Mindful?" introduces you to the basic principles of mindfulness and acquaints you with the many medical and psychological benefits of establishing a practice. It will introduce you to the power of the present moment for healing, and it will guide you in feeling comfortable with integrating the practice into your life, no matter your faith or belief system.

Part 2, "How Mindful Living Reduces Stress," provides a good grounding in the most current research about the benefits of mindfulness for physical and psychological health. We'll explain how mindfulness practice interrupts the body's stress response and restores the body and mind to a state of peace. We'll explain how mindfulness relieves chronic pain and examine how mindfulness can be a balm to our overtaxed, multitasked minds. Finally, we'll show how mindfulness cultivates compassion and promotes emotional healing.

Part 3, "Practicing Mindfulness Meditation," gives you instruction in the essential techniques of mindfulness, beginning with sitting meditation. We'll give you guidelines and ideas for walking meditation and mindful writing practice. We'll teach you breath awareness and the role of focal points, such as sensory awareness, visual objects, and chimes. We'll also touch upon the role of yoga in mindfulness practice.

Part 4, "Practicing Mindful Eating," examines the ways you can eat mindfully, extending that practice from the foods you eat to the way you prepare it, serve it, and participate in the sustainability of food production, whether it's as a consumer or a grower.

Part 5, "Practicing Mindfulness with Love," takes your practice of mindfulness into the context of your life, helping you see your relationships in new ways. We'll go into more depth about the benefits of mindfulness for navigating life's setbacks and frustrations, as well as its promise for alleviating chronic depression.

Part 6, "Living Mindful in a Mindless World," gives you solid advice about using mindfulness meditation practice to heal anger and quell anxiety. We'll teach you how to listen mindfully. As you experience your own transformation, we'll guide you in how to be more mindfully engaged in transforming the world around you.

In the Resources appendix, we give you a guide to further reading and other resources.

Little Gems

Throughout this book, we have added five nuggets of information in each chapter that will help you be more mindful.

def•i•ni•tion

These boxes illuminate key terms, giving definitions and explaining how they pertain to mindfulness.

Just Be!

Check these boxes for practical tips and related information about living and practicing mindfulness.

Breathe ...

Here you'll find cautionary pieces of advice, helping you head off challenges or guiding you in overcoming obstacles in establishing a mindfulness practice.

Live Mindful

These boxes offer little stories—often from our own journeys with mindfulness practice—that can encourage you on your journey.

Sutras

Each chapter in this book introduces a sutra that illumines the chapter's main concepts. These are excerpts drawn primarily from sacred texts of Buddhism.

Acknowledgments

From Anne:

I would like to thank Lee Ann Chearney for inviting me to participate in the creation of this book. It is an honor to be able to share the dharma with others, and I am grateful for this opportunity.

Thank you to Carolyn Flynn for her patience, persistence, and willingness to listen to all of my questions and wonderings about the right way to put these practices into words. And for her impressive ability to multitask!

I extend deep gratitude to the dharma teachers whose words continue to guide me on this path, especially to Rodney Smith of Seattle Insight Meditation Society, who taught me to meditate in the first place, and whose teachings have sustained me and continue to deepen my practice. I also thank my mentors, Cathy Henschel-McGerry and Ned Farley, who have shown me how to bring mindfulness into the practice of sitting with others, and who have helped me access inner resources I never knew I had.

Thank you to Michael, whose deep pain jolted me out of my slumber and showed me in a way nothing else can how precious and short life is.

And finally, thanks to Dave, for all that you are and all that you do.

From Carolyn:

I would like to acknowledge the clear, calm, steady presence of Anne Ihnen, who stood ready to meet this experience with me, no matter what came our way. Thanks for your commitment to the authenticity of this book—and your fast typing!

As always, I am ever grateful for the way book producer Lee Ann Chearney has opened up my world. This project touched my soul and transformed me—that's the power of mindfulness, if we are open to meeting what comes our way with kindness and compassion. Lee Ann asked me for more, and I gave, and I'm grateful for that.

Thanks to the wise and wonderful Lynn Northrup, who has been a guiding light on many Alpha projects; and thanks to Randy Ladenheim-Gil for believing in this project. Thanks to Jan Zoya, who saved me from my fast typing! Thanks to the many others at Alpha who made this book possible.

Special Note

This book is not a substitute for therapy, nor is it a substitute for medical care. Please seek professional help if you need it.

While mindfulness meditation practice can promote healing, if you have an illness or disease, the techniques should be practiced under the supervision of a physician or other appropriate licensed medical practitioner.

While we do discuss ways mindfulness can help with anxiety, depression, and other distressing experiences, we advise you to seek help if what you are experiencing is overwhelming or interfering with your ability to function in daily life.

Trademarks

All terms mentioned in this book that are known to be or are suspected of being trademarks or service marks have been appropriately capitalized. Alpha Books and Penguin Group (USA) Inc. cannot attest to the accuracy of this information. Use of a term in this book should not be regarded as affecting the validity of any trademark or service mark.

Part 1

What Does It Mean to Be Mindful?

Mindfulness is about being in harmony with your life. There is wholeness and serenity in dwelling in the awareness of the present moment. Mindfulness meditation is proving to be a powerful tool for enhancing health, promoting well-being, and adding meaning to your life.

You can practice mindfulness no matter your faith tradition. While it draws from Buddhist teachings, mindfulness techniques are separate and apart from religion. Instead, mindfulness is a way to live in the present moment, meeting your mind with open eyes and open arms.

Mindfulness Is More Than Meditation

In This Chapter

- Meeting each moment of your life
- Mindfulness-Based Stress Reduction
- A mindful therapist and a mindful writer
- The goal: present-moment awareness
- Anyone can practice mindfulness

Mindfulness is a way to meet your life. To live mindfully, with intentional awareness of the present moment, is to welcome your whole self back into your life.

Mindfulness meditation is steadily gaining attention in the West, from people of all backgrounds and circumstances, as a technique for healing and happiness. It's a deceptively simple technique, and it's powerfully effective in reducing stress, improving health, and adding meaning to your life. You don't have to be an expert, and you don't have to do it perfectly, according to someone else's program. It's an experience that you can have right now, no matter where you are in life, no matter who you are. With mindfulness meditation, the invitation is always open.

So, What Is Mindfulness?

Mindfulness is meditation and more. Mindfulness meditation is one of the most effective techniques to invite mindfulness into your life, but it is not the only one. Nor is sitting meditation the only way to meditate mindfully, though it is one of the cornerstone practices. Mindfulness is more than techniques; it's a way of being in the world.

Mindfulness is defined as clear awareness of the present moment. With mindfulness, you are open to the way things are in each moment without trying to manipulate or change the experience. To live mindfully is to meet each moment with kindness.

Mindfulness is a practice. It's not something you can learn from an expert; you learn to be mindful by practicing being mindful. We are here to open the door for you and invite you in. But the journey is one that you will live, and in living it, you will grow to understand the power of mindfulness. The more you practice it, the more you understand it—and the more you meet your mind. This is the magic. It's in you. You find it through the practice.

def•i•ni•tion

Mindfulness is the quality of dwelling in harmony with the present moment. The technique of mindfulness is cultivated by practicing meditation with an intentional, clear awareness of the present moment. Mindfulness meditation is practiced without judging your thoughts and feelings, neither grasping nor pushing them away, but rather, by being with your thoughts just as they are.

Mindfulness is not a religion, although meditation and contemplative practices can be found in Christianity, Judaism, Islam, and Hinduism, as well as in other world religions, as you'll learn in Chapter 2. We refer to Buddhism in this book because many people associate mindfulness with Buddhist meditation practices. Because the teachings of the

Buddha on meditation and mindfulness are precise and comprehensive, they provide an excellent path for learning mindfulness.

That aside, mindfulness meditation has been increasingly used in secular contexts in the West with remarkable results for physical and psychological health. In study after study, it seems to be a stress-reliever and a hope-builder. Mindfulness meditation has proven to be profoundly empowering for patients with chronic pain, high blood pressure, heart disease, cancer, and a multitude of psychological challenges such as anxiety, panic, and depression.

Mindfulness, too, is a life skill that's proving to have many benefits for people in need, such as low-income families, prison inmates, people who have experienced physical or emotional trauma, and people struggling with weight, food, and body image issues. It's been found to have remarkable results for depression and other mood disorders, as well as attention deficit disorder. Proponents have introduced it in the classroom to improve student learning and in the workplace to improve performance. Clearly, it's posting cutting-edge results for all kinds of people.

It's Popular, It's Effective, It's Changing Lives

While mindfulness has been linked with Buddhism in the minds of Westerners, that all began to change in 1979 when Jon Kabat-Zinn introduced Mindfulness-Based Stress Reduction (MBSR) in a clinical setting at the University of Massachusetts. Now more than 200 medical centers and clinics in the United States teach Mindfulness-Based Stress Reduction, and universities such as UCLA (University of California at Los Angeles), Stanford University, Duke University, and the University of New Mexico are advancing the research into more ways to use mindfulness for healing, coping, and abiding with illness. It's becoming a viable enhancement to healing, supplementing, or even replacing medication in many contexts.

MBSR has been shown to relieve chronic pain, alleviate stress, boost the immune system, and relieve depression. New studies are showing remarkable results with mood disorders, suicidal behavior, and binge eating. MBSR has also been shown to alleviate the symptoms of fibro-myalgia.

It's also been demonstrated to help war veterans manage post-traumatic stress disorder, and it's being used in the classroom to help schoolchildren improve their focus, performance, and overall contentment.

Kabat-Zinn, a molecular biologist, first achieved results in the area of medicine, showing that MBSR alleviated chronic pain and boosted the immune system. His first results were with patients who had breast cancer or bone-marrow transplants. His work has been featured on Bill Moyers's PBS television special, *Healing and the Mind*.

Kabat-Zinn requires that all practitioners who teach MBSR also engage in their own mindfulness practices. In his book, *Full Catastrophe Living: Using the Wisdom of Your Body and Mind to Face Stress, Pain and Illness* (see the Resources), Kabat-Zinn describes his own practice. Sometimes, when his children were young, he had to get up at 4 A.M. to practice. But he did.

Mindfulness has tremendous physiological benefits to the working of the brain, as Daniel J. Siegel, M.D., co-founder of UCLA's Mindful Awareness Research Center, has written about in *The Mindful Brain* (see the Resources). We'll go into more detail about the physiological effects of mindfulness in Chapter 5.

Scientists everywhere are exploring ways to use mindfulness techniques with a variety of populations, including adults with social anxiety (Stanford), fourth through sixth graders (also Stanford), prison inmates (UMass) and people who engage in binge eating (University of New Mexico and the Center for Mindful Eating).

Clearly, the growing body of research is indicating that the benefits of mindfulness are multifold. Imagine being able to reverse disease or mitigate its suffering. Imagine being able to live with pain rather than having it run your life. Imagine the sense of courage and hope that comes from living mindfully. When you feel connected to the full depth of your life, you feel its richness, and that empowers and equips you to face life's challenges.

Who We Are, Why We Practice

Just as Kabat-Zinn practices what he teaches and expects his teachers to practice, so are we practitioners.

Anne began practicing Centering Prayer, a Christian form of meditation, several years ago. As a graduate student in her 40s, she was introduced to Buddhist meditation practices, and she was drawn to the precision of the Buddha's instructions and the 2,500-year-long lineage of people engaged in these practices. In 2002, she shifted her practice from Centering Prayer to vipassana meditation, practicing with her husband in the mornings before breakfast. She currently meditates five mornings a week. For the past four years, she has kept a commitment to herself to go on silent meditation retreats twice a year. This combination of regular practice and longer periods of silence on retreat has been a wonderful journey for her, helping her through some extremely difficult times in her life.

Anne is a psychotherapist in private practice. Her therapy practice is a form of two-person mindfulness practice, in which she pays attention to what's happening in the present moment and guides her clients to do the same. To Anne, the relationship between a therapist and client mirrors the relationship she takes with herself when she meditates: she notices, names, and holds all that's seen with gentleness and compassion.

Carolyn is the editor of *SAGE Magazine*, a women's magazine about self-actualization and empowerment that appears in the *Albuquerque Journal*. She is the author of many books, including *The Complete Idiot's Guide to Creative Visualization* (with Shari L. Just, Ph.D.; see Resources), which employs a more intentional form of mindfulness meditation.

Carolyn practices mindfulness with a morning meditation ritual that can be sitting meditation or yoga. Her twins are accustomed to understanding that if they wake up before 7 A.M., they will need to engage in their own quiet time. Sometimes they meditate, read, or play with Legos. Occasionally they do yoga with her.

For about a dozen years, Carolyn has practiced mindful writing, teaching it in yoga/writing workshops, a format that pairs two forms of mindfulness. The practice of mindful writing is a technique known to many through Natalie Goldberg (*Writing Down the Bones;* see

Resources) or Julia Cameron's morning pages (*The Artist's Way;* see Resources). Goldberg holds silent writing retreats in Taos and practices zazen, a sitting meditation technique in Zen Buddhism. In mindful writing, you do a timed writing without stopping, spilling out your thoughts on the page. ("Keep the pen moving," Goldberg says.) You allow yourself to meet whatever arrives on the page with kindness; you do not evaluate or edit. ("Don't cross out," Goldberg says.) The thoughts that you are writing are neither good nor bad. You neither push them away ("This is crap!") nor grab at them ("Now I'm writing!"). You let yourself have the thoughts you're having; even if you have to write, "I don't want to write today" or "I'm so bored with this," you write it. As you write, you notice the chatter in your mind. You let the thoughts chatter away, even the censor who might say you should not write that because it might hurt someone. Still, you keep writing through the chatter.

For Carolyn, mindful writing began as a technique to overcome writer's block, unleash her creativity, and find a circle of supportive writers, but she has learned to appreciate its benefit for calming her mind and knowing herself better, as a person and as a writer. She can reflect back on her life for the dozen or so years she has practiced and see that mindful writing sustained her through turbulent times. Mindful writing trains you to not engage in the clamorous dialogue in your mind. It's a powerful tool for writing, but it's also a powerful tool for living. It helps you tap into a more essential part of yourself—whether what you hoped to discover is better writing or a better you.

Live Mindful

When Anne first began meditating, she discovered how often the busyness of her mind was filtering her experience. For instance, she realized how unaware she had become of the world around her—the sky, the trees, the late-afternoon sunlight reflecting on the buildings. As she continued to practice, she remembered more often to stop and look at the world, and she began to see beauty in the simplest things. What was once an uneventful walk to the grocery store became an opportunity to notice her surroundings. She began seeing the extraordinary in the most ordinary, everyday things.

A Simple, Singular Path

The goal of mindfulness is mindfulness itself. If you have previously explored meditation, you may have practiced guided meditation with a goal. Perhaps the goal was to focus your thoughts on an objective such as a state of enlightenment or state of calmness. Or perhaps the goal has been relaxation.

Mindfulness practice is not about achieving a goal. It's about being present with your experience from moment to moment. As you practice being present, you discover the richness of each moment, holding what you discover without judging it, clinging to it, or pushing it away.

When you practice mindfulness, you set the intention that you will pay attention to the present moment to the degree that you are able. You set the intention to return to the present moment when you find yourself wandering away. It seems paradoxical: mindfulness is not directed at a specific goal in the future, yet it does require setting the intention to pay attention to what's happening now. When you practice mindfulness, you focus on the process of paying attention rather than the goal of reaching enlightenment or achieving an insight. And in the process of paying attention, you will naturally begin to see yourself and your life more clearly along the way.

In practicing mindfulness, you are seeking the fine balance between effort and relaxation. You are engaged, not passive. It's an active way of being in the present.

Though there is effort, mindfulness is not striving. You don't need to strive for these understandings; they will naturally unfold as you practice. All you need to do is return, again and again, to each moment and open your awareness to what's happening now.

Breathe ...

Some people come in to mindfulness meditation as doubters, thinking, "I'll believe it when I see it." Others come in as true believers, seeking to achieve the next big spiritual step. Yet mindfulness is a practice, and you must live it to understand what it truly is. It is not something to achieve. It is a way to be. To come to it, you must not push away or grasp. You must simply be open.

The names that are used to describe mindfulness and meditation can lead us to believe that being mindful means striving for enlightenment. Mindfulness is often linked with Buddhist vipassana meditation, also known as insight meditation. Many people come to the practice of vipassana striving for insights, thinking that's the goal of the practice. Insights do happen, but the focus of vipassana practice, as in mindfulness practice, is on the present moment, not on reaching for insights.

Other forms of meditation are goal-oriented. These forms are often called concentration meditation, or in the Buddhist tradition, Samatha. The goal of concentration meditation is to empty one's mind or achieve enlightenment.

So it's important to remember what mindfulness is *not* about:

◆ Emptying your mind

◆ Focusing your mind

◆ Seeking insight

◆ Attaining enlightenment

The purpose of mindfulness is to meet the mind with openness and care. With mindfulness, you get to meet your mind and be with the constantly shifting landscape of thoughts, perceptions, and emotions that are passing through it. Think of your mind as the clear blue open sky, and the thoughts that pass through as weather patterns.

Good Thoughts, Bad Thoughts

The mind thinks all the time. That's just what minds do. Hearts beat, muscles contract, and minds think. We can get caught up in our thoughts. We often disagree with them, or we try to manipulate them, to push them away, or rationalize them. Or we love our thoughts, and we grasp at them.

You might think there are good thoughts and bad thoughts. Good thoughts might be defined as those that make you happy and that might induce relaxation. You might think with meditation that you need to have enlightening or insightful thoughts. You might also believe there are thoughts that you should not have, thoughts that aren't "spiritual," or thoughts that make you unhappy.

But none of this is the case. You simply have thoughts. With mindfulness, you simply observe them. You stay in the present moment with these thoughts.

The suffering comes when we try to manipulate these thoughts or when we try to change our experience of them. We evaluate them as happy thoughts, sad thoughts, or angry thoughts. We sort them out. We decide whether we will keep them, whether we will engage with them, or whether we will ignore them or push them away.

Whether our thoughts are painful or pleasant, we often create stories about them. We interpret the thoughts, and we give them meaning.

The Here and Now

It's important to know that you are not your thoughts. Many thoughts take us away from the here and now. They might be thoughts about the past or the future. Reflecting on the past, as wonderful as it might be, or dreaming about the future, both keep you a prisoner of your thoughts. It doesn't matter whether those thoughts are positive or negative. When you are thinking about the past or the future, you have not shown up for the present.

Think about your drive to work. Have you ever been driving and arrived at your destination without remembering what you saw along the way? We all have. We have all had those autopilot moments.

It's important to understand how not showing up for the present gets to be a habit. And it's important to understand how this habit diminishes your experience of life and continues the suffering.

Just Be! _____

Here's something to try the next time you drive to work: every time you stop at a light, take a moment to return to the present moment. Take a couple of nice, full breaths, and notice what's happening now. What do you see? What do you hear? Notice how your body feels in the seat: are you tense or relaxed? If you notice tension, try to release it. When the light changes and you begin to move forward, note to yourself, "Driving now."

Anyone Can Be Mindful

Meditation is one of the most effective techniques for mindfulness, but there are many paths. The cornerstone techniques of mindfulness include the body scan (which we'll introduce in Chapter 5), yoga (Chapter 6), compassion meditation (or *metta*; Chapter 7), sitting and walking meditation (Chapter 8), and breath awareness (Chapter 9).

Anybody can practice mindfulness. The Buddha said we can meditate sitting, walking, standing, or lying down. You don't need to sit on a cushion in lotus position to practice meditation or mindfulness.

The instructions are simple, yet the practice is challenging because it requires self-discipline and intentionality. It requires a commitment to be engaged with the effort, but not with our thoughts.

Prepare Your Mind

Committing to a practice of mindfulness requires acknowledging that mindfulness is not just a technique but a way of living. And though we can tell you about it in a book, you must practice it to know what it is. That's because the journey is unique to every person.

To engage in the practice with intentionality and self-discipline, just be open. Think of the clear blue sky. Let yourself trust the process. Invite yourself to be here for the experience, whatever it may be. Set an intention for the practice that sets the stage for openness, something like, "With an open heart, I invite in the experience of this moment."

> **Sutras**
>
> Each chapter in this book introduces a sutra that illumines the chapter's main concepts. In the context of Buddhism, a *sutra* is a nugget of wisdom from a discourse on the teachings of Buddha. The word *sutra* derives from the Sanskrit word for thread (or in Pali, the word is *sutta*). The root word means *to sew*. When you study or recite a sutra, you are weaving your mind with the teaching.
>
> *If you can find a friend to go with you who is steady, careful, and mature, together you can overcome all hardships with mindfulness and joy.*
> —The Buddha, *The Dhammapada*

Prepare Your Space

While you can meditate mindfully anywhere, it's good to set aside a place to meditate regularly. It should be a comfortable place, free of distractions, and protected from interruptions, if possible. It's good to set aside an area in your own home for regular practice, if you can. This can be as simple as a corner of your bedroom, or it can be a more formal meditation space. It's best to keep it simple to avoid getting too overstimulated. A comfortable chair or cushion, a shelf or table with flowers or a candle, and maybe some objects from nature can help define your meditation space and help you set your intentions.

Try It!

Let's try a meditation:

1. Sit in an upright position. You want to be alert and allow the energy to flow freely in your body. You can sit on the floor on a cushion or on a chair.

2. Close your eyes, and place your attention on your breath. We'll explore the role of breath in Chapter 9, but know now that the reason we focus on breath is not because it has magical properties. We focus on the breath because it's always with us, and it can return us to the present.

3. When your mind wanders away from the breath, which it will inevitably do, and when you notice that it's wandered away, return to the breath. If it's helpful, label what's happening, what you observe your mind doing, such as "thinking" or "wandering off" or "drifting." You can label what's happening as "thinking" if that's helpful. Just be careful not to clobber yourself with the label! Be compassionate!

4. Continue this as long as you want, either a designated time or just for a few minutes. Often we suggest five minutes for a first meditation.

You can carry this mindfulness with you. At any point in the day, regardless of what you're doing, take a moment to check inside. How are things going in your inner landscape? What do you notice? You can start by taking a few breaths and paying attention to how it feels to breathe. Then ask, "What am I aware of right now?" You can label your experience as "thinking," or use another word, to describe what you notice. How you label your experience is not important, so watch the tendency to get distracted by coming up with an accurate label. Another technique that can help is to use phrases such as "This is what it feels like to be _____." Or "This is how it is for me right now."

Also, a very effective technique for checking how things are going inside is to start by placing the attention in the body. In this way, it can become a tool to carry with you throughout the day.

Keep a Mindful Journal

Many people find it useful to keep a journal as they learn a new practice. This is a place where you can record your insights, and collect sutras or inspiring teachings. Or, it can be a place where you practice mindful writing. All you need is fresh paper, a fast-writing pen, and an open heart.

A Tool for Life

Mindfulness is a tool for living more fully. As you practice it, you will find more and more ways to experience it in your life. Come, experience the full texture of your life! Experience what happens.

The Least You Need to Know

- Mindfulness meditation is a practice of meditating in present-moment awareness without judging or evaluating your thoughts.

- Mindfulness-Based Stress Reduction (MBSR) is a secularized Buddhist meditation technique that has been used successfully in medical contexts to enhance healing.

- Mindfulness meditation is a way to improve health, boost your sense of well-being, reduce stress, solve problems, and add meaning to your life.

Chapter 2

Mindfulness and Spiritual Traditions

In This Chapter

- ◆ Mindfulness and faith: a tour
- ◆ Buddhism's mindful path
- ◆ East meets West
- ◆ "Coming home" meditation

You can live mindfully no matter what religious tradition you hold. Though mindfulness is drawn from Buddhist meditation practices, almost every religious tradition incorporates a form of mindfulness. You can practice mindfulness techniques no matter what your faith. And these techniques work for believers and nonbelievers alike.

Mindfulness is the threshold to exploring spiritual knowledge, which is why it is present in most spiritual practices. Together with your faith, or separate and apart from a faith, you can benefit from cultivating care and reverence for the present moment.

A Tour of Tradition

Throughout time, people of faith have sought deeper understanding of the guiding spirit in their lives. Over the course of human history, mindfulness has been practiced nearly universally throughout the world's many faiths as a way to achieve greater awareness and insight.

Mindfulness takes the form of *prayer* and *meditation* in many religions, but it is also an integral part of chants, vigils, and contemplation. The clarity of mind, relaxation, calmness, and quiet of mindfulness and meditation lend themselves to the deeper understanding of faith.

For Christians, it might be centering prayer, contemplation of scripture or the Divine Mysteries, chanting prayers to a rosary, or taking a vow of silence. Meditation takes center stage in the practices of Buddhism and Hinduism, while five daily prayers are the backbone of the practice of Islam. Many spiritual traditions have branches or segments that are devoted to meditation or contemplation, such as Sufism (contemplative Islam) or Kabbalah (contemplative Judaism).

Many of the foundational moments in the world's great faiths stem from moments of contemplation. Think of Mohammad in the cave, Buddha under the Bodhi tree, Jesus in the desert or in the garden of Gethsemane, Paul on the road to Damascus, Moses at the burning bush.

Many spiritual traditions also emphasize mindful living through service—through giving of yourself and helping others. Believers are exhorted to live mindfully by honoring each other and honoring the earth.

Another theme that runs through the meditation practices of various spiritual traditions is that of surrender—relinquishing the need to manipulate one's experience and yielding to a higher wisdom. There is a point at which the mind dissolves and is free of thought, in which the believer lets his or her mind rest in God, Allah, or Creator.

Often, the faithful meditator achieves a state of stillness that yields insight by concentrating on a religious object, such as a statue or prayer beads; focusing on a scripture, sacred text (sutra in Eastern thought), or sacred word (mantra in Eastern thought); or simply on the breath.

Sometimes the meditator focuses on a teaching story—in the Christian tradition, a parable; in the Buddhist tradition, a Zen koan.

Here's a closer look at the practices by tradition.

The Christian Tradition

In Christianity, the dominant form of meditation is prayer. Christian meditation is *concentration meditation*, in which the person praying contemplates a specific object, such as lines from scripture, the Divine Mysteries, or specific prayers recited as a chant. Catholics use a rosary to still the mind and bring it to focus.

def•i•ni•tion

> **Meditation** is generally the state of consciously relaxing your body and calming and focusing your mind. **Concentration meditation** is meditation with a focus, such as guided meditation or visualization—or, in a faith context, contemplation on a teaching for the goal of achieving spiritual insight. **Prayer** can be a form of concentration meditation or mindfulness meditation. Prayer is communication with a deity. When the goal of prayer is simply to commune with God and be aware of God's presence, it is mindful prayer.

The biblical basis for the directive to meditate is Joshua 1:8, which tells followers to meditate on God's word day and night. Many of the Psalms, such as Psalm 23, describe David's practice of meditation ("He makes me lie down in green pastures. He leads me beside quiet waters. He restores my soul.").

The oldest tradition of Christian meditation is the lectio divina, which believers began practicing in the fourth century C.E. In that era, it was mostly monks who meditated. Lectio divina is a ladder with four stages of sacred readings, beginning with reading the word of God aloud (lectio), moving to action (meditatio, or discursive meditation), then oratio, or affective prayer, with the fourth being contemplatio, in which the believer simply rests in God's presence. This last stage most closely resembles mindfulness meditation. Believers hold their awareness in the present moment, in which they experience God in a palpable way.

Centering prayer, which Anne has practiced, is based on lectio divina. Father Thomas Keating, a Trappist monk, developed it as a practice. It involves focusing on a sacred word that the believer receives from God during a guided meditation. The sacred word is kept secret; it's between you and God. As you meditate, if your mind wanders, you recite the sacred word to return to the moment. At some point during centering prayer, you achieve a state of stillness and peace and are said to be "resting in God."

Live Mindful

When Anne was learning centering prayer, she was taught to think of her thoughts as being like boats on a river. She was instructed to imagine herself sitting on the bank of the river watching the boats go by rather than getting on them. Whenever she discovered that she had gotten on a thought-boat, she used her sacred word to return to the riverbank. This practice calmed and stilled her mind.

Another way Christians experience meditation is through the ritual of the rosary or the contemplation of the divine mysteries. This tradition is largely Catholic, though Anglicans use prayer beads and Eastern Orthodox use prayer ropes. The believer meditates on the Mysteries of the Rosary, events that occurred during the lives of Jesus and Mary. It's a form of visualization and guided meditation that practitioners believe provides substance to and breathes life into their prayers. The rosary brings the meditator to mindful awareness.

Contemplation on a focal point is common to many forms of meditation, and it's one of the essential components of mindfulness. In many religions, the altar is the focal point. The altar directs the believer to direct his or her mind on God, Allah, or creator.

Silent retreats or prayer vigils are other forms of communal meditation practices in Christian denominations. Many contemplative Christians and saints in the early church are coming into popularity again as they are rediscovered, such as St. Teresa de Avila, who believed that the soul ascends through four stages of contemplation (*The Interior Castle*, see Resources).

Walking a labyrinth, such as the one at the Chartres Cathedral in France, is a form of Christian walking meditation. Labyrinths are gaining in modern-day popularity, too, as a form of meditation and contemplation, somewhat because of the influence of the book *Walking a Sacred Path: Rediscovering the Labyrinth as a Spiritual Practice* by Lauren Artress (see Resources), minister at the Grace Cathedral in San Francisco.

Pilgrimages—journeys to sacred sites or shrines—are another form of walking meditation. The long journey, which unfolds over time, prepares the mind and heart of the believer to receive deeper knowledge.

Like many other traditions, Christians believe they should practice mindful living through service. We'll discuss ways to live mindfully in Chapters 10 and 13.

The Jewish Tradition

Kabbalah is the Jewish contemplative practice, and it's based on the study of ancient texts with the goal of bringing the believer closer to God. The goal of the contemplative practice of Kabbalah is to empower the believer with higher insight into the inner workings of God's creation. The Hebrew word kabbalah means receiving. Like many traditions in which only a select few received revelations, it is considered a mystical branch of Judaism.

Interest in the contemplative practices of the Kabbalah has grown in recent years as Hollywood celebrities have explored it and authors such as Anita Diamant and Myla Goldberg (*The Red Tent* and *Bee Season*, respectively, see Resources) have written about it.

Yet Eastern European Jews have held the thread of mysticism in their practice. Through the ascendance of rationalism, the emphasis of Judaism has moved away from the contemplative texts, but rabbis such as Rabbi Aryeh Kaplan came out in the 1970s with books on meditation, ushering in an exploration of the ancient texts. Strains of the contemplative practice can be found in the Lithuanian Orthodox tradition of mussar, which illumines the root of suffering and focuses on the everyday experience of happiness. The Chasids meditate through melodies, practicing solitude with the goal of placing the mind in the awareness of God filling all things.

The Jewish meditative tradition has its origin in the description of the patriarch Isaac in the Torah going into lasuach in the field, which is understood to be meditation. One Jewish meditative practice is his-bodedus, a Hebrew word that derives from a word meaning the state of being alone.

> **Just Be!**
>
> If your faith has more contemplative roots than what you are accustomed to practicing, then this is a wonderful time to explore them. Also, try to be more mindful in your experience in your place of worship and with members of your community, noticing more in your prayers and practice, as if for the first time.

The Islamic Tradition

The most sacred place in Islam is the Ka'ba in Mecca. Five times a day, no matter where they are on Earth, Muslims turn in the direction of Mecca, a city on the western coast of Saudi Arabia, and pray. This prayer is a form of mindfulness—an intentional pause that takes the believer out of the day-to-day and into an awareness of a greater power working without and within.

In Islam, there are two traditions of meditation, but the one most closely akin to mindfulness is Sufism, which emphasizes muraqaba. Muraqaba is translated to mean "watch over," "take care of," or "keep an eye on"—essentially to notice, observe, or be mindful. There is a sense of yielding to Allah's will, seeking sincerity and consciousness, to allow Allah's hand to work in one's life. It is a quality of openness that is parallel to that of mindfulness, in which one does not try to manipulate the experience but allows it to unfold.

The Sufi tradition is mystical, and many Westerns are most familiar with it through the poetry of the thirteenth-century Persian mystic, Jelaluddin Rumi, whose works were translated in *The Essential Rumi* by Coleman Barks (see Resources). Here's an example:

Today, like every other day, we wake up empty

and frightened. Don't open the door to the study

and begin reading. Take down a musical instrument.

Let the beauty we love be what we do.

There are hundreds of ways to kneel and kiss the ground.

—From *The Essential Rumi*

Tafaukkur or Tadabbur is the other branch of the meditation tradition in Islam, and it's focused on contemplation of the universe with the goal of enlightenment. The believer receives divine inspiration and is liberated from the imprisoning thoughts that are part of the human condition. This insight enables the believer to live on a higher plane of existence with a sustained spiritual focus and a life of greater service— essentially, more mindful living.

The Hindu Tradition

Hinduism is the oldest religion with a tradition in meditation, dating back to the Bhagavad-Gita about 5,000 years ago. In the West, much of what people know about Hinduism is from yoga. In India, yoga is a method to achieve a balance of mind, body, and spirit and a means of spiritual self-mastery.

Though yoga is rooted in Hinduism, the meditation techniques of yoga have become secularized in the West, much as the mindfulness practices of Buddhism have. Yoga has many branches, including the Hatha yoga that is most popular in the West and focuses on postures that promote harmony of mind, body, and spirit. One of the most mindful branches of yoga is Raja, which emphasizes that the yogi (practitioner of yoga) must still the turbulence of his or her mind. Other forms of yoga meditation use mantras, the repetition of a sacred word, focus on a sacred object, or use the stimulation and relaxation of the senses (surat shabd yoga, which uses sound and light meditation).

One central idea in yoga is that of ending duality—quelling the conflict between opposing forces and achieving a state of harmony. This is similar to mindfulness in which the practitioner experiences the awareness of the present moment, without judgment. One concept that a yoga practitioner might explore might be the battle between good and evil. The key to inner peace is to end the conflict, to allow seemingly opposite concepts to exist in harmony and to transmute into one another. In the practice of mindfulness, we get out of the habit of evaluating thoughts as positive or negative, thus we end the inner conflict and enter into stillness. In doing so, we discover a more serene inner landscape.

Other Traditions

Meditation has flourished in the West since the 1960s, largely ushered in through popular culture.

Self-realization is the goal of the spiritual meditation tradition of Paramhansa Yogananda, who wrote *Autobiography of a Yogi* (see Resources). This meditation technique derives from the Kriya Yoga tradition, and its focus is on achieving an intuitive, inner awareness of God.

Transcending to a relaxed state of higher spiritual consciousness is the goal of Transcendental Meditation (TM), introduced in the United States in 1958 by Maharishi Mahesh Yogi. This is achieved through clearing the mind using a mantra, a word that the practitioner recites repeatedly in order to clear the mind. An estimated four million people have been trained in TM.

TM has been shown in numerous medical studies to have cardiovascular health benefits ranging from lowering blood pressure to reducing cholesterol level, as well as reducing anxiety and depression. It also has been shown to help people stop smoking and reduce alcohol use.

The Relaxation Response, pioneered by Harvard physician Herbert Benson in the 1970s, is based on the principles of transcendental meditation. Benson learned that meditation practitioners could slow their breathing by 25 percent, decrease their oxygen consumption by 17 percent, lower their blood pressure, and slow their heart rate.

Active meditation traditions include yoga, tai chi, qi gong, and those of Osho, formerly known as Rajneesh. With active meditation, you begin with activity, followed by stillness and silence, turning your thoughts inward, or you practice inner stillness through movement.

Native American spirituality practices meditation through contemplation of nature and communal experiences, such as a sweat lodge or drumming ceremony. In the shamanism traditions, the practitioner works with a master, who may be a shape-shifter, capable of transforming into an animal or another being. In some ceremonies, the practitioner achieves an altered state through a hallucinogen such as peyote.

In literature, classic writers such as Ralph Waldo Emerson, Henry David Thoreau and Walt Whitman practiced a nature-centered reflective mindfulness cultivating a relationship with the present moment with care and reverence. Contemporary writers such as Wendell Berry, Terry Tempest Williams, and Susan Chernak McElroy (see Resources) have furthered that tradition of nature-centered mindfulness in their writing, and a new therapy is emerging called Nature Connected Meditation.

Breathe ...

You may have hesitated to explore mindfulness or anything that sounds Eastern. But mindfulness is not narcissistic, not a cult, not out of touch, and not anti-Christian. Mindfulness-Based Stress Reduction (MBSR) creator Jon Kabat-Zinn says, "Meditation is simply about being yourself and knowing something about who that is." Devoting time to knowing who you are isn't self-absorbed "navel gazing." Instead, practitioners find that it's the foundation of building kindness and compassion toward others. Kindness to oneself—embracing *all* of your inner landscape—opens the door to having kindness to others, indeed to all beings.

Buddhism's Mindfulness Traditions

Meditation practice is at the heart of Buddhism, which believes that the path to wisdom, peace, and freedom lies in exploring your inner life. Buddhism guides practitioners in mastering the chaos of their outer and inner worlds, pointing them on the path of awakening to their own true nature. Buddhism rests on the Four Noble Truths and the Eightfold Path. There are two primary forms of meditation in Buddhism: mindfulness, also known as insight meditation (vipassana, in the Pali language), and concentration meditation, which calms and focuses the mind (samatha, in the Pali language).

Buddhism isn't strictly a religion—it's also a psychology. In fact, many scholars view the 2,500-year-old practice of Buddhism as a study of the nature of the mind rather than a theistic tradition. They see Buddhism as a technique that points the practitioner on the path to self-awareness and spiritual development.

Psychologists have begun to understand that some of the psychological principles of Buddhism, such as mindfulness and compassion, can be explored separately from the exploration of a deity or the divine, separate from theology. Christopher K. Germer wrote in 2005 that, "Reading early Buddhist texts will convince the clinician that the Buddha was essentially a psychologist."

The Four Noble Truths, for example, are a fundamental Buddhist teaching about the human condition. The Buddha taught that much of what we experience in life is unsatisfactory to us, and we create our own suffering by resisting the ways things are and grasping instead at the way we wish they could be. We can reduce our suffering by coming to accept the way things are, and mindfulness practice helps us cultivate this acceptance and wisdom. Mindfulness is one step on the eightfold path, a set of guidelines for living ethically and in the present moment.

The Eightfold Path is a guideline for ethical living—living in a way that fosters awakening and insight. The Eightfold Path is not a linear progression, but rather eight principles that are based on values. The steps on the Eightfold Path are right view, right intention, right speech, right action, right livelihood, right effort, right mindfulness, and right concentration. These are concepts that we will develop in the chapters ahead.

In the West, counselors and psychologists who use mindfulness work with their clients to uncover the ways they resist the truths about their lives, and the ways they create and perpetuate their distress. In therapy, people discover their own truths and learn how to make changes in their lives to live more fully and in accordance with their truth.

More and more, East and West meet. The effectiveness of mindfulness, separated from Buddhism and secularized, is just one reason for that. Psychologists Mark Epstein and John Welwood have written extensively about the intersection of Eastern and Western psychology, and many people are exploring it, as evidenced by the California Institute of Integral Studies and Naropa University, which offer advanced degrees in East/West psychology. The number of professional seminars offered across North America on East/West psychology, meditation, and mindfulness has exploded in the past decade. The Dalai Lama, the spiritual leader of Tibetan Buddhists, hosts retreats and seminars at the Mind & Life Institute in Colorado as a way to create a working collaboration between modern science and Buddhism.

Intersections: New Opportunities for Attuned Living

As East meets West and spirituality meets psychology, new opportunities flourish for creating a greater understanding of our lives. Through much of human history, the boundaries between East and West have been strict, largely because of geography and culture. With globalization, we have become much better informed about each other. And as the field of psychology has developed and become established, largely in the twentieth century, it has come to define itself in a way that can co-exist with spiritual practices. As you can see, mindfulness is a current that runs through these philosophies and has been practiced in a myriad of ways.

Mindfulness itself is a good grounding for arriving at these intersections, because the deeper awareness of self can give you the solid foundation that will inform the way you choose to explore them.

As these ideas converge, it's important to allow yourself to be open, to meet them with kindness, and to allow yourself to understand what value they might have for you. Explore them with mindfulness. Let this technique guide you, so that you can still feel grounded in the faith and philosophy that feel right to you.

These intersections are occurring everywhere—as Western religious traditions embrace their contemplative roots. East embraces West and West embraces East. And West remembers its roots. It's all part of an evolving American spirituality. Rabbi Lawrence Kushner, author of *Kabbalah: A Love Story* (see Resources) and scholar in-residence at the Congregation Emanu-El of San Francisco, writes that the choice for contemporary Jews in America is not between rationalism and mysticism, logic and spirituality, but both. His words echo those of St. Thomas Aquinas, one of the great Catholic theologians, who embraced logic and faith, saying that the believer could experience God both through reason (natural revelation) and faith (divine revelation). He said they were complementary, not contradictory. These convergences are an inevitable part of an evolving spirituality in the West as Western religions unearth their mindful roots.

> ### Sutras
>
> *Peace comes from within. Do not seek it without.*
> —The Buddha
>
> The Buddha discovered that when we explore our inner landscapes, we can discover a lasting peace and happiness. However you think about your inner landscape—your soul or spirit, your stream of thoughts—the journey inward can be healing and life-altering.

Coming Home Meditation

Now, as we are ready to begin our journey with mindfulness, we can use this meditation to bring us to center, to a sense of inner peace. From that place, we can set intentions for exploring a new practice. This meditation helps you see the possibilities in each moment. Notice the places within that need attending.

1. Sit comfortably. Take a few full breaths, and scan your body for any areas of tension. See if you can get these areas to relax. Feel the gravity connecting your body to the earth; your feet touching the floor; your body resting against the chair or cushion.

2. Observe the movement of breath in and out of your body. Don't try to manipulate it; just tune into the rhythm of your breath.

3. Call to mind a time in your life when you felt at peace within yourself. Maybe you were outdoors in nature, or maybe you were with someone who loved you unconditionally. Spend a few moments connecting with this memory: What do you see? What do you hear? Let yourself feel the sensations and emotions in this memory.

4. Notice that you didn't have to force the pleasant feelings and sensations; they arose naturally from within you. Notice that you didn't need distractions; you could just be present with what was happening. Remember how good it felt.

5. Now, know that *this* moment, right here, right now, is a perfect moment. It doesn't need to be manipulated. It is waiting to welcome you. This moment is waiting for you to come meet it. Vietnamese Zen Master Thich Nhat Hanh said, "We have more possibilities available in each moment than we realize." Know that the possibility for peace is present for you now in this very moment.

6. Accept that your mind is your home.

From Spiritual Threshold to Tool for Daily Living

Mindfulness is not religion, even though mindfulness practices are present in many religious traditions. And this makes sense, given that mindfulness provides a path for exploring our inner worlds and how we connect into the web of all creation.

With its many clinical applications, mindfulness is relevant to our present-day lives, and this has little to do with any specific religious tradition. It has anything and everything to do with living in harmony with yourself. How this fits into your faith and philosophy is something you have to explore for yourself. And mindfulness meditation can help you do that. As the Buddha told his disciples, "Be a light unto yourself."

Taming the Mind

The mind is like a wild horse. It doesn't want us to approach it or to know it. It wants to ride off into the wild blue sky. This is the challenge to living in present-moment awareness. When we start to notice the full range of our experience, we become aware of the mind's striving to tame our experience of life. Then we realize that all along, we are the rider, and the mind is the horse. We can simply observe the mind bucking, chomping at the bit, ready to race over the top of the next hill.

Mindfulness gives us safety around these agitated "wild horse" thoughts. We can look at them without judging them as good or bad, acceptable or unacceptable. By practicing mindfulness, we cultivate a calm center from which we can observe our experience in an open, accepting way.

As we open ourselves to the full spectrum of our experience, we engage in waking up to our true nature. In the light of awareness, we begin to remember who we truly are. This helps us see the extent to which our thoughts control us by creating stories around everything we experience, telling us who we are, who we should be, what's happening around us, and what's wrong with our experience. These thoughts are just the mind doing what it does, which is to try to protect us from pain.

As we engage in this awakening, we can remind ourselves of our intention—to stay in the present moment, just as it is. In this way, we reconnect—we come back to meet ourselves. It is in the meeting again and again that we are continually renewed. This re-knowing is very likely the substance of the healing power of mindfulness. Mindfulness centers us. The healing power of mindfulness may be that it returns us to what we already knew. It's like coming home.

The Least You Need to Know

- Meditation and mindfulness are present in every faith tradition.

- Prayer can be a form of mindfulness when its focus is on communing with God, Allah, or Creator in the present moment.

- Christian forms of mindfulness meditation include centering prayer, silent retreats, prayer vigils, labyrinth walks, and pilgrimages.

- Buddhism is a psychology and not only a religion. Many psychologists are incorporating the principles of mindfulness and compassion into their practice.

Chapter 3

Living Without Blinders

In This Chapter

- ◆ Eyes wide open
- ◆ Denial, aversion, delusion
- ◆ The pure present moment
- ◆ "Clear blue sky" meditation
- ◆ RAIN: Recognition, Acceptance, Investigation, and Nonidentification

To live mindfully is to live in full awareness of your life, acting with courage and openness. Over time, the practice of mindfulness builds a calm, safe center from which you can see the whole context of your existence without pushing it away, grasping at it, or numbing yourself to it.

The essential healing power of mindfulness may be that it brings you back into your whole self. Mindfulness liberates you from the relentless work of the mind to tame your experience of life through denial, aversion, or grasping. Mindfulness reminds you of what you already know—yourself—and the practice teaches you to trust it again. That may be why it's proving to be so easy for people from all backgrounds and life experiences to embrace it.

Living in Awareness

We live much of our lives with our eyes closed. As the Beatles sang in "Strawberry Fields Forever," when we—metaphorically speaking—close our eyes to much of our experience, we misunderstand all we see. Over time, we become accustomed to these constrained lives, confined to experiencing only a small part of ourselves.

The experience of mindfulness is an awareness of the present moment as open and spacious. Jon Kabat-Zinn says in *Full Catastrophe Living* that mindfulness "dramatically amplifies the probability that any activity in which you are engaged will result in an expansion of your perspective and an understanding of who you are."

That is part of the healing power of mindfulness—it opens us to so much more of our experience. And when we experience the full range of our awareness, we find ourselves more centered. The experience of being centered is like a portable sense of tranquility. It goes wherever you go.

The Foundations of Mindfulness

Insight meditation teacher Jack Kornfield (*A Path with Heart: A Guide Through the Perils and Promises of Spiritual Life*, see Resources) lists four areas that are the foundations of mindfulness:

◆ Awareness of body and sense

◆ Awareness of heart and feelings

◆ Awareness of mind and thoughts

◆ Awareness of the principles that govern life

So while we think of mindfulness as the exploration of the mind—our thoughts—it is actually something we experience through the body, emotions, and spirit as well as our thoughts.

We can experience mindfulness of the body through techniques such as the body scan, yoga, and walking meditation to name a few. We can experience mindfulness of our emotions when we begin to notice how we interpret and react to what's happening in the present moment. As we practice mindfulness, we discover for ourselves the principles that govern life; we see how our grasping at the world creates our unhappiness. We realize that things are always changing and that this is something we can count on.

We can release ourselves from grasping at the experience through the concept of *beginner's mind*, when we allow ourselves to experience a moment as if it is for the first time. With beginner's mind, we let the moment unfold as it is, without attempting to analyze it, describe it, or connect it with other past experiences. We don't interpret it. We allow ourselves to just be in it. We see it anew.

def•i•ni•tion

Beginner's mind is the practice of seeing an experience with fresh eyes, as if for the first time. We cultivate beginner's mind by staying in the present moment without evaluating it or prejudging it—that is, telling ourselves what it is before we even experience it.

Obstacles to Mindfulness Meditation

At first, mindfulness meditation may feel strange to you. It may seem like doing nothing. Or you may feel you are doing it wrong. The way through this is to keep practicing and stay committed to noticing your challenges. This *is* mindfulness—not a sense of calm, not a moment of insight. Those things *do* happen—calmness and insight—but the practice is about staying in the present moment. And the way you come to them is to keep practicing.

One common misunderstanding is that mindfulness meditation is about emptying your mind. "My mind is too busy and filled with thoughts for me to meditate," beginners often say. When people first start, they are often surprised to discover just how busy their minds are. It may feel like a spigot that they just can't turn off.

Another common misunderstanding is that you'll get an "Aha" moment or big insight when you start your mindful practice. Insights do come, but they're often small and subtle, and they can occur at any time, not just while you're meditating. They can sneak up on you and surprise you!

Beginner mindful meditators often discover how uncomfortable it can be to just sit with what's happening inside, experiencing physical discomfort, agitation, anxiety, or impatience. It's easy to fall into the trap of thinking that meditation is making you feel worse, and if you begin to practice with the idea that it's supposed to make you feel better, you may give up. It isn't true that meditation is "making" you feel worse; what is true is that meditation puts you in touch with the things going on in your mind that you've been working hard to distract yourself from, and you're feeling these experiences more now that you're paying attention to them.

People often think that mindfulness meditation will take away their unpleasant thoughts and feelings, and this leads people to take a sledge-hammer to themselves, squashing the experiences in an attempt to make them go away.

Often new meditators resist because they think they'll lose their sense of humor or will stop being themselves. They think they'll become detached and disconnected from life and will be like a stereotypical dis-passionate monastic, never feeling ruffled, upset, or engaged with the world. Mindful meditation helps you see yourself more clearly and can even pave the way for a new kind of humor, one that comes from joy. Buddhist monastics are some of the funniest people you'll ever meet. When the Dalai Lama laughs, he does so with full abandon!

People think they have to sit in an uncomfortable position on the floor. Not true—you can meditate mindfully in a chair, as many people do. Because of knee problems, Anne recently had to switch to meditating in a chair. Her body only allowed her to resist this switch for so long. She was pleased to discover that meditating in a chair works just fine for her, and not having knee pain anymore helps her explore other aspects of her experience even more deeply.

Just Be! _____

We take ourselves out of the experience of our lives when we think we know what it is ahead of time. This prevents us from seeing our experiences for what they are. Letting our experiences be what they are without judging or analyzing them enables us to experience them freshly. We are judging when we label or categorize our experience. When we do this, we filter out the breadth and depth of the experience. But when we tame the judging, we can see the extraordinary in the ordinary moments of our lives.

You can practice this by meditating or doing a 10-minute mindful writing on these statements:

The first time I [fill in the blank]

Now I am seeing [fill in the blank]

Out of Denial

Mindfulness brings you to seeing your life as it really is. You can heal the suffering that comes from shutting yourself off from the full experience of life. Mindfulness is a breath of fresh air in the tight, cramped mind space many of us live in; it creates a bigger space, enabling us to see ourselves with clarity.

The practice of mindfulness is training to live in "what is." Many times, we don't want our lives "as is" because invariably there are some parts of our lives that cause emotional pain.

Here's how denial works. We experience a physical sensation, and we identify this sensation as pleasant, unpleasant, or neutral. Let's say it's neck pain—very unpleasant! So we respond with an emotion; maybe we're irritated or anxious. Then the mind gets called in to solve the problem, and we start spinning stories. It can be very creative in its story-making, bringing in events from long ago, predictions of the future, and huge casts of characters.

What started out as a sensation of pain in the neck becomes the springboard for all kinds of stories about the neighbor's noisy lawn mower, the boss who makes us stay late at work, the bills that need to be paid, the state of the world … you get the picture. How about this: this is how we create suffering for ourselves. We spin our stories, the muscles spasm in our necks, the pain increases, the tension rises, and the mind is a wreck. We become stuck in a very unpleasant loop.

To be mindful is to cultivate the ability to watch this process unfold in all its variations, again and again. To be mindful is to just watch it without engaging with it. When we slow down to be mindful, we can see more and more how this process works. And we can see that we don't have to get involved.

Our stories become suffering. There are three ways, generally, that our minds respond to our experiences:

- **Grasping.** Grasping is engaging with the experience. We may think we need more of this or that, and so we grab at it. We evaluate the good thought as something we want. We've got to have it. But grasping comes from a sense of lack—the idea that we don't have it and we must get it. Until we get it, we are not good enough. This creates agitation and dissatisfaction, leading us to grasp even more. In this way, we squeeze the life out of the experience.

- **Aversion.** Aversion is pushing away. We simply don't want that thought or experience, so we want to get it away from us; we don't have to think about it or experience it.

- **Delusion.** Delusion is numbness. We pretend the thought or experience is not there, concealing it from our full awareness by putting a layer of protection around it. Doing this paralyzes us in a way; we cut ourselves off from full engagement with the world.

By getting to know our inner landscape, difficult circumstances start to feel less threatening. Being there with our experience in the moment reduces our suffering. On one level, we come to accept it. Remember, we give meaning to every experience we have by constructing a story around it. But these stories often exacerbate our stress and increase our suffering. They get in our way of seeing our life as it is.

Breathe ... _____

We can have denial about being in denial. We try so hard to put our painful experiences behind us, but often we end up suppressing the experience rather than letting it go. Later, when the pain starts to resurface, we may have difficulty recognizing it because it's old news. We respond by working harder to keep it in the subconscious. It's through observing the mind that we can become aware of our denial. We can face our pain directly, which allows it to heal.

Living in the Present

Mindfulness tunes us into the power of the present moment. Remember in Chapter 1 we talked about the balance between effort and relaxation? With mindfulness, there is not a goal, but there is effort. The effort is to stay in the present moment, as it is.

The practice of watching your thoughts, the willingness to meet your mind, reveals to you that you are not your thoughts; you are the one observing the thoughts. Your thoughts often take you away from the here and now. If you are thinking about the past or the future, you are letting yourself be a prisoner of your thoughts. Inevitably, you spin stories about these thoughts, and that keeps you right there in them.

But when you merely observe your thoughts, you begin to understand that if you have an awareness of yourself as an observer, *you cannot be your thoughts.* No more than you can be your heart, which is beating, or your lungs, which are breathing.

Now you can begin to notice the thoughts of the past and future that tug you away from the present.

It is helpful to view the past, which may be causing you suffering, as a series of present moments that have led you to this present moment.

Many of the stories we create around our experience take the form of "old tapes"—messages about ourselves we took in as children that continue to play over and over again in our minds. Often these stories have the theme of being not good enough. For example, "You're too sensitive," or "You're not smart enough." These vague, negative statements can cause us so much distress, and they just aren't true. "Too sensitive" compared to whom? What does "smart enough" even mean? When you hear these tapes play in your mind, try labeling them "old tapes." Notice what else is happening in your body and in your emotions. See how you react to them with grasping, aversion, and delusion. See if you can allow them to run in the background without taking over.

How do you do this, you might wonder? We are programmed to live in the past and the future. This is how the rational mind solves problems. We sort out the past to make sense of it; we worry about the future so that we can plan for it.

The secret lies in being open to whatever you might find when you come to meet your mind. Be open, and try not to evaluate it, judge it, or push it away, if you can. Know, however, that you *will* invariably react to your experience with grasping, aversion, and delusion, and when you do, just note it and return to the breath. This is how you train the mind. You begin to stop reacting with grasping, aversion, and delusion simply by noting when you catch yourself grasping, numbing, or pushing away.

It's not about forcing or directing your mind. It's about meeting your mind. This is more welcoming.

Soft Mental Notes

Soft mental notes are simple labels that you can use to redirect the mind when it's wandered off. This technique is useful for staying with present moment experience, as in mindfulness meditation, or returning to the object of meditation, as in concentration meditation.

"Soft" refers to nonjudgmental, as free of aversion or clinging as possible. We make these notes quietly to ourselves. We avoid getting caught up in trying to come up with the perfect word to describe our experience, instead using simple labels such as "thinking," "feeling sadness," "worrying," and "sleepy."

In mindfulness practice, softly noting our experience as it unfolds keeps us connected with the moment and not lost in story. When we notice we're thinking, we note, "thinking" to keep ourselves from getting caught up in the content of our thoughts.

In concentration practice, we use soft mental notes to let go of whatever has called our attention away from the breath and object of meditation and return to the breath and object.

Clear Blue Sky Meditation

A good starting meditation is this clear blue sky meditation, which helps you stay in the present moment using all your senses. To practice this meditation, take a few moments to center yourself by placing your attention on your breath. Say the phrases softly to yourself, pausing each time to notice what you're aware of. You can take a few minutes to practice this meditation whenever you want to reconnect with your experience, whether it's while you wait for a bus or in the middle of your workday.

My mind is the clear blue sky. My thoughts and emotions are weather patterns passing through. I experience these weather patterns, but they are not who I am.

I am here, hearing this _____.

I am here, seeing this _____.

I am here, feeling this _____.

I can allow whatever is here to be here now.

I can allow whatever is here to pass away.

I am open to whatever is happening in this moment.

Two Tempters

The past and the future are two very persuasive tempters. If the present is unpleasant, a happy memory may be more appealing. The future, too, comes wearing a beguiling disguise. It may seem dazzling, making all kinds of promises, luring you to dwell in fantasies and visualizations of what you believe might come.

On the other hand, if the past haunts you, then you may be unable to enjoy the present. Or, if the present is painful, fraught with suffering, you may place your hopes in the future where things will be better, and you may let your thoughts live there most of the time.

Insight meditation teacher Jack Kornfield compares the effort of staying in the present moment to that of training a puppy—an idea that Carolyn could really relate to as she and the twins were training their new puppy one summer. It goes like this: when you are cultivating the awareness of the present moment, your mind will wander off, much like a puppy. So you bring your mind back, as you would a puppy, gently but firmly, with friendliness and patience.

And remember, when we return to the present moment, no matter how long we have been away or how far we have gone, it is always there to receive us.

Sutras

Past and future veil God from our sight; burn up both of them with fire.

—Rumi, thirteenth-century Sufi poet and Persian mystic

The light of awareness can be like a fire that burns away all the stories about the past and future that keep us from clearly seeing what's happening now. This burning away puts us in touch with our true nature and with the way things really are.

The Perfect Moment

In this present moment, filled as it may be with pain and fear, there is also peace and ease. We don't often see it because our stories blind us to the whole experience of each moment. When we live in the past or future, we're trying to capture a quality of experience that's actually happening right now, if we can allow ourselves to see it. The fleeting happiness that comes from re-living the past or dreaming about the future pales in comparison to the joy that can be found in this very moment.

Perhaps you picked up this book because you want to correct something about your life. You might be facing something difficult, a physical illness or a psychological condition that bedevils you. You may have read news reports about the effectiveness of mindfulness with chronic pain, cancer, depression, or anxiety—and you want to fix that.

Or maybe you picked up this book simply because you want to enrich your life. You want more contentment around your relationship or your work or your finances. If that's the way you came to this book, you may be acutely aware of all the ways your life isn't what you want it to be.

Mindfulness won't take away the truth of your circumstances. It isn't a magic fix that will solve your problems for you. Humanistic psychologist Carl Rogers said, "The curious paradox is that when I accept myself just as I am, then I can change." When we open ourselves to the present moment, we open ourselves to the rich resources we all possess to respond to our lives with wisdom and care. We find ways to live with meaning and ease, regardless of our circumstances. In this way, we become free. Each moment is perfect; each moment is filled with limitless possibilities; each moment is filled with joy and peace along with the pain and sorrow we all experience.

"What, at this moment, is lacking?" is the question that Zen master Rinzai posed to his students. Just take a moment and answer this question for yourself.

Here are some examples: *I'm old. I'm alone. I'm hungry. I'm worried about money. I'm in pain.*

Let's work with "I'm old." If you talked to a dozen 35-year-olds about whether they think they are old, some would be focused on the first appearance of wrinkles or gray hair while others would be oblivious. If you talked to a dozen 70-year-olds, you'd find some who were focused on the limitations of their bodies while you'd find others who were out bike riding or swimming every other day. "Old" has only the power you give to its meaning.

We can't help but think of the line in the movie *When Harry Met Sally,* when Meg Ryan has collapsed in tears because she's getting old—40— but when Billy Crystal asks her when, she says, "Someday!" So, is Meg Ryan "old" in that present moment? Or is she *thinking* about being old?

Eckhart Tolle, in his book, *The Power of Now: A Guide to Spiritual Enlightenment* (see Resources), says that you cannot be unhappy and be completely present in the now. He explains this by sorting out your life—your living, right in this moment, now—from your life situation. Regrets about the past are about your mind resisting and not accepting what happened. When your thoughts dwell on regret, you are resisting what is in the present moment. If you are unhappy about an area of your life, but you think thoughts of hope, you are casting your thoughts into the future, which perpetuates your denial of the now.

Denying the present moment doesn't feel good, even if we're pushing it aside in favor of a thought we perceive to bring us more happiness. We feel cut off from the full experience of life, the wholeness of who we are. It's like losing pieces of yourself. You are missing the moments of your life, and these moments, when you experience them at their purest essence, are free of suffering.

Resisting

Are you resisting your here and now? Would you rather be somewhere else? Is your focus on getting to that place where you would rather be?

If Carolyn had to list what she was resisting to most in her present-day life, it would be two things: traffic and tumbleweeds. Carolyn lives on what she proudly calls "my acre of sand" in Rio Rancho, a thriving city on the west side of Albuquerque—on the opposite side of the Rio Grande from where she works at the newspaper. Traffic is a fact of life, and the roads get more congested every day.

Tumbleweeds are the other persistent annoyance. One good monsoon can make the plant known as Russian thistle sprout up all over any blank space in the sand overnight. They are prickly and invasive. After growing like gangbusters all summer through the monsoons, they die and dry up—and get blown around, snowballing in size.

These are two things Carolyn can't do much about, but they can easily give rise to unpleasant thoughts when Carolyn resists them. Each morning, at sunrise, when she takes the puppy out in the backyard, she has a choice: she can think the same thought she had the day before about her dislike of tumbleweeds—or she can notice it all—the sun rising in the sky at the northernmost edge of the Sandia mountains, the roadrunner tracks in the wet sand, her puppy, the weed-control carpet that didn't control the weeds, the New Mexico sunflowers blooming amid the tumbleweeds, the weathered wood on the play structure ... just noticing them without evaluating ("sunrise pleasant, tumbleweeds unpleasant, puppy pleasant, coyote unpleasant") … instead, just taking it all in her mind. And it feels peaceful.

It has taken years of mindful writing practice, yoga, and meditation to train her mind not to engage in this good, bad, and ugly game. Typically, Carolyn would have preferred to focus on the sunrise and the puppy, two pleasant thoughts. But the unpleasant thoughts would spring up like weeds in her mind. And the whole inner dialogue would crank up. Then she'd be on her way to work and carrying around the sense that her life was frenetic, and she wasn't really tasting it. Allowing the weeds *and* the rosy sunrise sky to dwell side by side in her awareness was the antidote for an agitated mind.

Live Mindful

One winter morning, a tumbleweed storm, as Carolyn calls them, blew a mass of prickly brown wicker onto Carolyn's back patio until the tumbleweeds were chest high, engulfing the patio furniture and barring the door. Carolyn and the twins took pictures and e-mailed them to family; then Carolyn ran the pictures with a column she wrote about "Radical Contentment." One late summer morning, Carolyn got out in the yard to scritch the hoe around the tumbleweeds, raking the sand like a Zen garden around them. During the hour she worked, it meant allowing the tumbleweeds to be in her awareness, staying with the unpleasant thought. Mindfulness is like this.

Recognizing, Accepting, Investigating, and Not Identifying

Jack Kornfield, in the magazine *Shambhala Sun* (2007), describes coming into the present moment with the acronym RAIN—Recognition, Acceptance, Investigation, and Nonidentification. We begin by recognizing what's happening now. Many people find it helpful to do what Carolyn just did—softly listing or naming to themselves what they see before them. This can be naming what you see, or it can be labeling the kinds of thoughts and emotions you're noticing, such as "thinking," "judging," or "sadness." And as you do so, you meet your mind. You accept what you find there. This is just how things are in this moment.

Investigation means noticing how we are experiencing this moment in the body and emotions. What does it feel like? We notice whether the experiences are pleasant, unpleasant, or neutral. We notice the interpretations we give to the experiences. With nonidentification, we let them pass their way. We neither adjust the interpretations nor accept them. We simply notice them.

No More Suffering

Whiskey-voiced blues-rocker Lucinda Williams has a take on our longing to empty the mind of the suffering thoughts with which we clutter it in her song, "Unsuffer Me." She sings, "undo my logic, undo my fear," as she asks to be unbound and unstained. She says she longs for bliss and knowledge. Logic and fear are two of the mind's clever ways of seeming very much on top of things—analyzing and categorizing the moments of our lives—but they can hinder our experience of the bliss of the present moment and the true knowledge it offers to us. It's through being willing to take off the blinders and be open to the experience—whatever it is—that we may find the essence of our lives.

The Least You Need to Know

- Living in present-moment awareness creates a sense of expansion of who we are.

- When we tame the wild horses of our minds, we enable them to rest peacefully with what is. This creates the sense of being centered.

- Beginner's mind is the intention to see each experience with fresh eyes, not preconceiving what it will be.

- Our minds respond to unpleasant experiences with denial, aversion, and delusion.

- We can calmly sift through our minds, clarifying what is past, present, and future.

- RAIN is a good acronym to remember the four steps of mindfulness—recognition, acceptance, investigation, and non-identification.

Part 2

How Mindful Living Reduces Stress

We are just beginning to understand the healing quality of mindfulness for catastrophic physical illnesses, chronic pain, depression, and anxiety. Researchers are finding that not only does it create a state of relaxation, it even seems to create permanent physiological changes in the brain and immune system. These states of awareness build hope and emotional resilience. Mindfulness meditation practice gives you a practice for living a life of clarity with lovingkindness and compassion. In this part, you'll also learn metta, the lovingkindness meditation.

Chapter 4

Mindful Multitasking? Hmmm ...

In This Chapter

◆ Distractions, interruptions, parallel tasks

◆ The downside of multitasking

◆ Is it possible to multitask mindfully?

◆ Rushing through the moment

◆ "To-do list" meditation

This is the modern dilemma. Mindfulness is the act of bringing our minds to what is happening in this moment, yet multitasking is the predominant life skill, whether you're a stay-at-home parent or a chief executive officer. Life and work in the high-wired world of the twenty-first century seem to demand that we multitask or die. Multitasking seems to be a survival-of-the-fittest skill—yet mindfulness is the way to survive and thrive.

In this chapter, we'll look at how mindfulness improves your fitness for surviving the gadget-frenzied life. We'll bring mindfulness to noticing what you do and how you do it. Then we'll give you ways to bring mindfulness to multitasking itself.

Your CPU

In computing, multitasking is what occurs when several processes share a common CPU (central processing unit). In humans, *multitasking* is what occurs when we perform two or more tasks at the same time, and the common CPU is our brains. A typical twenty-first-century example of multitasking is talking on the cell phone while typing an e-mail on the computer. You might be doing all of this with music in the background.

def•i•ni•tion

> **Multitasking** is performing two or more tasks concurrently. A person might do two or more tasks at the same time (talk on the phone while washing dishes) or might toggle between several tasks (dialing the phone while waiting for the computer to boot up, then typing in a computer password while leaving a voice mail). Multitasking also refers to multiple projects being performed on parallel tracks, requiring the person to switch contexts as he or she goes back and forth.

It's interesting to note that with computers, when multitasking is achieved, it's with the illusion of parallelism—that is, it's only an illusion that the tasks are occurring simultaneously. Computer programmers have to design the operating system so that the central brain can move from task to task without seeming to interrupt those tasks.

All of our gadgets make these parallel interactions possible. We can instant message (IM) while we're on the cell phone and watching a DVD—and we start early. Today, 82 percent of children are online by the seventh grade, according to the Pew Internet and American Life Project. A 2005 survey of Americans age 8 to 18 showed that kids were packing more media-enabled multitasking into a shorter amount of time. The survey by the Kaiser Family Foundation showed that kids spent an average of 6.5 hours a day with media, but because they could multitask—watch a DVD and IM at the same time—they were packing 8.5 hours worth of media exposure into the same amount of time.

The Landscape of Multitasking

As a single mother who keeps up-to-date with her electronic gadgets, Carolyn is a savvy but reluctant multitasker. On any given school night, she might perform the following tasks: 1. Start a load of laundry. 2. Boot up the desktop PC to print out a document. 3. Start water to boil for pasta. 4. Check voicemail. 5. Unload the dishwasher. 6. Print out the document. 6. Sort through mail. 7. Add the pasta to the boiling water. 8. Return a phone call to the twins' teacher. 9. Tell the twins to stop fighting. (Tasks 8 and 9 are generally cause and effect—Mom on phone, time to pick on sibling.) 10. Put the laundry into the dryer. 11. Make the pasta sauce. 12. Set out pajamas and towels for the twins' baths. 13. Pay a bill online. 14. Put dinner on the table.

If this feels familiar, well, we're so sorry. Multitasking has become an adaptation for many of us, yet Carolyn strives to be mindful, to notice what she's doing when she is doing it. The way she views a life filled with mundane tasks is that it presents infinite opportunities to experience the moment and to be grounded in the day-to-day ordinariness of physical tasks. This is the real stuff of life. This is visceral.

Carolyn often compares it to the carnival performer who keeps all the plates spinning. In order for the plates to keep spinning, they have to maintain a certain speed. If the plate-spinner lets any one plate slow down too much, it crashes to the ground and shatters. Our brains can monitor multiple plates—scientists say this is based on "highly practiced tasks." We can move laundry from the washer to the dryer while talking on the phone because we've done it a million times. But our brains can only monitor a certain number of spinning plates.

How Did It Get This Way?

Our lives run at a fast pace. They are full of distractions and interruptions. Gadgets have brought the world to us. If you're wondering how you missed the highway sign for the road to mindfulness, somehow taking a turn onto the Information Superhighway, not necessarily with your permission, you're not alone.

Breathe ...

Even though we are perfectly capable of performing a highly practiced task such as moving the towels to the dryer while talking on the phone, when we do so, we are shutting ourselves out from the freshness of the experience. We miss experiencing the extraordinary in this ordinary moment. We fail to notice the bright colors of the terrycloth towels. We fail to engage fully with the person on the phone. Instead of experiencing that person, we get to the bottom line: okay, I'll meet you at 2 P.M. Tuesday. We promise to be more mindful to the relationship *in the future*, which is only a possibility, when we always have the opportunity to be more mindful *now*.

In the mainstream middle-class Western culture, we value busyness, productivity, and getting ahead above the experience of just living. The present moment is rich and full of sensory experiences. Many of these experiences are painful or difficult, and many of them become stories that take us away from the moment. Many of us learn from an early age that being busy is a way to avoid these unpleasant or difficult experiences. For instance, many people say they deal with grief by staying busy. While it's helpful to have a structured schedule and productive activities to stay grounded in the first weeks after a loss, for too many of us, it becomes a way to avoid ever feeling the pain of loss.

So we take our culture's messages about the value of being busy and productive, and we combine that with our desire to be distracted from our suffering. And that sets the stage for multitasking. Filling our time with unnecessary activity—how often do you need to check e-mail, really?—is a strategy that works pretty well at first. Being busy gets an immediate payoff. We accomplish tasks, earn more money, and gain respect. But eventually it breaks down. The pain we are avoiding gets noisier and noisier, becoming more difficult to avoid. So we respond by getting busier and busier in order to get to the same level of distraction we had before. It's like an addictive drug. We get acclimated so we need more busyness.

We can stop doing this to ourselves, and we don't need to go cold turkey. We can practice mindfulness in small doses. We can incline the mind inward, leaning away from the distractions and to our inner experience. We can begin to see what's really important, what really needs doing, what can wait another day, and what cannot be done at all. Neither Anne nor Carolyn have televisions, and Anne lived without a car for a few years—two experiences that anchored them in the present moment of their lives. You'll learn more about those experiences in the chapters ahead.

Just Be!

It's important to remember that being busy is not necessarily being unmindful. We can be mindful of our busyness, which naturally leads us to making better choices about how to spend our days. These little changes can be quite wonderful because they spring from within. When we take the time to explore our inner landscape, we are coming from a more grounded place. It's so different from forcing ourselves to change from the outside—because it's something we believe we should do. But it's easy when the desire arises naturally from within. As Buddhist teacher Thich Nhat Hanh says, "When you are washing dishes, wash dishes. When you are talking on the phone, talk on the phone."

The Disadvantages of Multitasking

This is your brain. This is your brain on multitasking. If this reminds you of the anti-drug public-service announcements that showed an egg frying on a skillet to demonstrate the harmful effects of recreational drug use, then you get the message.

Multitasking has a big downside in not only diminishing the effectiveness of performing tasks but in the lasting effect it has on the brain—and the studies are piling up to prove it. The most notable studies have come out of the Brain, Cognition, and Action Laboratory at the University of Michigan. In 2005, Carolyn interviewed its director, David E. Meyer, for the *SAGE Magazine* issue about multitasking, which was also the topic of a public seminar the magazine sponsored.

The study demonstrated that people were less effective when they multitasked, but it also showed when people are multitasking, they are increasing the stress response in the brain. Multitasking activates the flight-or-fight response, which raises adrenaline—it's a survival instinct. Habitual multitasking raises your stress level, which increases the level of cortisol, and this has the effect of numbing your brain cells. Over time, the flooded, overtaxed brain cells die.

More recent studies have come out that demonstrate the diminishing returns of multitasking. When people try to perform two tasks at the same time—or toggle back and forth rapidly and repeatedly between two tasks—they make more mistakes. It often takes far longer—sometimes even double the time—to get the task done than if they do the tasks one by one, according to the Michigan study.

Overstimulation is a seemingly unavoidable aspect of twenty-first-century life. As our gadget options abound, and our ways of interfacing increase—click, type, tap, talk—we seem to crave more and more. There is a certain level at which stimulation increases performance and concentration, but at a certain point—Carolyn calls it "the fifth plate"—all the plates slow their spinning, and they all crash to the ground. The brain can't process it.

Another study out of Michigan created a bell curve that showed the relationship between stimulation and concentration. A little stimulation—a cup of java, blues-rock music—can boost performance. But too much is stressful, and there is a dramatic falloff in performance.

At the Rotman Research Institute in Toronto, Canada, new studies suggest that as we get older, we have more trouble turning down the background information. The study, done with functional MRI (magnetic resonance imaging), found that adults over 50 performed better while listening to instrumental music than music with a hard beat and lyrics, for instance.

Recovery Time

The Michigan study also showed that brains need a certain amount of rest and recovery time to reconstitute thoughts and memories. This is what occurs during REM sleep, when we dream and reprocess the day. The computer equivalent is defragmenting your hard drive. During the day, as you use your computer, information gets stored in different fragments on your hard drive. Running the "defrag" program consolidates related information in one place so that your computer can retrieve it the next time you want to access it.

The Michigan study examined young people in particular, who often are more gadget-savvy. It showed that those teenagers who fill every moment with a phone call or a text message don't give their brains enough rest and recovery time. It further suggested that habitual multitasking conditions their brains to lock into an overexcited state— so they have difficulty focusing when they need to. This has long-term implications for short-term memory and concentration skills.

Our Brains Don't Work That Way

We call it multitasking, but often what we're talking about is toggling back and forth between tasks. It's in this that the inefficiencies result. The scientific term for it is "context switching," which means that in order to drop one task and pick up another, our brains have to activate the part that was working on the first task. It takes longer to switch contexts, and that's the core of the ineffectiveness of multitasking.

To make computers into the multitaskers they are now, computer scientists have had to use various methods to improve the way a computer application talks to the CPU. In early computer operating systems (before Windows 95 and Mac OS X), programmers used cooperative multitasking. Tasks that were running at the same time had to "check in" with the CPU to gain time to process the task. One application would have to cede time to another. It's like asking your brain for the mind space every time you change from one activity to another. In the computer world, sometimes the CPU wouldn't cede time for one task to process. This is called getting "hung up." It's the inspiration for the tongue-in-cheek street name at Apple headquarters in Cupertino, California: One Infinite Loop.

Currently, the standard model for computer multitasking is "preemptive multitasking," which means that the CPU guarantees each process a slice of operating time. When you need it, you get it. It's like having a reserved table at your favorite restaurant. The operating system programs ways to block out certain tasks so that others can proceed no matter what other tasks are being performed; in other words, it shuts out distractions.

This strikes us as mindful computing. You allocate your mind the space to focus on what has greatest importance for you—the present moment, the authentic experience of your life. Mindful computing blocks out the distractions.

Live Mindful

"Are we multitasking yet?" the twins asked Carolyn the other day as they loaded the minivan (known as "the Money Van") with purchases in a very efficient, three-pointed effort. *"Where did you learn that word?"* she wanted to know. *"From you!"* said her son with glee.

Computers have adapted because programmers have recognized that a CPU can only process one task at a time effectively. Another multitasking study from the Human Information Processing Laboratory at Vanderbilt University put it more bluntly. As neuroscientist and lab director René Marois stated to *The New York Times*, "A core limitation is the inability to concentrate on two things at once."

The True Cost

Someone has measured the cost of ineffective multitasking on the economy. Jonathan B. Spira, chief analyst at Basex, a business consulting firm, estimated the cost of workplace interruptions on the American economy at $650 billion a year, according to a 2007 report in *The New York Times*.

But the real cost is more than that. When we multitask, we lose moments of our lives. The research shows that the quality of what we put into our lives diminishes. We lose the depth of thought. Multitasking and overstimulation hold us above the surface of our lives, and we are not quite experiencing them.

Elinor Ochs, a researcher at the University of California at Los Angeles (UCLA) and head of the Center on Everyday Lives of Families, who conducted a study on electronic multitasking, has voiced concern in media reports about what might happen to our society as we replace the richness of shoulder-to-shoulder and eye-to-eye human connections with quick, disembodied electronic exchanges.

Multitasking has become such an issue among college students, for instance, that the Master's in Business Administration programs at

UCLA and the University of Virginia have discussed blocking Internet access during lectures, according to a 2006 report in *Time* magazine. "I tell my students not to treat me like TV," University of Wisconsin professor Aaron Brower told *Time*.

Massachusetts Institute of Technology professor Sherry Turkle has noted that many students will write their blogs simultaneously while they are in the lecture hall. She told *Time* that these parallel discussions take people out of experiencing the world as it is. "People are going to lectures by some of the greatest minds, and they are doing their mail," she said.

The multitasking phenomenon has implications for how we learn, reason, work, and make sense of the world, but it has far greater implications for how we experience our relationships. What happens to family time when we are more tuned in to our devices than to each other? What happens when we believe the e-connection is the real thing and we lose sight of the possibilities that lie in experiencing the full depth of our relationships?

Can You Multitask Mindfully?

Sometimes we really are just busy. Carolyn accepts that this time of her life, raising her twins, is going to be jam-packed. That's mindfulness Step #1—accepting it, not resisting it. It's the topic she's exploring as she writes her book, *Straight to Heaven*, which originated from her desire to be present for her life. These years are sweet, wild, and wonderful, and Carolyn wanted to taste them fully. Resisting the busyness would have blocked her from fully meeting herself for the experience.

It's important to be mindful of distinguishing when our lives are full because they just are, and when we are filling up our lives in order to distract ourselves from experiencing our inner landscapes. We can notice when we are doing a lot of things versus doing them under such pressure that we are not focusing on the current activity. We can notice when our minds are racing on to the next moment and the next activity to be done—and we are being mindlessly busy. In *Transforming the Mind, Healing the World* (see Resources), Insight Meditation Society co-founder Joseph Goldstein urges us to notice when we are rushing.

If you find yourself rushing, notice that. If you must be busy, be mindfully busy.

Noticing rushing can be a mindful "bell" that can remind you to stop, take a few deep breaths, and take in the present moment. Ask yourself this:

◆ How does this activity serve me?

◆ Do I need to be doing this right now? (Notice busyness.)

◆ Do I want to be doing this right now? (Notice resistance.)

◆ If I wasn't so busy right now, what would I be feeling, doing, or thinking?

◆ What "shoulds" am I telling myself?

◆ What stories am I telling myself about this activity?

It's not even necessary that you stop what you are doing. Just notice what's happening while you do it.

We can live the path of right mindfulness even if our lives are full. We can engage in depth and self-reflection by having a regular meditation practice. It helps to designate a certain time of day and make that inviolable. For instance, for both Anne and Carolyn, if they don't meditate in the morning, it doesn't happen later in the day.

Another way to approach this commitment to being mindful is to have certain daily activities associated with mindfulness, such as a walk. Rodney Smith, the guiding teacher for Seattle Insight Meditation Society, instructs beginning students to practice mindful tooth brushing, for instance. Some other ideas are mindful dog-walking or mindful watering of the garden. (Chapter 8 will explore this idea further.)

Back to the Body

The simplest way of all to get back into mindfulness is through the body. As we go through our day, we are in our thoughts, our feelings, our emotions, our stories, and our plans. We are rarely grounded in our bodies.

Notice when you are rushing. Goldstein notes that rushing isn't always moving with speed; we can even be rushing when we are moving slowly. He defines the feeling of rushing as feeling as though we are toppling forward. Our minds are ahead of us. They are already out where we want to go instead of being settled in our bodies.

Let the feeling of rushing be good feedback, and let it remind you to come back into your body. Take a few deep breaths. Settle into your body again. If you are sitting, notice yourself sitting. If you are walking, feel the step of the walk.

The To-Do List Meditation

We can also notice what we are adding to the to-do list, and we can come back into the body to be mindful of the list. Go ahead and make your day's to-do list. Take a moment to stop, breathe, and ground your-self in your body. Ask: "What am I feeling right now? What am I aware of right now?"

Open your eyes and look at the list. What are you aware of? What stories come about you, the list, or your life? Notice these thoughts.

Now check back in with the body. Ask yourself the same questions. Notice how it feels in your body. Breathe. Look at your list again. Watch how you respond to the tasks on the list. Do you feel excited to have so many great things to do? Or do you feel overwhelmed? It's probably a little of both.

Mindfully evaluate your list. You may need to stop and breathe and come back to the body several times as you do this. Allow yourself the time to do this, and don't judge yourself if you need to come back to the body.

Now ask yourself this:

- ◆ What items do I need to do?

- ◆ What items do I want to do?

- ◆ Are any of these items here to distract me?

- ◆ Are any of these "shoulds"?

- ◆ What's important to me?

◆ What can be done another day?

◆ What can I ask someone else to do?

◆ What doesn't really have to be done at all?

Sutras _____

To the mind that is still, the whole universe surrenders.

—Lao Tzu

When we're caught up in busyness, it can feel like the world is fighting against us. But actually, we're the ones fighting the world. We stop fighting by mindfully engaging with each present moment.

Authenticity

Being mindful about the activities that fill your life means making authentic choices. You can create space in your mind to make these choices through time given to self-reflection and depth of understanding. In your inner landscape, you can find a more mindful path.

The Least You Need to Know

◆ In computing, multitasking is achieved through the illusion of parallelism. The operating system only seems to move from task to task without seeming to interrupt these tasks.

◆ Multitasking is possible and can be effective if you are performing a highly practiced task, yet even so, multitasking diminishes your engagement with the people and places in your life.

◆ The value that our culture places on busyness is at the root of our rushing.

◆ Studies show that when you multitask, you are less effective. The studies also suggest that multitasking may, over time, diminish brain function.

◆ To reduce multitasking in your life, notice when you are rushing.

◆ You can be mindful about composing your daily to-do list, choosing what's truly important to get done.

Chapter 5

The Physiology of Mindfulness

In This Chapter

- ◆ Relaxation and immune boosting
- ◆ Stress reactivity: the fight-or-flight response
- ◆ Mind-body connection
- ◆ Mindfulness and brain function
- ◆ A body-scan meditation

Mindfulness meditation has a healing quality—but just what is it? Numerous studies over the past 30 years have shown that mindfulness meditation relieves pain, accelerates healing, and eases stress. The technique is increasingly being used in medical contexts to boost healing from chronic and catastrophic illnesses. In recent years, evidence is accumulating that supports mindfulness meditation as a way to alleviate depression, anxiety, mood disorders, and eating disorders.

What is the nature of the healing power of mindfulness? In this chapter, as we delve into the growing body of research, we'll explain the inner workings of mindfulness to heal body, mind, and spirit.

The Benefits Are Many

The power of mindfulness meditation rests in the activation of the mind-body connection. Since the 1970s, Jon Kabat-Zinn and a colleague, Richard Davidson at the University of Wisconsin in Madison, have led the charge as medical doctors and psychiatrists contribute to a growing body of knowledge about its medical, psychological, and social benefits. Now, with more than 200 medical clinics in the United States holding Mindfulness-Based Stress Reduction (MBSR) clinics, more and more research is building, and the populations being served are widening.

The medical applications include relief from back pain and other chronic pain (which we'll go into more deeply in Chapter 6), psoriasis, many different kinds of cancer including breast cancer and prostate cancer, heart disease, and insomnia. Mindfulness meditation also has been used to support patients as they face stressful medical treatments, such as chemotherapy, radiation, or surgery. One study showed positive outcomes for patients getting bone-marrow transplants, for instance.

Studies also have shown that mindfulness meditation can have remarkable impact on psychological conditions such as anxiety, depression, borderline personality disorder, eating disorders such as binge eating or bulimia, substance abuse and addictive behavior, obsessive-compulsive disorder, and post-traumatic stress disorder.

In addition, mindfulness meditation has been demonstrated to have long-term emotional benefits. It boosts your emotional intelligence quotient, helps you achieve emotional balance, increases your capacity for empathy, and improves your relationships. It makes you more emotionally resilient.

It's clear that mindfulness meditation induces physiological changes in the brain and body, from lowering blood pressure and heart rate to improving insulin levels to improving brain function. For the past 30 years, the research has steadily accumulated that it may do more than temporarily induce the *Relaxation Response*. It may induce lasting physiological changes.

def•i•ni•tion

The **Relaxation Response,** a phenomenon identified by Harvard Mind/Body Institute founder Herbert Benson, describes the relaxation of the body induced by meditation, yoga, and other practices. The Relaxation Response is the body's returning to a normal heart rate, blood pressure, and adrenalin level after experiencing stress.

The Dalai Lama, the spiritual leader of Tibetan Buddhists, started the Mind & Life Institute, which is dedicated to establishing collaborative research partnerships that join modern science with Tibetan Buddhism. Since 1990, the institute has supported numerous studies that seek to explain the neurobiological benefits of meditation for people who practice it for the long term.

Here is a sampling of the cutting-edge research as scientists find more and more applications and come closer to explaining exactly how meditation alters brain and body. You can find a very definitive list online, including live links to most of the scientific articles, at livingmindfully. org/benefits/mindfulness_research.php:

◆ At the University of Wisconsin, researchers studied Tibetan monks who were longtime meditation practitioners, finding high-level brain activity and function unlike anything they had seen before.

◆ A 2006 article in the Archives of Internal Medicine showed that diabetes patients practicing meditation improved more than patients who were only treated with drugs and lifestyle improvements in diet and exercise. It was the first study that suggested mindfulness might help diabetes patients.

◆ A 2006 report from Massachusetts General Hospital psychologist and Harvard Medical School instructor Sara Lazar stated that patients who routinely meditate exhibit demonstrable physical changes in their brains. Much is known about the immediate benefits of sitting meditation, but this research, which was funded by the National Institutes of Health and the Centers for Disease Control, showed there are long-range benefits to the brain as well.

The list continues to expand: mindfulness meditation also improves perception, motor skills, and visual acuity. It reduces the rate of relapse in addictive behaviors. It supports lifestyle changes that prevent disease. And mindfulness enhances self-regulation, enabling people to temper binge eating and other eating disorders.

Breathe ...

As with any technique that is actively being researched, proceed with caution. Not all scientists are certain they can explain the physiological reasons that mindfulness meditation improves health. A 2007 report from Canadian researchers who analyzed 813 studies on meditation used in therapy cautioned that while many studies support this, more study is required with larger groups and better controls. The studies analyzed included mantra meditation, mindfulness meditation, yoga, tai chi, and qi gong. Before starting mindfulness meditation as a complement to a medical treatment, consult with your doctor.

Stress Reactivity

Reality is the leading cause of stress, goes the classic bumper sticker. But while we might argue with this cynical view (yes, even a cynical journalist like Carolyn might disagree!), we can say with certainty that stress is one of the leading factors common to major illnesses.

Mind*less*ness is the real culprit. It is not the reality itself that causes the stress, though many times our circumstances can be difficult. But rather, it's not paying attention to mind and body and not being aware that leads to stress-related illnesses. It's how you perceive the stress factor—or whether you allow yourself to perceive it consciously at all—that determine whether you'll respond to stress in a constructive way or a harmful way.

Mindfulness seems to have many benefits for slowing down the knee-jerk reactions to stress that keep us in the cycle of stress. In other words, mindfulness is a stress-buster. It breaks the cycle. Here's how it works.

Fight-or-Flight Response

When we experience stress, our bodies respond with the fight-or-flight response. We perceive a threat, and the body sounds this alarm. It gears up for a violent muscular action. It must decide, in an instant, whether to flee the danger or stand and fight. In the brain, the hypothalamus and pituitary glands kick in, and the adrenal glands flood the bloodstream with adrenaline, the fuel that gives us superhuman strength in the face of danger. Blood pressure rises, heart rate speeds up, and lungs accelerate breathing.

The difficulty arises when the mind locks into this fight-or-flight response, frozen between the two options. In this case, the body is geared up for stress but has no outlet for response and no resolution. The person stays in a state of chronic hyperarousal—ready for a fight, but not given the cue to fight or flee. The person stays in a vigilant mindset, poised to react, looking for danger. This state of chronic distress is the damaging factor of stress. It's not the stressful event itself, but the response to it that harms our bodies, brains, and psyches. Think of a cat with its hair raised and back arched, permanently frozen in this state. This is the picture of reactivity. Some of us are frozen this way and don't realize it.

Fertile Ground for Disease

In *Full Catastrophe Living*, Jon Kabat-Zinn describes five steps in the stress reactivity cycle, which creates disease and illness:

1. **We respond with fight-or-flight response.** Stress happens. It could be good, or it could be bad. We choose to perceive it as a threat. The mind interprets it, and the brain sends a signal out to all circuits in the body.

2. **We react to the stress.** Adrenals kick in. The body responds. Heart is pounding.

3. **We internalize the stress.** We attempt to inhibit the stress response. This lays the foundation for chronic states of hyperarousal, pain, insomnia, anxiety, irregular heart rhythms, high blood pressure, and a myriad of other conditions. This is the denial—the thoughts we push away. Kabat-Zinn calls this internalization.

4. **We don't cope well.** We make bad choices. We cope with the stress by defending ourselves or hiding the stress from ourselves. This can take the form of substance abuse, overworking, hyperactivity, overeating, and other addictions. Kabat-Zinn calls this maladaptive coping.

5. **We break down.** Finally, we hit bottom. We have a heart attack, develop cancer, lose our sense of purpose, lose our enthusiasm for life, collapse in physical or psychological exhaustion, or become immobilized by a psychological disorder such as anxiety or depression.

Mindfulness interrupts this cycle. First and foremost, it creates the state of awareness, which gets us out of the automatic reaction. Mindfulness gives us clarity, the ability to see the situation as it is, and insight, the ability to see it with wisdom (and we'll go into this more in Chapter 7). Studies show that a lifetime of unconscious reactivity significantly increases the likelihood of major disease or illness. Mindfulness keeps us conscious, heading things off at step one or step two. Mindfulness, then, is prevention.

Mindfulness also trains the meditator neither to push away nor deny the stress—which heads off steps three and four, internalization and maladaptive coping. Through mindfulness training, we learn not to push away or bury the painful thoughts. We learn to meet these challenges with an open and resilient heart.

Conscious Resolution

A practice in mindfulness meditation can give you a sense of what it's like to be in balance, something you might not have even known was possible. Either you've never felt it, or if you did, it was such a long time ago, you don't remember it's possible. Mindfulness meditation helps you define it so you know it's possible. That's why we say you have to practice it to know it.

This inner balance is called *homeostasis*, which is the state of the body returning to an inner equilibrium. When we perceive a stressful event, whether it's coming from the external or internal, the fight-or-flight response activates the autonomic nervous system (ANS). There are two branches of the ANS. One is the *sympathetic branch*, the one that speeds things up so we can respond to danger. The other is the *parasympathetic branch*, and it acts as the brakes to slow things down, returning us to a calm state. Both are directed by the *hypothalamus*, a gland in the brain that functions as a master control switch. The *hypothalamus* is part of the brain's *limbic system*, a region deep in the brain that is often called the "seat of emotions." It has two ways to get messages out into the body: nerve cells called neuropeptides and hormonal secretions.

We tend to think of life-threatening dangers as triggering this response, but what happens in everyday life is that it can be triggered by many situations, not all of them real and many of them not resolved. Most of them seem ordinary because they are so prevalent. We get used to not having enough money, not feeling good about ourselves, or not liking our work. So the source can be a chronic low-grade state of stress, such as money worries, an unfulfilling job, or an unsupportive family. Stress responses can be triggered by anything that reminds us of that state. Triggers can be something someone says—a threat to our social status or economic security, a challenge to a belief, or an unexpected disruption to our plan—in short, anything that we can't control or anything that doesn't go our way.

If we respond consciously to the threat, the body responds by winding down—homeostasis. But if we're not conscious of a problem, we can't fix it. If we have hidden it from ourselves, we can't know it's there to do something about it. But not being able to see the problem, we still sense it, and so we stay in a state of hyperarousal, sounding the alarm and awaiting a fix for the problem, but the resolution never comes.

This state can become permanent. In the day-to-day, it may show up as chronic muscle tension, often in the places that we tend to hold tension—shoulders, face, forehead, jaw, and hands. It can also show up as an elevated heart rate or irregular heart rhythm. We get so used to these states that we just live with them (or try to …).

Just Be!

Are you responding or reacting? Take the time to appraise your feelings the next time you perceive a threat. Notice in your body how you are reacting. Notice any muscle tension, and pay attention to your breathing. Your awareness of your awareness brings you into the full context of your life. This meta-consciousness—consciousness that you are a conscious being—enables you to more quickly recover an emotional equilibrium. From this state, you can see new options.

Interconnectivity: The Mind-Body Connection

At the core, mindfulness is effective because it activates the mind-body connection. Our entire biology, on every level of organization, from the cellular level to the organ level to the system level, works because of this information flow. When the flow is good—the mind and body are talking to each other—your cells are nourished, your organs function properly, and your systems operate optimally.

This connectedness of all systems, all organs, all cells, all the time, is crucial not just for physical integration but for mental, psychological, and social integration, too. It helps us learn, remember, and reason things out. It gives us the capacity to develop a supportive social network. We are sustained because we tend to each other and befriend one another. When we're connected on the inside, we're connected on the outside.

This interconnectivity helps us function in a way that makes us part of something. When our minds and bodies are connected, we can feel connected to each other, to the world, and to a greater power. Mindfulness weaves us intimately into the web of life.

 Sutras

> Just as a goldsmith gets his gold
>   First testing by melting, cutting, and rubbing,
> Sages accept my teachings after full examination
> And not just out of devotion to me.
> —The Buddha
>
> While studies and anecdotes about peoples' experiences are interesting and useful, you have to try these practices for yourself. Don't just accept these teachings at face value! The Buddha was very clear about this.

Wholeness and Healing

Mindfulness brings us back into the wholeness of our lives. We allow ourselves to meet what arises. We realize we have been denying ourselves all of the experience because it's stressful; with mindfulness, we return to it, coming to taste it more fully. Mindfulness enables us to see with the eyes of wholeness, and in this lies its healing power. With mindfulness, we achieve physical relaxation but also the ability to transcend our fears. Moments of stillness bring us to the clarity that we already are whole—body and mind integrated, self and spirit connected.

Kabat-Zinn describes it this way from his observations of patients in clinical settings who have used MBSR: Moments of experiencing wholeness "often include a palpable sense of being larger than your illness or your problems and in a much better position to come to terms with them." With mindfulness, we realize we are more than our minds, and in doing so, we no longer let our minds, with their frenetic, often erroneous thoughts, dictate how we perceive ourselves, each other, and the world. Sometimes this is called "meta-consciousness," the recognition that we can be aware of ourselves thinking and can understand that we are more than our thoughts.

Any illness, pain, or disease can drain our ability to experience the present moment. We can lose sight of our strength and power when our thoughts are troubled with pain and worry. There is power in the present moment—the power to transcend. There is the power to see ourselves in the context of a bigger picture, to see our foibles and our setbacks as wrinkles in time—but not the whole story.

When Carolyn was pregnant with her twins, she came down with a terrible cold. It was her first trimester in a high-risk pregnancy, and so the usual over-the-counter remedies were out of the question. She found herself left with hot tea and running the shower, hoping the steam would relieve the congestion. It was misery—had been for days—and she felt like she was fighting a monster. The experience of it was all-consuming, to the point of not having a reference point of herself as a healthy person. But she also had a really good reason to fight the good fight—the health of her babies—and find more strength. Under the steam of the shower, she started saying aloud, "Carolyn, you are bigger than this cold," over and over, letting herself be aware of the physical sensations of the steam filling up the room and her sinus passages opening up. She repeated this as many times as was necessary—to believe it and to relieve it. Her discomfort and distress from physical symptoms (and her thoughts about that) were so intense that it was all her mind could hold in awareness. The turning point was not in running the steam once more, but in allowing herself to perceive the wholeness of being, allowing herself to hold herself there in that moment that her mind wanted her to flee.

With mindfulness, we can understand, too, that we are not our illness or our pain. We are more than those conditions that make us suffer (or, indeed, any kind of label that defines, and so, constrains). In realizing this, we can begin to come to terms with our situation and transform it.

Live Mindful

It's a terrible irony that a catastrophic illness can cast us into living a more authentic, present-moment-oriented life, but that is often the case. Many people become clearer on how they want to spend the precious moments of their lives. They may take an Alaskan cruise, spend more time with family, or learn a new language—whatever unlived dream they might have. "It's not worth it," they may say about the high-level corporate job that consumed them. They become much clearer on what is fulfilling—and they focus on that.

Regulating Our Illnesses

Our minds have the ability to regulate our diseases and illnesses, as many studies have sought to prove in recent years. Prayer, for instance—a form of mindfulness—has been demonstrated to help people live longer and feel better, according to a 1997 study by Kenneth Pargament, professor at Bowling Green University in Ohio. The emerging field of psychoneuroimmunology examines the interconnectivity of the brain and the immune system. More and more studies are supporting the idea that the nervous system—essentially the mind—influences our susceptibility or resistance to disease.

Just as you train your muscles to perform, you can train your mind to be in this mindful state. Kabat-Zinn says, "You have the power to effect the balance point between your internal resources for coping with stress and the stressors that are an unavoidable part of living."

Attuning the Mind

Studies have shown that mindfulness has benefits beyond the in-the-moment relaxation that is achieved through meditation. According to scientist, psychiatrist, and educator Daniel J. Siegel, author of *The Mindful Brain* (see Resources), mindfulness changes the way the brain functions in a multitude of ways.

One of the most notable changes in brain function is that of attunement. Mindfulness seems to harness a specific social and emotional circuitry in the brain that transforms the moment-to-moment awareness achieved in mindfulness to a long-term state of emotional resilience. That means that practitioners of mindfulness are better equipped to handle life's emotional challenges than those who don't practice mindfulness.

Mindfulness seems not only to give temporary relief to life's stressors, it also seems to transform the very physiology of the way we interact and function in the world. Specifically, mindfulness leads to integrated brain function—in plain English, all areas of the brain communicate easily and freely with each other—and this fosters emotional balance, enhancing the parts of the brain that govern cardiac function and immune function. In short, mindfulness may make our hearts function better. It may protect us against invading viruses and bacteria.

A Better Brain

Studies are showing that mindfulness meditation improves the physical components of the brain. In Lazar's study of the effects of meditation on the brain, MRIs showed that the people who meditated for 45 minutes a day every day exhibited a significantly thicker *cortex*, which is the outer layer of the brain that governs thinking, reasoning, and decision-making. The MRIs also showed thickening of the *insula*, which Lazar called the "switchboard of the brain." This region essentially helps us make better decisions. It naturally thins as people age, but this research shows that meditation may keep this area thick. The more people meditated, the thicker this region was in their brains. Her research was reported in the November 2005 issue of *NeuroReport*.

A More Compassionate Mind

Davidson, the neuroscientist who has collaborated with Kabat-Zinn on many medical studies of mindfulness meditation, made the groundbreaking discovery that meditation can train the mind to react to certain situations with positive emotions. Meditation altered the circulation of activity in the brain that was critical for the development of emotion, suggesting that emotions such as happiness and compassion were characteristics that can be cultivated with training.

The Body Scan

You might think that mindfulness meditation means being in the mind. It does, but it also means being with the body, which is the home for your mind. Too often in our time, we are out of touch with our bodies. This arises from the cultural pressure to have the perfect body and our tendency to push away painful thoughts. The body, because it stores our emotional memories, is the bearer of truth. And if we don't want to see the truth because it doesn't match the expectations we have for ourselves, we cut ourselves off from the physical sensations of the body.

A body-scan meditation is a foundational component of mindfulness meditation. That's because coming back into our bodies is to come back into the present moment.

Remember, as we lead you through your first body-scan meditation, that you do not have a goal, such as relaxation. You're not trying to purify your body or glean information from your body, as the word "scan" might imply. Your intention is simply to "be" in your body, in this moment.

It's helpful to listen to these instructions as you practice the body scan. You can record them onto a tape, or purchase recorded body scan meditations (see Resources).

1. Lie on your back in a comfortable place where you can stretch out. We prefer a mat on the floor to the bed because we associate bed with sleep, and for this body scan, you want to be "relaxed awake."

2. Gently close your eyes.

3. Take in three deep, cleansing breaths. Notice the rising and falling of your belly with each inhale and exhale.

4. Experience the whole of your body. Notice what you are touching, the hardness and softness of the surface, the texture and sensation of the fabric or material.

5. Bring your awareness to the toes of your left foot. Direct the attention of your breath to your toes, imagining your breath traveling all the way to your toes as you take in a breath, and it rising from your toes all the way to your nose as you exhale.

6. Notice the physical sensations in your toes. Allow yourself a few moments to experience them. Feel your toes from the inside, wiggling them a bit if you like. Feel them from the outside, noticing the sensations on the skin.

7. When this feels complete, take in an intentional, deep breath. As you exhale, let the image of your toes and their physical sensations dissolve in your mind.

8. Direct your awareness to the sole of your foot, then to the heel of your foot, your ankle, your calf, your knee, and so on, continuing to direct the breath and observing the physical sensations in each area. Be fully present with each area.

9. Continue to move slowly up through the rest of your body, concluding with your face and head.

10. If you encounter painful areas, stay with them through your breath, if you can. Don't react; just notice. If you notice that your breath has become shallow and your body is becoming tense as a response to the pain, try to breathe more deeply. See if you can get the body to relax again. Then let the image of this painful area dissolve, and move to the next area.

Once you have completed the body scan, lie quietly for a few minutes, and allow your attention to take in your body as a whole. Take your time getting up from the floor.

Back to the Essence

While mindfulness meditation has many healing qualities, we don't meditate to conquer a disease. We meditate to be in the moment, to live life more fully, whether we are suffering from heart disease or we're completely healthy. Fully lived moments, lived one by one, are the essence of healing power of mindfulness.

The Least You Need to Know

- ◆ Mindfulness meditation slows down the fight-or-flight response.

- ◆ Mindfulness meditation induces the Relaxation Response, when the body returns to normal after reacting to stress.

- ◆ Many studies are showing long-term physiological benefits of a meditation practice.

- ◆ Studies are demonstrating that meditation increases emotional resilience and compassion.

- ◆ The mind-body connection is activated during mindfulness meditation, and this wholeness ushers in healing to the systems, organs, and cells in the body.

- ◆ One of the essential techniques of mindfulness meditation is the body scan.

Chapter 6

Mindfulness Lessens Pain

In This Chapter

- The origin of pain
- How we think about pain
- Pain as a messenger
- Pain meditation
- Dealing with emotional pain
- Yoga: being in your body

Chronic pain can be so relentless that it can become your identity. When pain is always there, it defines your existence, and therefore it defines you. A growing body of research definitively supports the idea that mindfulness not only relieves physical pain, it also frees you to regain a more joyful and engaged sense of yourself.

Increasingly, mindfulness is being documented as a tool for mitigating emotional pain and depression, as well, giving birth to new forms of psychotherapy that incorporate mindfulness into their practice. In this chapter, we'll show you how mindfulness can help you deal with emotional pain. Additionally, we'll introduce yoga as another essential component of mindfulness practice.

The Beginning of the Road

Lingering physical pain can be disabling, restricting our bodies and starving our spirits. Pain can be a continual drain on our energy and our mental outlook, distracting us from enjoying life. Over time, it can erode our quality of life. It has a way of grinding us down bit by bit.

Pain alters our sense of self. We may feel we have lost control of our bodies. We may have temporarily, or even permanently, lost our ability to make a living, and this may affect our self-worth. It's challenging, sometimes devastating, to lose the sense that we are making a contribution to the world. It feels like being walled off from participating in the commerce of life.

If our pain is chronic, it becomes a daily filter for our thoughts. That limitation is always there. Every twinge and spasm reminds us of what we cannot do. Our thoughts about pain begin to attach to *everything* that happens—pain seems to become the filter for our experiences, everything we think, feel, and do. And so we don't enjoy our relationships fully, and we decide to curtail activities we enjoy. Or, we keep trying to plug away, and we push it too much, making the pain worse. The pain can become global. We can start to feel a growing sense of helplessness; we are confronted with our limitations and our need to depend on others. Over time, it can leave us with a sense of hopelessness. We may lose a sense of what our lives mean.

Mindfulness teaches us a way to make contact with our whole lives—yes, with the pain, but also with the whole picture, including the pieces we've lost. Through mindfulness, we learn not only to live with the pain, but to find the heartbeat of joy still there beneath it. Present-moment awareness takes us beyond our mind's response to pain, and our mind's attempt to control and contain it. It takes us beyond the story we create about the pain (*I can't do this because* … or *I am not a useful person because* …). It leads us gently and compassionately to see ourselves beyond the pain. It's an effective lifelong practice for many people who suffer from chronic pain. Mindfulness sets us free from the pain by allowing us to see that we are not our pain. We are more than our pain.

In modern medicine, generally, when we learn we have a condition that causes chronic pain, we might be told we just have to live with it—but we're not given the tools to live with it. Our aversion to pain naturally leads us to conclude that the only way to live with the discomfort is to ignore it, distract ourselves from it, or find some way to numb our experience of it. Mindfulness and lovingkindness practice are tools that help us to release our aversion to pain and to stop struggling against it. Instead of pushing away the pain, which is what we want to do, we can greet the pain with compassion and lovingkindness. And so being told that we must live with chronic pain is not the end of the road, as Jon Kabat-Zinn says in *Full Catastrophe Living;* it's actually the beginning of the road.

Mindfulness Gets Results

There's a reason that people who suffer from chronic pain tend to maintain the practice on their own, years after learning it in a clinical setting: mindfulness gets results.

Mindfulness-Based Stress Reduction (MBSR) instructors at the Stress Reduction clinic at the Center for Mindfulness at the University of Massachusetts Medical School use the McGill Melzack Pain Rating Index to have patients quantify their pain. In one study, 72 percent of patients achieved a 33 percent reduction in pain over the eight-week period, while 61 percent reported a 50 percent reduction. The study also measured how patients changed their perceptions of their bodies—meaning whether they viewed parts of their bodies as limited, painful, or problematic. At the end of the program, patients said they perceived their bodies as 30 percent less problematic. Patients also reported a 30 percent reduction in how much pain restricted their normal life activities such as preparing food, eating, driving, sleeping, and sex.

Another study compared pain patients who received MBSR training with those who did not. Both received the same medical treatment. Those who did not meditate in addition to treatment showed little change during the 10-week period of study. Meditators, however, quantified a 36 percent improvement in pain. They also reported a 37 percent improvement in their negative feelings about their bodies, an 87 percent improvement in mood, and a 77 percent improvement in psychological distress. Nonmeditators reported only a 22 percent improvement in mood and an 11 percent improvement in distress.

Most interesting, pain patients appear to be "sold" on mindfulness meditation, continuing to practice years later, indicating an internal motivation to commit and maintain the discipline. About 93 percent reported they continued to practice meditation in one form or another. Almost everyone reported still using breath awareness. About 42 percent reported they were practicing formally, at least three times a week for at least 15 minutes a day. This was three years later.

> **Just Be!**
>
> Respond to your pain with phrases like, "May this pain be held in kindness" or "May all who feel pain be held in kindness." It's a way of connecting with others who feel pain. This technique also reminds us that at any given moment, somewhere in the world, someone is practicing *metta* and sending lovingkindness to all beings—including us!

What the Studies Say

Countless other studies demonstrate the effectiveness of mindfulness meditation as a complementary therapy. It can train patients to live with pain as they go through drug treatments, surgery, chemotherapy, and radiation. It also seems to be a curriculum in self-care.

Numerous studies have supported MBSR as an intervention for chronic pain, supporting research that explores whether MBSR can reliably alleviate pain without drugs. The National Institutes of Health (NIH) has endorsed it as a therapy for chronic pain caused by a variety of reasons, including rheumatoid arthritis and back pain, among others.

In addition to being able to alleviate pain, MBSR has been shown to be a viable complementary therapy for patients facing stressful illnesses and diseases. Some studies suggest MBSR may do more than that: it may influence the outcome. A controlled study of 90 cancer patients found that those who practiced mindfulness meditation reported a 31 percent lower rate of stress and 67 percent lower rate of mood disturbance. Some studies have also suggested that more meditation improves the chance of a positive outcome, according to the American Cancer Society.

Among the new and notable studies, a 1999 study reported in *Alternative Therapies* showed that patients who suffer from fibromyalgia, an extremely painful disorder, experienced decreased pain, decreased anxiety, decreased depression, decreased impact of fibromyalgia symptoms, and improved global assessment when they practiced MSBR. A 2007 report in *Psychotherapy and Psychosomatics* showed that female patients experienced significant long-term (three years later) relief from pain, anxiety, and depression.

Mindfulness meditation also attunes the mind to relationships and activities that restore enjoyment to life. Mindfulness seems to be a hope-builder.

The Way We Think of Pain

There are two kinds of pain—acute pain and chronic pain. Acute pain is intense, and it goes away quickly, either on its own or because we seek treatment right away. Acute pain comes on suddenly, and it's often caused by an injury. Chronic pain persists over time, and it isn't easily relieved. It can be constant—an aching or throbbing—or it can come and go—a twinge or a spasm. Chronic pain varies in intensity. Sometimes it's dull and aching; sometimes it's excruciating.

Modern Western medicine is unparalleled in its ability to treat acute pain. Usually it's easy to identify the cause of acute pain, so we can treat it at the source and make it go away. But sometimes our most common modern ways of treating pain—drugs or surgery—don't make it go away. Sometimes the pain lingers. Sometimes it's not well defined or we can't pinpoint a pain source.

It's understandable if the way you have generally thought about pain is that it's something you make go away. You fix it, if you can, and pain is eliminated. In the twentieth century, advances in medicine fostered this view; pain and illness were things that could, and should, be conquered.

And so this became the established way of thinking about healing as well. But this paradigm hasn't proven to be so clear-cut. An understanding of pain, its sources, and its resolution is an emerging focus of twenty-first-century medicine.

Pain Is the Body's Messenger

Pain gives us very important messages. If you touch a hot stove, pain tells you to take your hand off the stove. Acute, intense pain tells us something is wrong, and we need to change it. Pain tells us what to avoid. It's a very effective teacher.

Kabat-Zinn says that aversion to pain, though, is a misplaced aversion to suffering. It's important to make a distinction between pain and suffering. Pain is the body's natural way of informing us that something is the matter; suffering is only one possible response to the pain.

It's important to see pain as neutral. It's a signal to us. We may respond by taking action—getting away from the pain. It's how we respond to the pain that creates the suffering. Suffering is created in our thoughts and feelings about the pain.

Here's an example: Let's say we experience a minor pain at the base of the skull. It's enough to get our attention but not enough to make us black out. But it doesn't feel like an ordinary headache. The pain itself may be relatively tolerable. But if we believe it's caused by a brain tumor, and if we go to the doctor, have an MRI brain scan, and we're waiting for the results over the weekend, we can experience a great deal of agony as our thoughts are oriented to the possible diagnosis of brain cancer. Let's say we find out on Monday that the tests are negative. Then we turn our awareness to the pain itself. It feels like something we can treat with an over-the-counter pain reliever. We're still aware of the pain, but it's not as troubling to our thoughts. It doesn't color our awareness—not the way it did over the weekend!

Why It's Not Mind over Matter

Why not just ignore the pain, then? Couldn't we use meditation to activate the mind to overcome the pain? One, this kind of top-down awareness, in which the mind arm-wrestles the body into submission, is not the thrust of mindfulness. Two, the short answer is that we can't. Pain is too distracting. Ultimately, it will be querulous until it gets our attention. Of course, this assumes you have a medically diagnosed pain; if you experience a new pain, please get medical attention.

Live Mindful _____

One of Carolyn's regular magazine contributors received news of a medical test that needed further inquiry. The doctor told her to come in a week from Monday. It meant 10 heavy days of worry. The writer decided that in those 10 days she would apologize to everyone—and of course, write an essay about it. (This is just what writers do. Diagnosed with cancer? Pick up a pen.) "Apologize for what?" Carolyn asked. "For everything," the writer said, "for every time I didn't send a thank-you note, for every message I didn't return, for any time I let another person down." The test came back negative, but in the meantime, the writer had made amends with everyone on her list. And of course, she did turn in an essay.

Pain is the messenger that brings the mind to mindfulness. There are too many times when ignoring pain or distracting ourselves from pain hasn't worked. While it's considered noble to endure pain, doing so requires two things: the pain must end at some point, and we must separate our mind from our body to reach that moment, which is some-where in the future. It's an act of wholeness to tune into your pain, noticing the sensations it creates. Tuning into pain is counterintuitive, and it's not where we want to go. But it's a noble response. It's the path of pain without suffering. With mindfulness, we end the resistance and separation that create our suffering.

Additionally, we believe that the reason those who live with chronic pain retain the discipline and commitment to practice mindfulness is that mindfulness meditation practice can lead us to new levels of insight about ourselves. This is something that escape, distraction, or mind-over-matter can never do. Mind-over-matter *is* the struggle that creates suffering; mindfulness softens the struggle in the gentlest, kindest way possible.

Mindfulness is all about understanding the mind and allowing our experiences to be what they are. Through mindfulness practices, we cultivate the ability to open to pain, allowing it to be there. When we practice mindfulness, we observe the unfolding process of feeling the pain and creating our story about it. We become less caught up in our stories and more able to allow the pain to be there. Often, we discover that when we experience just the pain itself, it isn't nearly as bad as we thought it was.

Pain Meditation

As you do a pain meditation, the idea is to notice the pain, not bore into it. Place your attention on the pain, breathe into it, and see if you can relax this part of the body a little. If the pain is intolerable, see if you can place your attention around the pain. Find the edges of the pain.

Meditation teacher and psychologist Tara Brach guides people to place a hand over the pain (or if they're not comfortable doing that, to place a hand on their cheek) and then send a message of compassion and care to the pain, such as "I care about this pain." With clients who meditate, Anne will sometimes guide them to send themselves lovingkindness and compassion while focusing on the pain.

Before beginning this pain meditation, it's important to reframe your experience of the pain. Remember yourself as a whole person. You are not your pain. The part of your body that hurts is not your whole body. Remember moments of joy you have experienced. Remember activities that you enjoy and people you love. See yourself as whole—more than this pain.

Here's how to do a pain meditation. It's helpful to do this lying down, as you did with the body scan in Chapter 5:

1. Begin by reframing your story about the pain and who you are. State, "I am (your name), and it is my intention to feel joy and pleasure in my life."

2. Set an intention to meet your pain, as it is, with friendliness and compassion.

3. Do a body scan.

4. When you encounter painful areas in your body, breathe into the pain. Stay in it as long as you can. Notice how the rest of your body is reacting to this pain—are you tensing, clenching, or holding your breath? See if you can relax, even for just a moment.

5. Make soft mental notes to identify what you're experiencing. Note what sensations you're experiencing—heat, prickliness, aching. Do this gently without judgment. You're just noticing the experience, not trying to change it. Remember to breathe normally.

6. Notice the thoughts that visit you as you practice this body scan. Are you are judging the pain? Notice the statements that form in your mind, such as "This is killing me," "I don't know how much more of this I can take," or "I'll just hold on a little while longer. This won't last too long." Remember that these are just thoughts about the pain; they are not the pain itself.

7. Allow yourself to be aware of the physical sensations RIGHT NOW. Are they tolerable RIGHT NOW, in this moment? If you find yourself tensing this area, notice that. But bring yourself back to this moment only, noticing the physical sensations that are present RIGHT NOW. Often when we experience intolerable pain, it's because we are anticipating the next moment, and we tense up, believing that the next moment will be more painful.

8. If this moment is tolerable, stay in this moment and breathe through it.

9. Let each moment unfold, experiencing the pain from moment to moment.

10. Do this for as long as is tolerable or when you feel complete.

Stay aware during this meditation. Note your physical sensations. This tender moment of compassion opens the door to understanding that not only are these thoughts not the pain itself, but you are not your pain. It's the beginning of seeing that you are more than your pain. The compassion gives you a new definition for pain.

Emotional Pain: The Roots of Chronic Pain

MBSR has a tremendous effect on the emotions that crowd around physical pain. But it also has demonstrated in a myriad of studies that it can alleviate emotional pain, which is at the root of many chronic physical and psychological conditions. Mindfulness meditation gets to the heart of the emotional pain, which is masked by mind*less*ness.

The body of research showing ways to use MBSR and other mindfulness awareness practices grows every day. A 1992 study published in the *American Journal of Psychiatry* showed that MSBR decreased panic attacks in patients with anxiety disorders; it also demonstrated a 25 to 65 percent decrease in depression and anxiety. More recently, a 2000 study in the *Journal of Consulting and Clinical Psychology* showed that depressed patients who received Mindfulness-Based Cognitive Therapy (MBCT), an outgrowth of MBSR, experienced a 66 percent gain in stability. Many of these studies also demonstrate a remarkable rate of sustainability—meaning that patients rarely relapse.

Liberation from Pain

A part of you is aware that not all of you is in pain or is ruled by pain. That part is activated during mindfulness meditation. When we allow ourselves to observe the pain with this awareness, we can see that a part of our mind is free of these thoughts of pain.

When we meditate, we can drop below our thoughts into the thread of the present moment. We can test our thoughts about pain this way. We can test our physical sensations this way. We can experience the present moment without having to make choices about how to analyze or think about the pain. We can even be liberated from trying to solve the problem of the pain and all the problems that we have built around the pain, such as the limitations of work, ability, money, activities—whatever we perceive as a limitation caused by the pain. We can be in the present moment and know we do not need to make a choice about that NOW. In this moment, we can let go of all that.

Just Be! _____

To allow yourself to become more mindful of your pain, you must know what your story is about the pain. You must know, then, that that's all it is—a story. And you must learn how to be with it, with compassion and lovingkindness.

Try doing three 10-minute mindful writing practices on these topics, using these prompts:

I suffer because of this pain.

The origin of this pain is …

My story about this pain is …

Tenderly, softly, I greet this pain.

Think about what you no longer need about this story. See beyond the limitations you believe exist in the moment when you feel the familiar throb or spasm. See the whole picture of you with the pain as only part of it.

Even though I feel this pain now, I can …

Even as I feel this pain, I know …

Mindful Therapies

Mindfulness-based forms of psychotherapy are coming more and more into the mainstream. MBCT grew out of MBSR, and it's been shown to be effective for treating depression. Dialectical Behavior Therapy (DBT), developed as a treatment for Borderline Personality Disorder, includes mindfulness training. Acceptance and Commitment Therapy (ACT) uses experiential exercises to develop mindfulness, helping patients find a way to allow experience to come and go and find ways to live more meaningful lives.

Humanistic psychotherapy, with its focus on the present-moment experience and foundational belief in our capacity to heal and develop regardless of our circumstances, has a lot in common with Buddhist psychology and mindfulness practice. Psychodynamic and psychoanalytical approaches focus on the stream of experience and are based on the belief that awareness is necessary for change.

Contemplative psychotherapy and Hakomi are two forms of therapy that combine principles of humanistic psychology with fundamentals of Buddhist psychology.

Yoga: Mindfulness in Action

Yoga is an essential component of mindfulness because it gives you a practice of being in your body. Two foundations of mindfulness taught in Buddhism are breath awareness and contemplation of the body, and yoga embraces both of those. Yoga attunes you the physical sensations of moving and being in your body. It can be thought of as an active body scan because during a 30-minute or hour-long yoga practice you generally bring your attention to most every part of your body. It's for this reason that many refer to yoga as an internal massage. Most yoga sessions close with shavasana, commonly called the corpse pose because it's a lying-down position in which the body is completely relaxed.

Yoga activates the mind-body connection, and so it's an important practice in wholeness. Because many of the poses require concentration and balance, the discipline of yoga brings you to mindfulness. You must listen to the body with tenderness and care as you move through the poses.

Yoga is not like other forms of exercise, in which the athlete pushes himself or herself to improve performance. Yoga is a practice in holding yourself between effort and relaxation, just as mindfulness meditation is. That's why yogis emerge from sessions saying they feel both invigorated and relaxed.

As you move through yoga poses, you move with moment-to-moment awareness of the physical sensations of the body, using breath to work through them. Yoga is more than a way to stretch and strengthen the body, which no doubt has its benefits; it's a way to attune the breath and mind to the body.

Many people who start off learning MSBR begin with yoga. That's because they experience the wanderings of the mind during sitting meditation, and they realize they are quite distracted when they first begin to examine the activity in their minds. Yoga's discipline of being in the body keeps them in present-moment awareness and gives them a taste of the experience.

> **Breathe ...**
>
> In yoga, one of the basic principles is to do no harm. (It's one of the *yamas*, the "don'ts," along yoga's Eightfold Path, delineated in *Yoga Sutras*.) This yama is called *ahimsa*, and it means to do no harm in your actions, words, and thoughts. In yoga, we move with gentleness and reverence for the body and what it is capable of doing. We do not stretch ourselves beyond our limits. As we move through poses, we do them mindfully, staying present in the body, with the breath, noting what feels like too much. We never push ourselves to the point of pain.

Yoga teaches you to dwell in the space between the limits of what the body will do and pushing it too far. It teaches you to *be* in the body. Too often, our experience is all about *doing* something with the body. The emphasis in many forms of exercise is to get the body to perform. We do laps. We beat the previous time. We compete against others. We monitor our heart rates. We keep score.

In yoga, we challenge ourselves. But we use the breath to explore what the body can and will do. It can be different on different days. You explore what that is for you. As we explore, we explore with lovingkindness and compassion. We meet the body as a new friend.

A friend of ours experiencing chronic pain decided to begin a yoga practice. In any poses that involved stretching, her hamstrings proved especially difficult and painful, so naturally her first impulse was to fall out of poses to avoid feeling even more uncomfortable. "Lean into your discomfort, not away from it; breathe into the pain and release it," the teacher would tell her. It took many months of yoga practice for our friend to recognize the experience of painful hamstrings as a release. She came to realize that the pain proved a catalyst, a call to attention. Honoring that call did, truly, help her gently over time to release the pain and achieve balance. Instead of drowning in the pain, she felt it diffuse and begin to fade.

> **Sutras** _____
>
> *Praise and blame, gain and loss, pleasure and sorrow, fame and disrepute come and go like the wind. To be happy, rest like a great tree in the midst of them all.*
>
> —The Buddha
>
> The vicissitudes of life are the storms that pass through our landscapes, that "come and go like the wind." When we can be like a great tree, rooted and present in the moment regardless of what's happening to us and around us, we can find true happiness and peace.

Pain and You

Let pain be the messenger that leads you to a more complete you. Use the pain as a teacher and a guide, leading you to cultivate more and more moments of mindfulness in your whole life, beyond the regular practice you are establishing with mindfulness. Let the pain lead you to the experience of calmness that can result from acceptance, the stillness that comes from letting go, and the insight that comes from present-moment awareness. Let pain lead you to seeing your intrinsic wholeness, your essential self that is liberated from the pain. Skeptical? Sound too good to be true? Give it a try.

The Least You Need to Know

- ◆ Living with chronic pain can alter your sense of self; mindfulness restores your sense of self.

- ◆ Studies have shown a myriad of applications for mindfulness meditation to relieve pain.

- ◆ Your thoughts can create suffering around your pain. Use mindfulness practices to see beyond the suffering thoughts.

- ◆ Many forms of mindfulness therapy have been developed, including Mindfulness-Based Cognitive Therapy and Acceptance and Commitment Therapy.

- ◆ You are more than your pain.

- ◆ Yoga teaches you a way to fully inhabit your body with mindfulness and compassion.

Chapter 7

Mindfulness Brings Clarity, If Not Peace

In This Chapter

- ◆ One-pointed meditation vs. mindfulness
- ◆ Clarity and compassion
- ◆ A lovingkindness meditation to practice
- ◆ Soft mental notes

Present-moment awareness brings you to the truth of the moment—not a hard truth, but a soft truth that comes with the practice of clear-seeing with kindness. As we practice mindfulness meditation, we begin to see how liberating the truth can be. We begin to lay a foundation in our lives for a practice of living in clarity with courage and compassion.

Though the truth may be painful or frightening, it ultimately opens the door to new choices that free us and usher in beneficial changes. Through the practice of mindfulness meditation, we can bring about lasting changes in our lives. In this chapter we'll explore how to make those changes.

Choices in Clarity

Each moment presents a choice. Do we live here and now, or do we dwell some other place? We have a natural inclination to want to escape from what seems boring or ordinary—or worse, painful and frightening. It seems counterintuitive to face it directly, acknowledge it, and accept that it's there. We even get pretty good at telling ourselves we are present with our experience when we're actually hiding it from ourselves.

Zen Buddhist Larry Rosenberg defines insight meditation as "the practice of liberation. By making friends with our old wounds, fears, anger, and loneliness, we free ourselves."

When we are fully present with ourselves, it is as if we are flying on a great bird, Buddhist psychology tells us. And the wings of this bird are clear-seeing and compassion. With clarity, we see what's happening in each moment, and with compassion, we meet what's happening with tenderness, friendliness, and sympathy.

Concentration Meditation vs. Mindfulness Meditation

Newcomers to mindfulness meditation sometimes equate it with concentration meditation because that's the form of meditation most people know about. When meditation was introduced to the Western world on a large scale in the 1960s, the prevalent practice of meditation was concentration meditation. In concentration meditation, the meditator focuses on an object, word, chant, sacred text, or sound to the exclusion of other objects. Each time the mind wanders away from the object of concentration, the meditator returns to the focal point. This form of meditation calms the mind and develops stability that is necessary for cultivating mindfulness. When we focus on the breath, we are practicing concentration meditation.

When practicing concentration meditation, our minds can become very still, stable, and settled. We can go on a meditation retreat and feel wonderful. It's a very useful practice—both of us have experienced it—but when the retreat is over and we return to our lives, the inner stillness fades, and the old, familiar habits of our minds return.

The one-pointed attention of concentration meditation is useful as an entry point during the practice of mindfulness meditation. When we practice mindfulness meditation, we begin by concentrating on the breath. But as our minds settle and we develop stability and focus, we begin to allow our attention to focus on experiences as they present themselves in the mind. We investigate the whole of our experience, watching how our minds respond to it. For example, we may start with the breath, and then our attention is drawn to a pain in the leg—so we allow our attention to rest on the leg pain and what our mind is doing with it. This process leads to insight and understanding of our minds.

Filtered Focus vs. Denial

People can confuse the calm, settled state they achieve through concentration meditation with mindfulness, thinking that they've let go of their pain, fear, and unpleasant emotion when in fact they're avoiding it by being in a blissful state.

The filtering that occurs during one-pointed meditation is not denial, by the way. With concentration meditation, we leave those thoughts behind for a while; with denial, we are hiding from thoughts perpetually. When we practice concentration meditation, we are training the mind to be still. Returning to the breath is not a denial of what's happening; it's simply refocusing attention.

Denial is a trickster. It can be such a perpetual state that even when we practice concentration meditation—for instance, achieving a blissful state of relaxation—we believe we have released painful and frightening thoughts.

In mindfulness meditation, denied truths are right before our eyes. They hide in plain sight, believing we would never simply just acknowledge them. When we practice mindfulness, we meet these denied truths directly, with friendliness and compassion and without trying to run away or push them away.

Breathe ...

If painful truths arise during mindfulness meditation practice that flood you with fear or despair, know that you must go easy. If you have experienced a severe emotional or physical trauma, emotions that come up may feel big, powerful, and overwhelming. Give yourself comfort. Go gently. Acknowledge only what you feel ready to meet. And don't do it alone. Find a trusted friend or therapist to be your ally.

Gentle Compassion

Like the two wings of a great bird, clarity and compassion work together to bring us to mindfulness. Just as a bird with one wing cannot fly, awareness without compassion—or compassion without awareness—cannot cultivate mindfulness. It's unbalanced.

Gentle compassion builds a reservoir of resiliency that enables you to grow into mindfulness meditation practice. In her book *Radical Acceptance* (see Resources), Tara Brach describes this process as saying "yes" to our experiences. By saying yes to our experiences, we create a loving, accepting relationship with our minds.

Sometimes our first attempts to say yes can flood us with fear. It's important to stop and comfort this fear with sympathy. We may have to stop and do this before we can practice saying yes to more. We don't have to say yes to all of it, all at once. As Brach says in *Radical Acceptance*, "For the time being, saying no to what feels like too much and yes to what simply works to keep us balanced is the most compassionate response we can offer ourselves."

When we are gentle with ourselves, we limit our exposure to painful thoughts that arise in the mind. In this way, we keep our practice workable. A few years ago, Anne left a meditation retreat a day early because she felt like she was losing her mind. She had not yet learned how to keep her practice workable. Sometimes on retreat, she experiences significant anxiety that makes it extremely difficult for her to practice meditation indoors with her eyes closed. When this happens, she sits outside with her eyes wide open looking at the sky as she watches her mind. This calms her and creates enough space for her to sit with her fear without becoming engulfed by it.

Metta: Lovingkindness

A mother loves her baby, giving all her heart, mind and soul, without conditions. She acts with kindness, wishing health, happiness, well-being, and safety for her baby. This is *metta*, the Pali word for loving-kindness. It is love in action. Metta is one of the four Brahma-Viharas, or Heavenly Abodes, along with compassion, sympathetic joy, and equanimity.

Though *metta practice* is a concentration meditation, it is similar to mindfulness in that it embraces all parts of ourselves, others, and our world. It is the practice of becoming friends with our mind, embracing it with love, kindness, and unconditional acceptance.

def•i•ni•tion

Metta means lovingkindness. Because it's a selfless love, given without conditions, it's often compared to the love of a mother for her child. Metta is one of the four Brahma-Viharas, which are qualities of the heart that can be cultivated through specific concentration meditation practice. **Metta practice** is the meditation practice that cultivates lovingkindness; in this form of practice, the metta phrases are the object of concentration.

There is a parable about metta that Sharon Salzberg tells in *Joyful Mind* (by Susan Piver, see Resources) that illustrates how metta penetrates our illusions and fears. The legend goes that Buddha sent monks off into the forest to meditate, but the tree spirits so resented the monks' presence that they wanted to scare them away. They shrieked, they transformed themselves into ghouls, and they filled the forest with disgusting smells. The monks fled. They begged the Buddha to let them meditate somewhere else.

But the Buddha sent them back to the same forest, saying, "I will give you the only protection that you need." Then he taught them metta meditation, the practice of lovingkindness. So the monks went back to the forest, and the tree spirits were so moved by the lovingkindness that they welcomed the monks to the forest, offering to serve and protect them.

A Metta Meditation

Metta practice is generally practiced as a sitting meditation with eyes closed. When we say the metta phrases, we are cultivating a quality of heart rather than praying for ourselves or others. This is an important distinction. The mind can get caught up in the idea that metta practice is a prayer; please know that while praying for ourselves or others is a wonderful practice, it isn't metta practice. We say the metta phrases to open our hearts and develop lovingkindness for ourselves and our fellow beings.

Begin by getting comfortable, taking in three deep, cleansing breaths. Then breathing normally, place your attention on your heart, and spend a few moments recalling a time when you felt happy and peaceful. Allow the warmth and joy of this memory to arise in your heart.

Continue to breathe normally as you say to yourself the metta phrases. Begin by directing the phrases to yourself:

> May I be safe and protected.
>
> May I be happy and peaceful.
>
> May I be healthy.
>
> May I have ease and well-being.

Continue to repeat these phrases over and over again, directing them to yourself. If you like, you may tie the phrases to your breath, saying one phrase per breath. When you notice that your mind has wandered, place your attention back on your heart, recalling the warm feelings you began with, and begin again by repeating the phrases to yourself.

In metta practice, we start with ourselves and then move on to others. You may stick with practicing metta for yourself for as long as you like. You may decide to practice metta for yourself for the rest of this meditation session or even for the next several sessions.

When you feel ready, think of someone to whom you feel grateful or someone who has extended kindness to you. Call this person's presence to your mind, and place your attention on your heart. Repeat the metta phrases with this person in mind:

May you be safe and protected.

May you be happy and peaceful.

May you be healthy.

May you have ease and well-being.

When you feel ready, move to a neutral person, someone you neither like nor dislike, perhaps someone who is an acquaintance, or someone you see daily but don't really know. Call this person's presence to your mind, and place your attention on your heart. Repeat the metta phrases with this person in mind.

When you feel ready, move to someone with whom you have had conflict or someone who has hurt you in some way. Call this person's presence to your mind, and place your attention on your heart. Repeat the metta phrases with this person in mind.

Finally, direct metta to everyone everywhere, with no distinction as to whether you like all of them or not, whether they have helped you or hurt you. Include all beings, not just humans. Allow an image or images to arise that bring to your mind all beings all over the world. Place your attention on your heart, and repeat the metta phrases using these words:

May all beings be safe and protected.

May all beings be happy and peaceful.

May all beings be healthy.

May all beings have ease and well-being.

Enemies, Near and Far

It's especially important to be gentle and keep our practice workable as we practice metta. With metta, you may experience the near enemy of desire and the far enemy of aversion.

Salzberg says we may think we're feeling lovingkindness and compassion for someone when we are actually feeling attachment and desire. She says desire is the "near enemy" of metta because it is so well disguised. Because it feels similar, it can masquerade as metta—until it reaches its limit. But metta is boundless, Salzberg says in *Lovingkindness: The Revolutionary Art of Happiness* (see Resources). "It is open and freely given. Metta does not create a duality between subject and object; it does not try to control or hold on; it is not subject to the same fears and frailties of betrayal. Metta is based on desirelessness."

We experience desire during metta practice when we become attached to certain outcomes for ourselves or others. When this happens, we can meet this near enemy with mindfulness. We can notice the attachment arising and then return to our metta meditation.

The far enemy of metta is aversion. We call it the far enemy because it is the opposite of lovingkindness. We experience the far enemy as anger, fear, grief, disappointment, anxiety, or despair—all things we know we don't want. The far enemies are mind-states that keep us from experiencing metta. Many people—Anne included—experience a great deal of aversion when they first start doing metta practice. When we experience these far enemies during metta, we need to be very gentle and kind to ourselves. It may mean staying in the practice, greeting these enemies with compassion, or if it's overwhelming, it may mean we need to stop and do something else that's soothing and restorative. As you continue to practice, the far enemies will dissipate, paving the way for lovingkindness to unfold.

Live Mindful

The memory of Carolyn's father can be the near and far enemy in her writing. He was the near enemy when she first attended a mindful writing workshop nine months after his unexpected, tragic death. His encouragement was the reason she became a writer, and the grief was palpable. He can be the far enemy, too, when she pushes his memory away, as she did in spring 2007 in order to focus on a writing project. But her "far enemy" showed up in the form of a sign bearing his name on a construction sign at a writer's conference on Father's Day 2007. "Okay, there you are again," Carolyn said. "What do you have to tell me?" In greeting him with love and compassion, she tapped into a higher octave in her writing.

Out-of-Control Thoughts

Anne often works with clients who experience the out-of-control thoughts that define obsessive-compulsive disorder (OCD). These thoughts can be highly disturbing, filled with emotions such as rage, shame, or terror, and they can be frightening and very distressing. Such obsessive thoughts can be words or mental images, and they always feel completely uncontrollable. Anne's clients with OCD have tried all kinds of ways to make their thoughts go away, but these invariably fail. The content of the thoughts is so compelling that it's tempting to argue with them, to prove them wrong. But you can never win an argument with an obsessive thought! Other clients try to distract themselves through hard work, substance abuse, or other addictive behaviors.

Anne works with these clients by guiding them to start welcoming their thoughts in by naming them rather than arguing with them. When thoughts arise, they practice saying, "Obsessive thinking is happening." At first, they may only remember to do this occasionally, but as they return again and again to the mindfulness of these thoughts, it becomes easier and easier to remember to do.

While not everyone has obsessive-compulsive disorder, many of us experience troubling, out-of-control thoughts. It can be helpful to think of these thoughts as nasty houseguests who barge in and monopolize the conversation, shouting over everybody else and eating all your food. We can say to such guests, "I see you." When a judging thought arises in the mind, we can say, "Thank you for your input" or "Thank you very much for your thoughts, judging voice; now go sit over there."

As Anne's clients reduce their resistance to their obsessive thoughts, the thoughts begin to quiet down. Maybe the thoughts become less frequent, only popping up in moments of high stress. Or maybe the thoughts are always there, but they begin to feel less threatening, even becoming more comical than frightening. This welcoming in of obsessive thoughts is a welcoming back of some aspect of themselves.

Troubling or unwanted thoughts, as distressing as they are, are actually our wounded places calling for us to attend to them so they can heal. A Course in Miracles, a spiritual teaching, terms this "a call for love" and would say that the only thing that can be missing from any situation is love. We can think of these thoughts as a mother does when she tends to a sick or injured child. When we can embody these thoughts with the mental image of a hurt child, it changes the way we respond. We can intentionally meet them with compassion, with the wish of metta that all beings be safe, secure, happy, healed, and content. When we attend to our wounds in this way, we are practicing compassion for ourselves. Practice tending to these unwanted thoughts as you would a sick or injured child, visualizing yourself nursing the wounded places.

Uninvited Guests

We love the poem, "The Guest House," by thirteenth-century mystic Jelaluddin Rumi, which speaks of each day bringing a new arrival. Some of our thoughts come as guests of joy, others as sorrow. Some are unexpected; some bring us turmoil.

We must remember that every thought is a guest—some of which we can allow in the mind because they are familiar or pleasant; others of which are not so easy to allow into our conscious awareness. These are the aspects of our experience that we have cut ourselves off from: troubling thoughts, unpleasant memories, judging voices. Imagine them as guests knocking at the door because they want and need to be acknowledged and attended to. The more we keep these guests out, the louder they knock at the door.

Sutras

Right meditation is not escapism; it is not meant to provide hiding places for temporary oblivion. Realistic meditation has the purpose of training the mind to face, to understand, and to conquer this very world in which we live.

—Nyanaponika Thera, *Power of Mindfulness*

When we practice mindfulness, we are training our minds to face life and all that it offers us directly, meeting it with friendliness and acceptance. Mindfulness is not a drug that gives us relief from the world; it's a practice that helps us live fully engaged in the world.

Opening the Door

Mindfulness practices are a way to start opening the door and letting these guests in. Maybe the guests are so troubling that we can't really open the door at first—that's okay. As long as we're approaching the door, acknowledging that they're there, we're practicing mindfulness and inclining ourselves in the right direction for healing to happen. Here are five steps for opening the door:

1. **Set an intention.** Commit to being willing to meet your mind— all guests, friends, near enemies, far enemies.

2. **Note the thought.** Making a soft mental note is one of the ways we can welcome these guests.

3. **Come to the body.** When we place our attention in the body, we are also removing ourselves from the thoughts as well as noticing other aspects of our experience. We are taking ourselves out of the story we build around these difficult sensations and experiences.

4. **Disengage from the thought.** Making a soft mental note and coming back into the body are ways to disengage from the thought.

5. **Let it pass.** By noting "thinking" or "judging," we are acknowledging the thought, allowing it to be in the mind without resistance, giving it space. This allows it to pass through the mind.

Thoughts in and of themselves have no value. They only have as much weight as the meaning we give them. With the clarity gained through mindfulness practice, we know we are free to release thoughts that are not concrete reality or absolute truth.

Both making a soft mental note and placing our attention in the body create space around the experiences in the mind. It reduces resistance, allowing the thoughts and experiences to pass through. These practices are ways of witnessing our experience without engaging with it, resisting it, or making it stronger.

Free to See Clearly

It is through the practice of meeting your mind with friendliness that you gain clarity about which thoughts serve you and which thoughts are not necessary. Before mindfulness, we pushed away thoughts because they were painful, and we called that letting go. But the ability to disengage from a thought that holds us and let it pass comes from the practice of mindfulness. We set ourselves free to observe our inner and outer reality without commentary. We are free to be in the truth. We can rest peacefully in the truth. We've practiced it.

The Least You Need to Know

- ◆ The two wings of mindfulness practice are clear-seeing and compassion.

- ◆ Concentration meditation is focusing your thoughts on an object, word, chant, sacred text, or sound. While mindfulness practice may use concentration, it is the practice of focusing on the present moment that sets it apart from concentration meditation.

- ◆ Meet painful truths that arise during meditation with lovingkindness and compassion.

- ◆ Keep your practice workable. You don't have to say yes to it all at once. You can say no to what feels like too much.

- ◆ Metta practice is meditation practice that cultivates lovingkindness.

- ◆ Desire is the near enemy of lovingkindness; aversion is the far enemy.

Part 3

Practicing Mindfulness Meditation

The essential components of mindfulness meditation practice are sitting and walking meditation, yoga, and breath awareness. In this part, we'll instruct you in mastering those techniques for your mindfulness meditation practice, and we'll introduce ways to expand your practice—from mindful driving to mindful writing. Through practicing these techniques, you'll lay a strong foundation to make being mindful simply the way you live.

Chapter 8

Sitting, Walking, and Writing: Nourishing Mindfulness

In This Chapter

- ◆ Sitting meditation
- ◆ Writing mindfully
- ◆ Walking meditation
- ◆ Practicing mindfulness while driving
- ◆ Focal points

Sitting meditation, one of the foundational components of mindfulness meditation, is a practice in being. It's a way to nourish your practice by dwelling in your mind and body. With sitting meditation, you train yourself to experience moments of peacefulness and stillness amidst activity.

And, as you see when we discuss walking meditation and mindful driving, you can experience tranquility even if you're the one doing the activity. In this chapter, we'll show you how to be where you already are.

The "Doing" Mind vs. the "Being" Mind

The activity of the mind is incessant and relentless, or at least it seems that way. We spend much of our lives doing, striving, planning, deciding, and problem-solving. We accomplish things. But we do a lot of this robotically, and we fail to realize how much of our activity is driven by our minds.

Jon Kabat-Zinn calls this "unbridled doing." We can live for years this way, without taking time to observe the mind and all of its thinking—thinking about doing. Our lives lack the reflective quality that neuroscientist and psychiatrist Daniel J. Siegel points out is vital for nourishing the function of the brain, improving the quality of our relationships, and fostering learning and creativity.

Our awareness of the mind's raucous activity tends to quell its illusion that it rules. Once you are aware of mind*less*ness, it enables you to fix the problem. It's a bit like the mother who returned in *The Cat in the Hat* after an afternoon of mayhem, with Thing One and Thing Two put away. "What happened while I was gone?" Mother may have asked the children. "Oh nothing …."

Guidelines for Sitting Meditation

Sitting meditation is the heart of mindfulness meditation practice because it enables you to "nourish your being" as Kabat-Zinn puts it. But you might ask, why sitting—why not lying down if you want to achieve relaxation? Sitting is a way of staying active, balancing effort with relaxation, staying in intention. Mindfulness meditation is not passive, as you know; you stay engaged in observing the activity of the mind. Even if your eyes are closed, you are wakeful. Sitting in an erect but comfortable posture is a way of achieving that balance.

Let's get started:

1. **Choose a place.** It's important to have a quiet place, free of distractions and protected from interruptions. Beyond that, you may want to place objects in the space that reinforce your meditative

purpose. You want it to feel like a sacred and peaceful place. You may want to create an altar with a flower or sacred image. Do this with joy. This is a way of nourishing your domain. What you experience on the outside reflects your inner reality.

2. **Set an intention.** Let your intention be simple: "I am meeting my mind, acknowledging whatever arises."

3. **Choose a time.** Only you can choose the time that works for you. If you are a morning person, that's great, but if you are a night owl, you may have to experiment with different times, perhaps during the day, before dinner, or before bed. Ten minutes is a good duration for starting out. Forty-five minutes is a good duration for regular practice.

4. **Take a good posture.** You may sit on the floor on a cushion, or you may sit on a chair. Sit forward on your sit bones with straight but not rigid posture. If you choose a chair, choose one where you can keep both feet flat on the floor. You may want to use a pillow on your lower back for support. If you sit on the floor and use a cushion, keep your sit bones on the front third of the cushion. This tilts the pelvis at a good angle for aligning the spine. Sit cross-legged with your knees on the ground or supported by pillows. Your hips should be higher than your knees.

It's important to keep your spine aligned, with your head, neck, and back aligned vertically, because this allows your breath to flow easily.

Kabat-Zinn describes taking your sitting meditation posture as a "dignified posture," something that is "mountainlike in majesty and solidity." A good posture speaks of stability and signals your intentions for your practice. Zen teacher Suzuki Roshi has equated taking "right posture" with enlightenment. To take this kind of posture is itself right mindfulness.

5. **Rest your hands comfortably** on your lap or on your knees. Relax any areas of tension you notice in your body.

6. **Be with your breath.** Start with three deep, cleansing breaths. Scan your body for areas of tension. Resettle yourself. Send your breath to those areas. Breathe naturally, paying attention to your

breath. Don't manipulate your breath in any way. When you notice your mind has wandered, gently return to the breath. You may make a soft mental note, such as *Thinking*. Some people prefer not to use labels because that's another form of thinking. If you can notice without labeling, try it for a while to see if that works for you.

Expanding Your Awareness

You may work with the breath alone for as long as you like—the first few minutes of each sitting or the first several weeks (or longer) of your practice. When you're ready, you can begin to work with other experiences in the mind.

When you're ready to work with other experiences, you can expand your awareness to all sensory perceptions, noting what you're experiencing. Opening your awareness to hearing is a good way to start. Just notice the hearing, if you can, rather than what's being heard: *hearing.* If your attention is drawn to the temperature in the room or a tingling sensation in the leg, note that, too: *chilly, tingling.* Continue to note what you're receiving through your senses. At any point, you can return to the breath as an anchor, a way to steady your practice and calm the mind. Also, whenever your sense perceptions quiet down and nothing's calling your attention, return to the breath.

You will no doubt notice discomfort in the body. Pain and physical discomfort are wonderful objects of mindfulness practice because we tend to have so much aversion to them. If the pain isn't unbearable, try working with it mindfully, noting the sensations of pain: *heat, numbness, pulsing.* If the pain is unbearable, shift your body quietly and then notice how the sensations change. Remember, this is a gentle practice.

If you feel anxious or agitated at all, try opening your eyes and letting your focus soften on a spot on the ground. You can also use awareness of hearing or the sensations in your hands as an anchor if focusing on the breath feels too threatening.

As you continue to practice with labeling your thoughts and sense perceptions, you'll begin to notice the ways your mind creates a story. You can label these experiences, too: *future, past, story, judging.* You can try noticing how these thoughts and perceptions feel: *pleasant, unpleasant, neutral.* The words you use to label your experience aren't important. Simple labels like *thinking* and *feeling* work just fine.

It may take time and practice for mindfulness to become strong enough to embrace a wide array of thoughts, feelings, and sensations. If you have not regularly meditated or meditated at all, you may feel overwhelmed when you open the door and allow yourself to experience the full spectrum of your mind. So go slow and start with breath awareness, letting your awareness gradually ripple out to embrace more. Remember, keep it workable. As Kabat-Zinn says in *Wherever You Go, There You Are,* "try it for a few years and see what happens."

When Carolyn first attended a Natalie Goldberg writing retreat in Taos, New Mexico, she had goals. She wanted to complete a short-story collection and a novel—in a week. Now, writers are easy to get to know because all you have to do is ask, "What are you writing?" When Carolyn asked one devotee of writing and meditation what she was writing, the answer was that she wasn't. She was just doing the practice. She had committed to doing writing practice for two years before she would even think about starting a book. Carolyn simply did not get it. She was accustomed to the daily discipline of journalism, in which you get the near-instantaneous gratification of seeing your words in print. The other writer said she would know when it was time. It's only through years of practicing, writing her way through the hills and valleys of life, that Carolyn has come to understand that this was not clever procrastination on the writer's part. Through writing practice, Carolyn has come to meet and understand her mind—her personal inner landscape. Some writers call it "voice" when they discover this fresh, vital energy that guides their writing.

Mindful Writing

Mindful writing is closely akin to sitting meditation; workshops with Natalie Goldberg emphasize sitting meditation as a prelude to the practice and sometimes include weeklong silent retreats. With sitting meditation, you train yourself to sit and be with your thoughts, even when you'd rather run and hide. With mindful writing, you train yourself to sit and be with the page, even when you don't like what you're filling up the page with. For writers, it's the key to busting through writer's block; for journal writers, it's the key to transforming the thoughts that cause suffering.

In mindful writing, you spill your thoughts on the page as they come in. The practice reminds Carolyn of the line from the Beatles' song, "Across the Universe," which John Lennon wrote after practicing meditation in the 1960s. He described his words like rain spilling into a paper cup. When he tapped into them, they were endless. Some were positive ("waves of joy"); some were negative ("pools of sorrow"). He described the feeling of not being able to—or even wanting to—control them when he wrote about them drifting through a mind he had allowed to open to all these thoughts. He described the words as "possessing and caressing" him.

Mindful writing is useful as a tool to supplement mindfulness meditation because it's a way to record our honest, unfiltered feelings. Or, alternately, we may notice as we are writing that we resist recording certain feelings. But because we are mindful as we write, noting body sensations and breath as well as the thoughts that spill forth, we notice the resistance. We notice what we struggle with, what we don't want to commit to the page, or what we'd like to cross out from the page. We notice when our minds unleash a torrent of distractions—sending us wild, creative thoughts that have to do with anything and everything but the present moment (or the present moment of the moment we're writing about). We can also notice grasping—the self-congratulatory thoughts that have us "off to the races." These are the times when the words spill onto the page. We can't write it all down fast enough. The commentary of the mind sounds much like a sportscaster calling a thoroughbred race, narrating a stunning photo finish.

This is different from inspiration, which is what John Lennon described as his songwriting process in "Across the Universe." He was describing a moment when he let the muse flow without commentary.

Monkey Mind

Probably the first revelation for people in Carolyn's workshops is the endless chatter of their minds. Carolyn often refers to the first 10-minute warm-up write as "deep diarrhea," a play on the words "deep diary" and, well … you get the idea. Your mind runs on.

But it's also striking how quickly people get to the heart of the matter. Even in a 10-minute free-write, they get below the surface chatter of the mind to the true essence of the moment they are writing about. We call these gems. They are often the topics that will guide the writer as he or she writes to discover his or her voice and true purpose.

We get to the heart of the matter because we quickly get bored with the incessant chatter of the mind. We call that "monkey mind." It's the reason that we teach the discipline of keeping the pen moving as the abiding principle of mindful writing. We write the next sentence no matter what it is. Just as with sitting meditation, we acknowledge the next thought no matter what it is. Generally, in mindful writing, it only takes two sentences of "I'm so bored with this" or "I'm distracted by the hum of the air conditioner" before our minds cease with the incessant small talk and go below the surface to what truly intrigues and inspires us.

In writing workshops and writing practice groups, Carolyn typically begins with a 10-minute writing session to cleanse the mind, followed by a 15-minute writing session, and a longer 20- to 30-minute writing session. Some writing sessions can be 45 minutes and can yield powerful writing.

The Mind as an Editor

Because it is writing practice, not just sitting meditation, mindful writing brings out the evaluator in our minds more strongly. It is the practice itself that quiets the editor in the mind. The evaluator wants to censor the writer, "Don't write that," "You can't write that; it's embarrassing," "That's not good writing; you're not a writer" or—Carolyn's personal favorite—"This is crap."

Keep the pen moving. If you have to write the words, "This is crap" (and Carolyn has many times), then write that. You will write through it. Carolyn has written a lot of crap and has the notebooks to prove it, but she has also written seven published nonfiction books, two memoirs, many published literary short stories, several essays, a monthly column in her magazine for eight years, and most of all a novel. You will push back the monkey mind, which wants to take you out of the present moment and into the mind's stories, interpretations, judgments, and strivings. Come back to the page. Feel your hand grasping the pen. See the ink flowing onto the paper. Notice the paper absorbing the ink. Notice the loops and swirls of your handwriting. Come back into the room. Hear the rattle in the air conditioner, the puppy barking, the folksinger on the intercom. Spill it onto the page.

With mindful writing, your task is not to write a piece of the most fabulous writing any writer has ever penned. It is to be in the present moment, here with your mind.

Your mind also says wonderful things about you, such as, "That was a smokin' line. You're such a good writer" or "Now, that's something interesting to write about. Let's write more about that. You always write well when you write about that." These thoughts, too, take us out of the present moment. We leap into the future when we imagine our sterling prose gracing a published page in a book, inspiring readers with our insights. Or we leap ahead into what we're going to write instead of letting the creative process unfold, as it is, in this moment, flawed, filled with awkward images and cluttered sentences.

> **Breathe ...**
>
> Self-congratulatory thoughts ("No one has ever done a finer job") are pleasant little friends. But they transport you to the future—the reward, or approval, or the big payoff for your effort. Follow these thoughts with a more genuine: "I so enjoy creating this moment." Stay here with it now—not as it will be, but as it is.

That's why a vital component of mindful writing practice is reading aloud. At the end of a free-write, group members share their writing aloud. The purpose is neither to embarrass nor glorify the writer. It is merely to allow the writing to *be*. Other members of the group do not comment unless the group has agreed on "recall," which we'll describe in a moment. Just as you do with sitting meditation, when you greet your thoughts, acknowledging them with an "I see you" or "Thank you for your input," so do the other members of the writing group.

This aspect of the practice has the effect of bringing the writer back into the present. By simply allowing the writing to be without manipulating it, interpreting it, or evaluating it, this newly created being—a piece of writing—is allowed to breathe. In a typical writing group, writing is shared in order for the writer to receive encouragement. The writer wants to hear, "I like your writing." Not so with mindful writing.

It's difficult to snap out of this expectation. Just as with sitting mindfulness meditation, we are accustomed to wanting a result—a trophy that marks the achievement, such as saying we've accomplished 45 minutes of sitting meditation and reduced our blood pressure, or doing three free-writes and completing a piece. But writing, whether it's for the purpose of developing a piece or whether it's for the purpose of self-knowledge, needs to simply be what it is for a while.

Recall: The Resonating Power of the Present Moment

Recall is a form of mindfulness that Carolyn often uses in writing workshops and can be used to enhance other forms of mindfulness such as mindful listening. The group is instructed to play back key images or lines from the piece that is read aloud. It keeps the listeners mindful, and it's useful feedback for the writer. It gives the writer valuable information. Recall points the way to the lines that resonated—and *always* the lines that resonated are the lines that were the most present.

Recall shines light on the mind's wanderings; when the mind wanders back into the present moment, the moment feels alive and with purpose. A fully realized piece—Carolyn calls them *pebbles*—is a piece that has this quality of a resonating present moment. Even if the event the writer is describing is an event in the past, it's clear that the writer (or the character) was present in that moment as it was lived and as it was imagined.

Over time, the mindful writer becomes trained to hear this in his or her own writing. The mindful meditator can use mindful writing and mindful listening, which we'll discuss in Chapter 19, to hone this technique.

Walking Meditation

Buddhist teacher Thich Nhat Hanh says, "Peace is every step." Sitting in mindfulness meditation may not be for you, but you may find you can get deeply into mindfulness through walking. If you experience a lot of chronic pain, it may be hard to sit for a long time and stay mindful. If you have a lot of bottled-up anger, sitting may make you feel too agitated.

The key to walking meditation is how you keep your mind. Just as in sitting meditation we focus on the breath, in walking meditation we focus on the sensations of walking. We are not walking to get to a certain place or to get a workout. In formal walking meditation practice, we choose a lane 10 to 20 paces long and walk back and forth in this lane.

Begin your walking meditation by standing and taking a few nice, full breaths. Place your attention in your body and notice what it feels like to be standing. Shift your weight slightly to see what that feels like. Begin walking, keeping your awareness on the walking itself. Walk at a speed that enables you to stay present with the movement of your body; you may find that walking slowly allows this, or you may need to walk at a more regular pace. Notice each footfall. Keep your eyes on the path in front of you. (Don't look at your feet, if you can help it.) Allow your arms to swing freely and naturally. Notice the shifting of weight between your left and right legs as you walk. If you're walking slowly, notice the actions of lifting, moving, and placing each foot. It's helpful to make a soft mental note as you do this: "lifting, moving, placing." When you notice your mind has wandered, gently return your attention to the walking.

Nature Walk

Transcendental writer Henry David Thoreau spent two years in retreat at Walden Pond. Kabat-Zinn calls it a "personal experiment in mindfulness." Nature brings us to the wonder and simplicity of the experience of life. It can bring us back into the freshness of the present moment as if experiencing it for the first time.

Walking the Labyrinth

The labyrinth is a path that leads you to the center, folding back on itself. It is a symbol found in nearly every religious tradition in the world—Chartres Cathedral in France; the Celtic knot, often called the Never Ending Circle; in Native American spirituality, the Medicine Wheel; in Tibetan Buddhism, the mandala. As a symbol, it can be a powerful tool on which to focus a concentration meditation or insight meditation. As a path to walk, it can be a powerful tool for mindfulness.

Labyrinths can be found in churches, at retreat centers, and on college campuses, among other places. Some labyrinths are indoors, and some are outdoors. You can find a directory online at wwll.veriditas. labyrinthsociety.org.

Unlike a maze, which has many tricks and dead ends, the labyrinth leads only one place—to the center. When you walk a labyrinth, you enter at the same place you will exit. The path is in full view, which enables you to focus within. You are walking, which keeps you in the present moment.

In walking the labyrinth, you practice as you do with the walking meditation. You let your mind come to the present-moment sensations of walking, noticing your breath, quieting your mind, and noticing your footfalls.

Mindful Driving

We lead hectic, busy lives. For many of us, the car has become a place to have precious alone time. Some people like to listen to music in the car, some like to sing, others like to pray or "think out loud," and some like to listen to National Public Radio or books on tape. But we can use our driving time to practice mindfulness. And like following the breath and walking, driving is something we're always doing when we're at the wheel, and it's something we often do on autopilot.

Just Be!

Stuck in traffic? What a waste of time, we may think. When we are spread thin and traffic throws off the plan for the day, it can fuel our thoughts into a rage. Road rage has become such a problem that the Vatican has issued a Ten Commandments for the road. The guidelines say that driving is a matter of virtue. In addition to practicing charity (courtesy to other drivers), prudence (no cell phones), and justice (obey the traffic laws), the guidelines suggest that while stopped in traffic, faithful Catholics pray using the rosary, essentially a form of concentration meditation.

Practicing mindful driving means paying attention to the act of driving and the feelings of movement—both the small movements of the body in operating the car and the overall forward movement and speed of being in a vehicle traveling down the road. You can roll down the windows and feel the movement of air around you. Just notice what's happening for you as you drive. Pay attention to your attitude about driving—are you rushing, or are you taking your time? What thoughts and stories are you aware of?

A variation of this is to use stoplights as a meditation bell for a mini-sitting meditation. Follow your breath as you wait for the light to change.

Sutras: Focal Points for Mindfulness

The sutras that we introduced in Chapter 1, you'll notice, have been sprinkled through the chapters. Sutras can serve as focal points for mindfulness meditation to bring us back to be fully present with our life as it unfolds. They can bring us back to the wisdom beneath the chatter of the mind, which distracts us from the wholeness of the present moment.

The word *sutra* means "threads" in Sanskrit, and it derives from the verb *to sew*. It literally means a rope or thread, and it can be a lifeline in your mindfulness meditation practice—the rope that pulls you back into present-moment awareness. We like to think of the sutras as the stitches that weave your mind into the present moment. As you study them, you will gain in aptitude—you'll be more fully united with the present moment.

Reciting a sutra at the beginning of any mindfulness meditation practice, whether it's sitting, writing, walking, driving, or another activity, can help you set an intention for the practice. It can illuminate and inform the way you stay in the present moment. You can recite it aloud as a focal point that returns you to the present moment. We'll go into more depth about the various ways you can use breath and other focal points in your practice in Chapter 9.

Sutras

He who knows that all things are his mind
That all with which he meets are friendly
Is ever joyful

—*The Hundred Thousand Songs of Milarepa,* translated by Garma C. C. Chang

As we begin this journey of meeting our minds, we can be uncomfortable or frightened with what we find there. Remember, these are just thoughts and perceptions passing through your landscape; they aren't your enemy. Meet them with friendliness.

The Least You Need to Know

- ◆ Developing sitting meditation as a disciplined practice is a way to nourish your being.

- ◆ As you practice sitting meditation, let your awareness gradually expand from the breath to sensory perceptions.

- ◆ Like sitting meditation, mindful writing is something that seems like nothing. It's only by practicing it that you know what it is.

- ◆ With walking meditation, notice the actions of each foot, making soft mental notes: lifting, moving, placing.

- ◆ Many people find mindful driving helpful because this is a time when we often are rushing and shutting ourselves off from the experience of movement.

- ◆ Think of the sutras in this book as lifelines for your mindfulness meditation practice, pulling you back into present-moment awareness and compassion.

Chapter 9

Mindful Breathing

In This Chapter

- ◆ Breath awareness
- ◆ Effective breath techniques
- ◆ Full-sensory writing
- ◆ Nature, stones, beads, and chimes

Breath awareness is essential to mindfulness. It serves as a focal point, bringing you back into your body, returning you gently to the present moment. But its power is greater than that: breath restores us to wholeness.

This simple tool, which is always available to us, has the power to transform our thoughts of craziness, fear, shame, and sorrow. In this chapter, we'll show you how breath points the way to the healing power of mindfulness.

The Secret Weapon of Mindfulness

Breath, in and of itself, is nourishing to the body. Every time you take in a breath, you are filling your lungs, which nourish the blood. The blood delivers this sustenance to every cell of the body. Breath is regulated by the brain, as well as neural cells in the heart (yes, it's true, there are neural cells in the heart—in fact, 65 percent of the neural cells in the body reside in the heart). This places breath right at the intersection of the mind-body connection.

Neuroscientist and psychiatrist Daniel J. Siegel (*The Mindful Brain*) says it well when he says, "Breath awareness brings us to the heart of our lives." Breath brings us to the place where conscious effort and automatic activity meet.

Breath awareness is more than a focal point that gets us started on the journey of mindfulness. It *is* the map. And it's the sustenance. Breath nourishes us. It brings us back into wholeness, igniting interconnectivity through all systems and all levels of the body. Breath has the power to integrate our experience on the physical, mental, emotional, and spiritual dimensions. For this reason, it's more than a technique for activating the mind-body connection or managing pain. It's a tool for transformation.

Breath awareness creates a sense of home in the body that enables us to welcome in the full range of thoughts that pass through the mind. It awakens us to feel alive in our bodies and at home in our lives, even with the pain. It creates the openings that allow for compassion, loving-kindness, and the forgiveness that transmutes disease, illness, and pain. The practice doesn't make them go away; it points the way for us to dwell more peaceably with them.

Pranayama as a Practice

In yoga, breath awareness practice is called *pranayama*, which uses breathing to influence the flow of life force through the body. In Sanskrit, *prana* means vital energy or life force, and *ayama* means extension or expansion. When yogis talk about the vital energy of life, they see it as the force of a greater power—what we might call God, Allah, Yahweh, Creator, or Source. It's one of the eight million names of God.

def•i•ni•tion

Pranayama is breath awareness. In meditation or yoga practice, breath awareness is a focal point that calms the mind and activates the mind-body connection. Pranayama literally means expansion of vital energy.

So pranayama is the expansion of the dimension of the life force. It activates the life force, enabling us to go beyond the limitations of flesh, bone, and blood to attain a higher state of vibrating and attuned energy.

Ancient yogis knew something about the healing power of the breath. They equated slow breath rate with longevity, noting that turtles, pythons, and elephants had longer life spans than birds, dogs, and rabbits. They knew that pranayama restores tranquility to the mind, and they used it as an essential prelude to spiritual practice.

Shallow Breathing, Shallow Existence

Many of us, much of the time, use only a fraction of our lung capacity. We stay in a state of shallow breathing, which deprives the body of oxygen. We are not fully nourished. What's happening in our bodies with each shallow breath is parallel to the chattering mind that holds us above the surface of our lives, not allowing us to fully experience them.

Just as shallow breathing deprives the body of oxygen, the distractions of the chattering mind disconnect us from important resources in our inner landscapes. The noisy thoughts can make it difficult for us to know how we're feeling in this moment or what's really happening around us. When we return to the present moment, we can reconnect with our inner resources and make more authentic choices about our lives. We can notice the shallowness of our breathing and make the choice to breathe more deeply.

Breath Techniques

The effectiveness of many breath techniques lies in their ability to break through the fight-or-flight response that creates shallow breathing. They bring the mind back to the focus of the present moment. *Alternate nostril breathing* is one of the most common breath techniques practiced with mindfulness meditation for that very reason. It is one of five basic breath techniques in yoga, along with *natural breathing*, which is practiced in sitting meditation or yoga's shavasana, the closing relaxation pose; *abdominal breathing; thoracic breathing;* and *yogic breathing.*

Ujjayi, or victorious breath, is often used in mindfulness meditation or during yoga as the yogi is moving into a pose. Ujjayi is invigorating, increasing focus and concentration. It is often called ocean-sounding breath.

Cooling breath is the other breath-awareness technique we'll introduce here. And finally, we'll close with a variation on the "glittering sand" meditation, which Carolyn developed with Erica Tismer in their book, *Empowering Your Life with Massage* (see Resources).

> ### Sutras
>
> *So don't be in a hurry and try to push or rush your practice. Do your meditation gently and gradually, step by step. In regard to peacefulness, if you become peaceful, then accept it; if you don't become peaceful, then accept that also. That's the nature of the mind. We must find our own practice and persistently keep at it.*
>
> —Ajahn Chah
>
> When we practice mindfulness, we relax into what's happening in the moment, honoring ourselves by not forcing or rushing our experience. Being mindful is about dropping into the present moment, just as it is.

Alternate-Nostril Breathing

Alternate-nostril breathing is a technique that deftly brings you into the present moment. It's a simple but effective way to practice breath awareness to come to mindfulness.

1. Take a good posture either sitting on the floor or in a chair. Hold the fingers of your right hand in front of your face.

2. Rest your index and middle fingers gently between your eyebrows. Keep the fingers relaxed. Your thumb should be above your right nostril, and your ring finger should be above your left nostril.

3. Close the right nostril with the thumb.

4. Breathe through the left nostril through five inhalation and exhalation cycles. Stay aware of each breath.

5. Release the pressure of the thumb on the right nostril.

6. Press the left nostril closed with your ring finger.

7. Breathe through the left nostril through five inhalation and exhalation cycles. Stay aware of each breath.

This breath awareness exercise can feel very cleansing. You may use it to return to a more alert and engaged state of mind.

Victorious Breath

Ujjayi, or victorious breath, is a good technique to use at the beginning or close of a sitting meditation to come into focus. Because it's good for concentration, it's also a good companion to yoga's standing (Warrior) and balance (Tree, Eagle) poses as you may use it as you pause during walking meditation. Ujjayi breath is named so because it means to conquer; ujjayi is liberating.

1. Bring your awareness to the breath, inhaling through the nose. Allow your breathing to become calm and rhythmic.

2. Move your awareness to your throat. Contract your throat as you inhale. Some people find it helpful to bunch up the tongue in the back of the throat or to whisper an "h" sound. For others, all they need to be told is to breathe like Darth Vader in *Star Wars*. If you are doing it correctly, there will be a corresponding contraction in the abdomen.

3. Keep your breathing long, deep, and controlled.

4. Concentrate on the sound made by the breath in the throat.

5. Do this for as long as necessary to feel complete.

This breath technique is believed to soothe the nervous system and tap into the intuitive level, unlocking the mind into more subtle states. Many people have found that it relieves insomnia.

Cooling Breath

Cooling breath, or sheetali pranayama, restores balance to the body. It cools the body and the mind, regulating its functions, calming the stress response, and encouraging a free flow of prana through the body. Many yoga and breath practitioners believe it reduces blood pressure and aids insomnia.

1. From a comfortable sitting-meditation posture, close your eyes, and relax the whole body.

2. Extend your tongue outside your mouth as far as possible without straining.

3. Roll up the sides of your tongue so that it forms a tube.

4. Inhale, drawing breath through this tube.

5. At the end of the inhalation, draw your tongue in the mouth, close your mouth, and exhale through the nose.

6. Repeat nine more rounds for a total of ten.

The noise you make as you're breathing should sound like the rushing wind. Notice the sensation of icy coolness on the top of the tongue and the roof of the mouth.

Abdominal Breathing

In Mindfulness-Based Stress Reduction (MBSR) clinics across the country, abdominal breathing, or diaphragmatic breathing, has proven to be beneficial to the practice. This is breathing into the belly.

The diaphragm is the umbrella-shaped muscle at the base of the rib cage. It's a wall between the chest cavity and the abdominal cavity. When we breathe from only the top part of our lungs, we aren't allowing the diaphragm to expand the chest cavity so that we can take in more air. When we relax the belly, we allow the diaphragm to push more air into the belly, allowing the lungs to expand more.

1. Start by lying on your back. You may lie on a bed, couch, or on the floor with a mat or pillows.

2. Close your eyes. Place one hand on your belly. Your hand should rest just below your belly button.

3. Bring your awareness to your hand, and feel it move as you breathe in and out.

4. Continue for three to five minutes.

If this is gentle and subtle, you are doing it right. Your belly should rise only a little. Do not try to force the movement. This breathing exercise may be practiced with a body scan, or it may be practiced in yoga's shavasana pose.

Breathe ...

"Just breathe" is the advice people often give when others experience nervous anticipation about an event, such as speaking pub-
licly or going to the dentist. Instinct tells us to take a deep breath when
we face a conflict or prepare someone for bad news. Breath nourishes
us and grounds us.

Glittering-Sand Breathing

This breath-awareness exercise is a hybrid of concentration and mindfulness meditation, using visualization to direct the breath. It's a good
prelude for a mindfulness practice because it brings you back into the
body. It creates a visual focal point that can anchor you in mindfulness.
Every time your mind wanders off, bring your awareness back to the
sensation of breath and the image of the glittering sand.

1. Take a good sitting-meditation posture.

2. Breathe in and out of your mouth three times with three deep,
   cleansing breaths.

3. Bring your awareness to your spine. With the next inhalation, see
   in your mind's eye a glittery thread of sand rising up the left side
   of your spine.

4. As you exhale, see the glittering sand cascade down the right side
   of your spine.

5. Maintain this focus on the inhalation and exhalation for eight minutes. (Set a timer.) Maintain the rhythm of your breath. As your
   thoughts come, note them, and send them on their way.

6. Bring into your awareness the sense of this glittering sand within
   you. See the sun shining on the sand. Let this dazzling light represent the now. Feel the sparkle in your body, igniting with each rise
   and fall of the breath. Imagine the glittering sand massaging you
   on the inside.

7. Dwell in the glow of the now, keeping your awareness on the rising and falling of the breath. Continue for three more minutes.

The image, which uses the left and right sides of the spine, is parallel to that of alternate-nostril breathing. It can serve the purpose of restoring an inner balance between both sides of the body, between logic and intuition, between past and future, resting peacefully in the space between—the now. The "now" is the place of perfect balance.

When you find your thoughts wander to the past, see in your mind's eye the release of the exhalation down the right side of the spine. When you find your thoughts veer off into the future, imagine the inhalation drawing the breath up the left side of the spine.

Fully Realized Moments

In Carolyn's yoga and mindful-writing workshops, she trains writers to hear the fully realized moment in their writing. It's the moment when the writer was fully present in the story. The knowledge that one is writing about a moment can be a focal point, like the breath, bringing us back to observing the moment as is, for its true quality, pure of preconception. It can spur us to activate our senses, so that we experience the moment on all dimensions, noticing sensations that we might otherwise filter out if not for the commitment to the intention to write about this fully realized moment.

The intention to write about a moment also can be liberating. We allow ourselves to see and notice what we might otherwise have rushed past or shut out. Often in mindful practice, we use prompts such as, "What I am seeing right now is ..." or "In this moment, I am feeling ...." Each time the writer hits a snag or lull, the writer returns to this phrase. The phrase is a focal point, like the breath, that brings us back to our sensory awareness of the present moment.

Breath awareness brings us back to our senses—what we're hearing, what we're seeing, what we're tasting, touching, and smelling.

Our senses are the bridge between our inner and outer landscapes. They bring us to wholeness. Jon Kabat-Zinn says it well in *Coming to Our Senses* (see Resources): "The senses overlap and blend together, and cross-pollinate. We are not fragmented in our being. We never were. Our senses shape our knowing of the world, and our participation in it from moment to moment."

Our senses bring us into the present moment, into our bodies, and into a connection with the natural world. And as we connect with the natural world, the boundary between our inner landscapes and the external physical world softens and becomes less rigid.

Live Mindful

On a recent retreat, Anne was struck by the ease with which she could wander through the woods allowing her awareness to take in her surroundings. She wondered how it could be so easy to open her senses to her outer landscape and so frightening to open her awareness to her inner landscape. Her first thought was that it was because the woods were peaceful and nonthreatening, but then she remembered the decapitated mouse her cat had left on her doorstep that morning. She realized she had been filtering out the ugliness so that it wouldn't trouble her. As she opened to the reality of the outer landscape and accepted it without resisting, she realized she could open to her inner landscape the same way.

Mindfulness is paying attention to what we receive through the senses and then paying attention to what our minds do with what we perceive. Our sensory perceptions, including breath awareness, are the foundation upon which we build our stories, from which our emotions arise.

Focal Points for Mindfulness

Nature can be a focal point for mindfulness. Like the breath, it brings us to the present, and it activates our senses. Likewise, objects such as amulets, trinkets, flowers, stones, beads, and charms can bring us back into present-moment awareness. Sounds, such as chimes, can return us into the present when we drift off into the past or future. (Carolyn often uses chimes to punctuate mindful writing practice.) Focal-point words, called mantras in Eastern meditation, can bring us back. "Om" is one of the most commonly known mantras in yoga and meditation, but you can use your own word—a word you chant or a word you visualize.

Just Be! _____

Om (also spelled aum) is the most commonly known mantra, or chant, from yoga. Its purpose is to place you in clear awareness of where you fit into the web of life. Each letter, and the pause between chants, represents a vital strand in the web. "A" represents the self in the material world; "U" represents the intuitive or subconscious realm, that which can't be known through logic or rationalism; "M" represents indwelling in spiritual light. The pause between chants is the stillness that reminds us of the perfection of the present moment. Try chanting it at the beginning of your meditation practice to experience this unifying power.

Matching Maps

When you see an object, hear a sound, hold a pen, touch a pebble—whatever it is—take a moment and notice your breathing. Breathe fully into your belly. Check within to notice your inner landscape. What's happening in this moment?

Coming back to the breath—whether it's through the practice of breath awareness, nature, the senses, or the anchors and cues we create for ourselves—is the foundation of the practice of mindfulness. As breath awareness activates the mind-body connection, it creates clarity and insight—a convergence of focus of the mind, the body, and your intentional state. Matching up your intentions with the sensory awareness of the present integrates your map of the world. This creates wholeness and a sense of harmony within.

The Least You Need to Know

- As a focal point during meditation, breath nourishes the practice.

- Pranayama, the breath-awareness practice in yoga, literally means "expansion of vital energy" in Sanskrit.

- Breath techniques break through the fight-and-flight response and activate the mind-body connection.

Chapter 10

Being Mindful

In This Chapter

- What it means to live mindfully
- Extraordinary moments
- Anchors, bells, cues
- The essential you

Mindfulness is available to you in every moment of every day of your life. While mindfulness meditation practice can provide you with a set of techniques for healing, in truth, the practice gives you a new way of being in the world.

A mindful life is a fully engaged life. It comes step by step as we allow ourselves to let go into the domain of being—simply being. This comes little by little, thought by thought, day by day. In this chapter, we'll give you techniques for living with your mindful, essential self.

Living the Mindful Life

For most of us, the shift to being mindful throughout the day is gradual. Maybe we start catching ourselves being reactive, noticing more of what's happening when we find ourselves lashing out at someone or reaching for yet another cookie. When our judging internal voices begin chiming in, we may be more aware of their presence, as well as how we react to them. We resist these voices less, knowing that we don't have to argue with them or make them go away.

Little moments of peace alight in our minds, in which we notice the beauty of the simplest things—the sun sparkling on the dishwater, the catchy rhythm of the rain on the roof, or the feel of the sun on our face as we wait at a stoplight. It can at times feel like time has slowed down, enabling us to experience discrete moments.

Right Intention

To start being mindful throughout the day, begin by setting an intention. In Buddhism, this is called Right Intention, one of the steps on the Eightfold Path. It is important because it inclines our minds toward awakening, toward the end of suffering. If our intentions are incorrect—for example, if we practice mindfulness because we believe it will bring us wealth and fame—then we have turned away from the end of suffering.

If, on the other hand, we set our intention to face whatever happens in each moment of our lives, we are on the path to awakening. We are opening ourselves to the domain of being, where we can experience the wholeness.

Making New Choices

We can start being mindful throughout the day by noticing how we make decisions. We can choose based on our actual experience and our own truths rather than on our stories. We can listen to our conscience, trust our inner wisdom, and make choices in accordance with that.

We can be more aware of the people around us, seeing them more as the unique beings they are rather than stand-ins for our projected stories. Then we become less reactive. Reactivity comes from our stories, not from our actual experience. As we begin to see our stories for what they are, we release the emotional reactions that arise from them.

You can start with small decisions. Instead of ordering what you always order for lunch (or what your partner thinks would be a good choice), you check in with yourself and notice how hungry you are and what you feel like eating today. Instead of picking up the phone and chewing out the phone company, you may take a few moments to gather yourself first in order to use wise speech to express your concerns and request a resolution.

Breathe ...

Being mindful throughout the day means being aware of the times when you're rushing, upset, or flustered and staying present with yourself during these trying times. Rather than trying to force yourself to an artificially induced state of calm, you notice the rushing feeling, knowing that it will eventually pass. Rather than getting all caught up in your frenzy, you make choices to take care of yourself as you complete the tasks that need doing. You might allow yourself a break or take deep breaths as you ride the elevator to yet another meeting, holding your experience with kindness rather than judgment.

Taking a Pause

We can take a mindfulness pause at any time during the day. Taking a pause means stopping what you're doing, taking a breath or two, and then asking yourself, "What am I aware of right now?" or "What am I feeling?" Notice what you're feeling in your body and what emotions are arising for you. It may seem, especially at first, that you aren't aware of anything. That's just fine. Keep practicing in this way and see what happens. See what you start to notice about yourself and your experience.

It's especially interesting to take these kinds of pauses when we notice ourselves feeling distressed or annoyed. It's at these moments that our stories often kick into high gear, which makes them more noticeable. At moments like these, we can more easily see our stories for what they are—just stories. And these stories take us away from ourselves at times when we really need our inner resources! By pausing, we move closer to reconnecting with our inner resources, closer to our own true nature.

Think of the challenging times in your day. Set the intention that you will take a pause during these moments and take a minute or two to check in with yourself. Leave yourself a note as a reminder.

Finding the Extraordinary in the Ordinary

Every moment of your life is worth living. Every moment is filled with the extraordinary, if only you will allow yourself to be present for it.

Jon Kabat-Zinn says that finding the extraordinary in the ordinary moments of our lives points the way for us to see how changing our minds can change the way we live. It's when we get out of the routine way we look at things that we can see this. "A dog is just a dog," he says. But one day we can look at the dog as a nuisance ("barking dog"), and another day we can look at the dog as a faithful friend ("cuddly dog"). The dog hasn't changed; the way he thinks about the dog has changed.

Carolyn often experiences days when she has a glimmer of where this one day fits into the whole fabric of her life. These glimmers often come to her as she is crossing the bridge through the *bosque* (Spanish for woods) over the Rio Grande, when she looks up and notes whether the river is full and flowing, red and muddy, dry and sandy. These glimmers are moments when Carolyn can see the fullness and connectedness of her whole life *as well as the individuality and singularity of that one day*. These glimmers enable her to sit peacefully in each day.

Live Mindful _____

One morning, stuck in traffic, Carolyn decided to practice mindful driving. The Rio Grande brimmed its banks. She noticed the horses frolicking on the farm, and the morning sunlight on the green Hopi beads hanging from her rearview mirror. The sunlight reminded her of sunrise on Balloon Fiesta day, when 800 hot-air balloons go up. She realized she associated early-morning sunlight with the balloons—a special event. It occurred to her that in approximately 17,063 days of living she had not been paying attention to sunlight—except on those special event days. A new definition came to her for early-morning sunlight. It wasn't "special moment of my life." It was "now."

Mindfulness, Anywhere, Anytime

No matter where you are or what you are doing, you can practice mindfulness. While sitting meditation provides a good grounding in the techniques, you can practice mindfulness throughout the day by using focal points. We can find focal points through our senses, and nowhere is this more immediate and palpable than in nature.

When Anne is agitated or anxious, she takes a walk in the woods. She feels the trees are actually holding her, and she allows this feeling to comfort her. She allows her eyes to soften and take in the patterns of light and shadow. She opens her ears to the sounds around her and notices the sensations of walking, the rhythm of her steps along the path. This opening to nature creates a space in which her agitation seems less overwhelming, making room for her to allow it to be there.

The natural world is our natural habitat. As animals, we are part of nature. Being in nature, or looking at it through a window, can be calming and soothing. It invites a spaciousness for the thoughts and feelings coursing through the mind. Some people resonate by being near water, at a lake or seashore. Others feel energized by being among trees. Maybe you're a desert or mountain person. Most people have environments in which they feel most at home, and it's good to seek out those environments and spend time in them when we can. But we can practice mindfulness of nature in any environment, even in the city.

Whenever you can, go out into the natural world. You can do this in a city, too—there's earth under that pavement and sky overhead. The sunlight plays across buildings as well as trees and mountains. So, be in the natural world, or if that's not possible, look out a window. Let your focus soften and allow your eyes to receive the patterns of light and color. Pay attention to the sounds you are hearing, whether you're hearing "nature sounds" like birds and a river or "city sounds" like conversations and construction. It's all sound—you can let your hearing soften and pay attention to the experience of hearing. Notice whether you find these sense perceptions pleasant or not.

Another way is to pay attention to your fellow beings—the people and animals around you. Just notice them and your reaction to them. If you feel like smiling and saying hello, do so, and notice what that feels like. If you feel like turning away, go ahead, and notice what it feels like to do so.

Sutras _____

> I regard the eye, eye-consciousness, and things cognizable
> through eye-consciousness thus: "This is not mine. This I am not.
> This is not my self.

—The Buddha, *The Dhammapada*

All that we take in through our eyes, through all of our senses, and the
thoughts we form around these sense impressions, neither belong to us
nor do they define us. They are just sense impressions and the thoughts
that arise in response to them. We can say to ourselves, "not me, not
mine, not who I am" whenever we catch ourselves clinging to sense
impressions and thoughts.

Anchors

Objects such as amulets, trinkets, flowers, stones, beads, and charms
can bring us back into present-moment awareness. Traditions ranging
from Christianity to Tibetan Buddhism to Islam have incorporated
beads in their prayer rituals: Christians use the rosary to pray, with
33 beads to symbolize the years of Christ's life on earth; Muslims use
99 beads, reciting all the names of Allah; Tibetan Buddhists use mala
beads, carrying them in their pockets to remind them to recite a mantra or affirmation. All of these are practices of mindfulness.

Thich Nhat Hanh urges followers to carry a pebble in their pockets.
Each time a thought of suffering (usually a thought about the past or
the future or a thought of judgment or striving) comes into your mind,
reach into your pocket. Cup the pebble in your hand. Say, "I am suffering." Then, "I am doing my best." Then, "Please help me." Use the
pebble to come back into the present.

We can carry objects in our pockets to remind us, place them on an
altar in our homes (in our meditation spot!), or hang them from the
rearview mirror of the car. We can even use our computer passwords to
bring us to mindfulness. They can remind us of our intentions.

Sounds

Sounds, such as chimes, can bring us to present moment awareness.
Sounds have a way of capturing our attention—evaporating distracting

thoughts. Perhaps it's the training of the school bell or the morning alarm clock, but sounds do have power. Often Carolyn closes mindful writing practice by sounding Tibetan chimes, letting the vibration of the sound wash over her heart.

Any sound can bring us to mindfulness. It doesn't have to be a beautiful sound like a chime. It can be the cell phone ringing at the table next to you in the restaurant. Watch what your mind does with the sound. See if you can just experience hearing—this can be extremely challenging with some sounds, such as music and conversation. Notice what stories are arising for you around the sounds. See if you can release the stories and return to the hearing itself. This may be why bells and chimes are nice—they're simple sounds; we can more easily attend to the experience of hearing with such sounds.

Just Be!

Five times a day, take your pulse. Whatever you are doing, stop for a moment, and place your first two fingers on the inside of your wrist. Feel your heartbeat. Bring your thoughts to your heartbeat and all the sensations around it. Take in a full, deep breath. Hold your fingers there for one full minute. Notice your thoughts.

Words

We can also use words to bring our focus to mindfulness. Each year, as Carolyn sets her intentions, she distills them down to one word, such as "Flourish" or "Sing." When she gets off track—when the harmful thoughts dominate and she loses sight of the present moment—she recites this word. Or, she "draws" the word, writing it out in an elaborate or decorative font and doodling patterns and pictures around it. "Flourish," for instance, might be abundantly intertwined with vines. The act of creating this piece of art is an act of mindfulness, letting the art of the word unfold as it comes, and staying in the presence of that word. The true sense of purpose in her life is something she can taste in just that one word. The word brings her back into the sweetness of the moment.

The Essential You

Living mindfully creates new definition for your life. Practicing throughout the day being in the present moment ushers you into the domain of being—and in that, you find your essential self.

Practicing mindfulness throughout the day can cue you in to the narrative you overlay on your life. You learn to quickly identify this narrator when it steps in and starts defining who you are and what your life is. Practice gives you the experience of "bare awareness," seeing your life stripped of this narrative voice. It's been called *ipseity*, reconstructing a definition of yourself that is your essential way of being, beneath the layers of thoughts and stories that have become your adaptation to life.

def•i•ni•tion

Ipseity is your essential self. It's the real you—no stories, no overlays of narrative, no justifications, no judgments, no reactivity, no acting out another's expectations, no excuses about why you are the way you are. Ipseity is the bare awareness stripped of the chattering mind that tells all the stories about who you are. Ipseity is something you grow to sense as you practice mindfulness meditation.

The word "essential" conveys a quality that isn't altered, the unchanging core. It's your way of being, no matter the situation or context. This is the real you, not the automatic you.

Scientists such as Daniel J. Siegel (*The Mindful Brain*, see Resources), as well as longtime meditators, say that mindfulness gives us a hint of this state. They say that dissolving the automatic patterns created by the narrative you—the story-making you—often liberates you to develop a sense of self-regulation. It's counterintuitive—you may think the story-maker you is regulating your thoughts and actions, and you may think you need it. But this story maker is covering up the essential you. Knowing who you are frees you to take charge of your life.

Speaking to the Page

The essential you will speak to the page every time you practice a mindful free-write. *This is the purpose of mindful writing.* When you keep the pen moving, you let the words flow so fast onto the page that the narrator can't stop them. The real you *will* show up. It *will* burst through.

As we discussed in Chapter 8, mindful writing allows the narrator to have his day. He speaks his lines and walks off the stage. Let him. Don't judge him. Let him pass, then let the real you show up. It will, invariably. This is the you that writes about all the thoughts you have pushed away. When they land on the page, it takes the charge out of them.

One good prompt to push the narrator aside is: *This is not what I want to say. What I really want to say is …* It often happens that the unpleasant, cluttered, and ugly thoughts will emerge on the page right beside the gems. This is no accident. The unwanted thoughts are the very thoughts we leave to guard the door so we will not have to "go there," to those places where we have thoughts of uncertainty or fear. By allowing the unwanted thoughts to be born on the page, we unbarricade the door. We end the resistance to the thoughts and allow uncertainty and complexity to surface in our minds. The uncertainty leads us to what feels like the unknown, but it is our essential self. This is what writing teacher Natalie Goldberg describes as the places "where the blood has dried." It's the places where the writing is alive with freshness that we find our essential self. These lines resonate because they are the essential you. There you are, right on the page.

The Small Self

We are not separate from the rest of life, yet our thoughts often keep us that way. They keep us separated from our true selves, and they place distance between ourselves and others.

When we practice mindfulness throughout the day, we see new opportunities for wholeness. We end the illusion of our separateness. In the present moment, we can widen the circle of our compassion to embrace all living creatures and all the beauty of the earth.

Compassion—and joining—are the way we do this. Joining means to hold in your awareness both the similarities and differences between yourself and others. You neither deny the differences nor push them away. You allow them to be. A "joining" statement might be, "I'm glad you're here" or "I hold you in my awareness."

The more you practice, the more readily you come to this. The more you practice, the more you build a foundation for inner security.

Albert Einstein pointed out that when we neglect the perspective of interconnectedness, we only see one side of being alive. Our pain and our challenges become supreme and block us from the awareness of others. It's through compassion that we can restore this awareness and put our pain and our problems into the web of life.

Taking It into Your Life

You have to experience it first before you can see that there is another way to feel and be. When in a state of mind*less*ness, you have no frame of reference; you don't know what you're shutting out. You don't know what experience you're denying yourself. It's like going about with numb taste buds. You don't even know how fresh asparagus tastes if you have always eaten canned asparagus.

Your life becomes bright and flavorful. Your eyesight is clear. Relationships are whole. From this place, you can make better decisions.

This comes over time, and it asks of you that you be creative and imaginative in the way you integrate it into your life. *There is no one way* to live mindfully.

The Least You Need to Know

◆ Learning to live a mindful life is gradual. Just start to notice your thoughts throughout the day, catching yourself when you are rushing or reacting.

◆ Whatever experience presents itself in your day, be with it. Find the extraordinary in the ordinary.

◆ Practice compassion—and joining—with others you encounter in your day. This ends the illusion of separateness and deflates the sense of your problems being bigger than everyone else's.

Part 4

Practicing Mindful Eating

Food gives us pleasure and pain—pleasure in the taste, but sometimes pain in the anxiety about eating right in a world rife with eating hazards from sugar and fat to hormone-laced beef and mercury-laden tuna. As we explore how to eat mindfully, we'll show you how to prepare and serve your food with lovingkindness and compassion. And we'll discuss ways to extend that kindness to the earth that grows the food that sustains us. Tending to the earth is just one of many ways to engage in mindful service, making a conscious contribution to the sustainability of all life.

Chapter 11

A Mindful Relationship with Food

In This Chapter

- ◆ Harnessing the spark of life
- ◆ The messages behind the food you eat
- ◆ Caffeine, alcohol, sugar, and other bugaboos
- ◆ Making a mindful eating plan
- ◆ Forging a new relationship with food

Food nourishes our bodies, minds, and spirits, but in today's culture, what we think about food is not nourishing: it's fattening. It causes cancer and heart disease. We can't trust the ingredients. We can't trust the people who manufacture the food. And on and on … Add a frenzied lifestyle to the mix, and it amounts to not having much time or energy to give much thought to what we eat.

A lifestyle based on mindfulness practice, though, brings a deeper intention to the way you experience eating and the way you make choices about food. It takes you beyond what you've undoubtedly done a lot of—informed eating—to a new, vibrantly alive and engaged way of integrating mindful choices into your life.

In this chapter, we'll show you how to have a full-spectrum awareness of the context in which you eat—why you eat, who you are, and what kinds of foods are right for you. In Chapter 12, we'll guide you in the present-moment awareness of preparing and eating those foods.

Extending Mindfulness into Your Life

No doubt about it, there's a glut of information out there about nutrition and healthy lifestyle. One week it's "cholesterol-reducing foods." Next it's "50 slimming foods." At any given moment, you can hear that you should eat blueberries for the flavonoids, cabbage to fight cancer, green tea for the antioxidants, bran for fiber, and almonds for a high-protein snack. This is all good advice, but it can be one thing to know it and another thing to know what's right for *you*.

If we are what we eat, then it's getting so we hardly know ourselves. That's the central idea in Michael Pollan's *The Omnivore's Dilemma* (see Resources), a book that sounds alarm bells about the way we think about food in the twenty-first century. It's time for us to rethink this—to see food as a way to restore the deep connection with ourselves, the people with whom we share food, and the earth that yields the food.

Here's where the power of a mindfulness practice enters in. As you practice, you gain insight into shaping a lifestyle informed by your practice. The practice then ripples into every aspect of your life. Your lifestyle choices are supported by your mindfulness practice. This works in a reciprocal way, too, because as mindfulness ripples into your life, you begin to live mindfully, and this supports your practice.

"The way we eat represents our most profound engagement with the natural world," Pollan says in *The Omnivore's Dilemma*. Eating mindfully is about recognizing the wholeness of our connection with the natural world. It's about recognizing the connection we have with ourselves and honoring that. We are an energy force. Our bodies are a channel for that energy force. Eating mindfully is about harnessing that energy and holding it in balance.

To a large extent, our bodies define who we are. You are you because of the raw materials you ingest. You may notice that when you eat a certain way, your skin is more vibrant, your vision is clearer, your mind is sharper, and you have more energy. You may also have noticed that when you eat certain other foods, you are irritable or fatigued. Over the course of your life, if you are like most people, you may have noticed the difference between when you eat healthfully and when you respond to stress by eating out of your normal routine. In fact, you probably already know what foods are "bugaboos" for you. And you're probably aware of what kinds of life events can throw you off track.

With mindfulness, you start to notice all the connections between what you ingest and how you function. We can begin to see the connection between how we nourish ourselves and how that creates our energy force. We can begin, then, to think of food as the spark of life.

Sutras

The dharma that is taught and the dharma that is experienced are descriptions of how to live, how to use your life to wake you up rather than put you to sleep. And if you choose to spend the rest of your life trying to find out what awake means and what asleep means, I think you might attain enlightenment.

—Pema Chödrön, *Wisdom of No Escape*

The teachings of Buddhism—the Eightfold Path, the Four Noble Truths, as well as many others—are practical instructions for living in a more fully engaged way. When we study and practice these teachings by practicing mindfulness and by making choices in our lives that reduce suffering, we begin to wake up; we step onto a path toward enlightenment. It's a path we can stay on for the rest of our lives, if we choose.

The Way to Eat: Your Way

In our diet-obsessed culture, food is fraught with messages. Food isn't just food anymore. It's guilt. So we look for "light" on the label, wanting to feel liberated from the sense that we might be doing harm to ourselves. Food is fear, so we seek out "healthy" or "antioxidant" on the label to hold away, far away, the awareness that someday we will die.

Food is uncertainty, so we scan the news reports for "safe," wanting to regain a sense of trust in the people who grow, harvest, and process our food. As we make choices about what we eat, our minds can be bombarded with questions. Is it safe—free of *e. coli*, growth hormones, or mercury? Is it nourishing? Is it harmful or healthful to our bodies? Is it plentiful in vitamins, antioxidants, flavonoids, or omega-3 fatty acids? How much should we partake? Is this portion too much? And, finally, how does this bite affect the planet?

There is plenty of advice about what to eat and, more often, what not to eat, but not a lot of advice about how to think through your personal choices in a way that upholds *your* way of being in the world and brings you fully to the experience. Our minds are cluttered with "shoulds," some of which may be useful to us, and others of which divert us from our true way of being.

Just Be!

You can find a list of 130 of the World's Healthiest Foods at a website run by the nonprofit George Mateljan Foundation (www.whfoods.com/foodstoc.php). This list takes in more criteria than nutrition. It favors foods that are nutrient-dense—that is, have a high amount of nutrients compared to calories—but it also takes into account the affordability and availability of these foods for the average person. The list emphasizes whole foods, which are foods that are not highly processed and do not contain synthetic, artificial, or irradiated ingredients. You can use this list to create an individualized list to emphasize in your mindful eating plan.

Finding the Balance Point

Each of us has a particular point of balance with food. This is unique to every individual. For some people, more protein is the right balance point. For others, fewer carbohydrates is the key. Some of us have a fast metabolism; others have a slow metabolism. If we are really looking mindfully at what we need, we are noticing what our bodies require. We notice that certain foods enliven our natural balance, while others work at cross-purposes. Some of us may notice we thrive on fiery foods, while other people may notice they need alkaline foods, high-water content foods, stick-to-your-ribs foods, and so on.

When you find this balance point, you'll feel it in your body. Your thoughts will be sharper, your energy level will be right on, your eyesight will be clearer. Your body tells you. You just have to listen! When you function at optimum, well-being ripples from there; your relationships with other people will change because you'll engage with people differently.

Finding your balance point is about being attentive to what your body needs. Mindfulness practice can give you the vision to see the whole picture, noticing the areas in which you have a disconnect.

Taking a pause is a good way to find that balance point. Stop what you're doing, whether it's looking at food in the grocery store or standing in front of the refrigerator to decide what to eat. Place your attention in the center of your body, and take two full breaths. Feel the breath entering and leaving your body. Feel your connection to the earth by placing your attention on the soles of your feet (if you're standing) or on your sit-bones (if you're sitting). Let yourself be aware of how gravity is holding you to the earth.

Now, check in:

- ◆ What are you feeling right now?
- ◆ What do you want to eat right now?
- ◆ How does your body feel? Are you hungry?
- ◆ What is your energy level right now?
- ◆ What foods appeal to you right now?

Yes, No, and Maybe

Choosing what foods you eat with mindfulness means undoing a lot of "shoulds." You can discover your personal "shoulds" by first noticing with complexity what is "hot" for you. If you have agitation around any area, it's a signal for you to engage in inquiry. For instance, if you feel you need to diet and lose weight, you are going to notice agitation around body image, and you may suppress physical sensations in an attempt to regain will over your body.

When you notice agitation around food, take a pause. Then place your attention on the body—on the physical experience of the agitation. Allow it to be there. Resist the urge to analyze it or make it go away. Notice everything you can about this feeling, and see what else is coming up for you—the thoughts and feelings that arise, the beliefs you hold around food. Allow these insights to come from the feeling of agitation rather than your thoughts about the experience of agitation.

What do you tell yourself about what you should be eating? Have you divided foods into "good" and "bad" categories? Are you avoiding certain foods or quantities of food or eating at certain times of the day because you want to lose weight? Maybe you have beliefs about food that come from your family or culture, ideas of what you should and shouldn't eat.

Pay attention. Are you eating something that you don't particularly like because it's what you've always eaten? Are you avoiding eating salad because it's "rabbit food"? Are you interested in vegetarianism but believe that you'll become a "granola roller" if you start eating tofu?

As you begin to pay attention to the "shoulds" that arise for you when you eat, you may begin to notice which ones are based on truth and reality and which ones are reactive—that is, coming from grasping, aversion, or delusion. The following table gives you examples to help you begin to define the difference.

Reactive "Shoulds"	"Shoulds" Based on Truth or Reality
Unexamined stories about who you'd be if you ate certain foods	Dietary requirements
Eating something you don't really like because it's what you've always eaten	Restrictions that a doctor recommends (such as for diabetes or heart disease)
Avoiding all "bad" foods in an effort to lose weight	Food allergies

As we identify which "shoulds" are reactive, we can begin to let them go, and we can see the stories behind them. We can ask ourselves if we really believe these messages we tell ourselves by asking "Is this true?" "Shoulds" based on truth and reality become clearer and more solid, and reactive "shoulds" are seen for what they are.

We can also notice the aversions we have to certain foods because we believe they represent poor health or extra pounds—french fries, potato chips, or milkshakes. These would be the "outlaws" of healthy eating. But we must watch for the "enemy in disguise," too: high-fructose corn syrup, the sugary sweet ingredient that goes into many processed foods and increases our sugar cravings. This enemy in disguise creeps into everything, as presented convincingly in *The Omnivore's Dilemma.*

When we bring mindfulness to pausing before eating, when we ask our bodies whether they want to eat, and when we reflect on our experience of eating, we will naturally begin to make wiser choices about what to eat. In place of the "shoulds," we begin to make mindful choices about what to eat.

The "shoulds" and "should nots" are just our stories. They can take us out of the experience of eating to the point that we're not tasting our food. We can completely miss the experience. We can forget that a tangerine is not Vitamin C or a cancer-fighter, but simply a tangerine. As Buddhist monk Thich Nhat Hanh says, "Every time you look at a tangerine, you can see deeply into it. You can see everything in the universe in one tangerine. When you peel it and smell it, it's wonderful. You can take your time eating a tangerine and be very happy."

Live Mindful

Carolyn's sister believes that you should allow yourself one "vice" a day, choosing from sugar, alcohol, caffeine, and other temptations. Basically, you're okay as long as you don't have a slice of cherry cheesecake and a glass of wine on the same day. Other people believe in simply choosing one vice and sticking with it. Seriously, when it comes to "vices," it's all about finding your individual point of balance with it. It's worth it to find out why you're tempted by that food in the first place!

Foods That Bedevil Us

If you have foods that bedevil you, you probably already know what they are. You already know you need energy, so you rely on caffeine. You already know that you have trouble unwinding, so you take the easy fix of alcohol. You already know that when faced with disappointment, you bury your emotions in sugar. You may not *want* to know that because it's uncomfortable, but you always sense that it's there.

Mindfulness practice helps you explore these thoughts without letting your "inner scold" take over. When you take a mindful pause, you can drop down below the thought level—the "shoulds" and "should nots"—and investigate what else is happening for you. You can begin to see what it is you think you need from these foods. Are you getting that?

Begin by allowing yourself to sit with the questions. It may lead to surprising insights. You may come to realize you were compensating for low energy with caffeine, but when you eat protein, you have that energy. You may realize, then, that no amount of caffeine is going to fix the problem. But if you're mindful about protein, you don't need caffeine. Or you may come to realize that adjusting the balance of protein and carbs tempers your craving for sugar. Beyond that, "more protein, fewer carbs" means you can rest more calmly around the feelings that lead you to turn to sugar. When you are no longer trying to compensate for the protein-carb balance point, you can see your feelings purely for what they are and as they are, uncolored by the energy you were needing. You are then better equipped to uncover them.

Our cravings for foods that bedevil us often come from a desire to control our emotional experience or energy levels. After taking a pause, set the intention that you'll notice any thoughts that arise about your need for these foods. Allow yourself to eat them, and pay attention to the kinds of things you say to yourself as you eat. Ask yourself these questions:

◆ How aware are you of what you're eating?

◆ What do you want?

◆ Are you getting that?

◆ What are you feeling right now?

It's important to come to this without judgment and with compassion—and with curiosity.

Your Mindful Eating Plan

As you continue to pay attention to your experience of eating, you may find yourself making different choices about what to eat. At some point, you may find it helpful to create a written eating plan that incorporates these choices.

We encourage you to bring mindfulness to what you're eating *as you're eating it* before you sit down to write an eating plan.

When you make an eating plan, be mindful of what works for you. You want to stay in body awareness but also in awareness of your health, your lifestyle, your level of activity, your family, your community, your culture, your climate, and your taste buds.

Make notes here:

Your Body

Practice the body scan or abdominal breathing regularly three times a week over a period of three weeks. Notice what grumbles, what's needy, and what's satisfied. Notice your energy level.

_____

_____

Your Health

As you practice the exercises in this chapter, notice the messages that come up about your health. What are the stories you tell yourself about what you need to eat?

_____

_____

Your Lifestyle

With an open-minded inquiry, collect information about your story, about your lifestyle, and how that defines what you believe you need to eat.

_____

_____

Your Activities

Why do you do what you do? What do you tell yourself you should do, and why?

_____

_____

Your Family and Community

How do these factors influence what you choose to eat?

_____

_____

Your Climate

Though we'll discuss this further in Chapter 13, start to notice how the weather, seasons, and agricultural viability in your area affect your body, what you choose to eat, and what's natural for you to eat.

_____

_____

Your Taste Buds

Even though this is last, it's by no means the least important! Notice how foods authentically taste. Notice what tastes sweet or sour to you.

_____

_____

A New Relationship with Food

A mindful eating plan guided by _Right Intention_ is a living plan that is constantly changing. You use mindfulness to adapt the plan to what's happening each time you eat. As you continue to practice mindfulness of eating, you'll see more and more what leads you to make the choices you make; each new insight illumines the choices you make in the eating experience that follows.

def•i•ni•tion

Right Intention is one of the steps on the Eightfold Path, the guidelines for ethical living. When we practice Right Intention, we make choices that cultivate a more aware, engaged way of being with food. We notice all the things our minds do around our experience of eating, all the beliefs and fears and unmet needs we've wrapped around food. We do this not to discover all the ways we're wrong or bad, but to learn more about what it is for us to be human, to see ourselves more clearly, and to hold what we see with friendliness and compassion.

Your eating plan is not fixed. It's a plan that arises from practicing mindfulness. As the energy force that is you shifts, so does your eating plan. It's fluid, changing, and adapts to your experience in the moment. This concept resonates with the Eightfold Path: the choices you make in this moment affect your experience in the moments that follow.

When we practice mindfulness of eating, we set the intention to open ourselves to what it is for us to eat, and we do this in order to discover all the ways we create suffering for ourselves around food and the experience of eating. We discover how we take ourselves away from the rich sensory experience of eating and how we use food to numb and distract ourselves. By paying attention, we begin to see how each of us can create a new relationship with food.

We can begin eating mindfully with Right Intention. This inclines our thoughts and actions in the direction of awakening to what is wholesome and correct for us. We can start to see with new eyes, redefining what constitutes true nourishment. The news about good foods and bad foods changes like the direction of the wind, but what feels right to your body, your lifestyle, and your climate is something you can only know through practicing mindfulness.

In *Ordinary Magic: Everyday Life as a Spiritual Path*, a compilation of writings by Buddhist teachers (see Resources), Marc David says what remains constant is our mindful relationship to food and our inner world. How we eat is a reflection of how we live.

Breathe ...

You don't have to embrace a whole new eating plan and radically turn around your lifestyle to have a new, mindful relationship with food. It's a day-to-day series of choices. Mindful eating doesn't mean only eating certain kinds of food, such as eating a vegetarian or organic diet. It doesn't mean cooking everything from scratch and not using any prepared foods. Mindful eating and mindful food preparation mean knowing what you're doing when you're doing it. Above all, let that guide you in making the right choices for yourself.

The Spark of Recognition

Eating is a moment-to-moment, meal-to-meal experience. It's a fluid, aware relationship with food. With each bite, you are mindful of your personal point of balance with food. It's the way of Right Intention, step by step. These experiences, over time, bolster your inner wisdom.

In the movie *Phenomenon*, John Travolta plays an ordinary man who is hit by a blinding light that leaves him with a transcendent intelligence. Toward the end, he knows that he has a brain tumor and is dying. He's on his lover's farm—his lover is played by Kyra Sedgwick—with her two children, and he has to tell them that he's dying. He takes a bite of an apple, then hands the apple to the kids, and they take a bite, too. He tells them that now they are all together, because "everything is everything." The bite of the apple represents a bite of the life force, the energy that creates and forms us all. And this is how we can use mindfulness, to see every bite as a bite into the spark of life.

The Least You Need to Know

- ◆ Your body is a channel for an energy force. When you eat with mindfulness, you do so with attention to optimizing that energy.

- ◆ Notice what foods are "shoulds" and "should nots" for you by noticing agitation and reactivity.

- ◆ Your relationship with food is constantly changing. It's a moment-to-moment, meal-to-meal experience.

Chapter 12

Learn to Prepare, Serve, and Eat Food Mindfully

In This Chapter

- ◆ Finding flavor
- ◆ Preparing and serving: slowing down
- ◆ Portion control
- ◆ Seeking new traditions

With every meal, in every moment, we have the opportunity to taste life again. Too often, in our multitasking world, we often accept and eat the food that is there, hardly noticing what went into preparing it and sometimes not even tasting it. But food is sustenance. It is life.

Preparing, serving, and eating food is a moment-to-moment experience—and a call to attention. Every bite, every nuance of flavor beckons us to the present moment. In this chapter, we'll awaken your taste buds.

A Burst of Flavor

In Mindfulness-Based Stress Reduction (MBSR) training, which we first discussed in Chapter 1, participants are asked to taste three raisins. It's incredible how delicious one sweet, juicy raisin can be. Jon Kabat-Zinn and other MBSR teachers often use this exercise at the outset of a class series because it's an immediate way to experience mindfulness. It's an experiential definition of mindfulness that goes beyond a dictionary definition. It's a burst of flavor, not just literally; it leads to a leap of awareness that can inform how a person begins to practice other techniques of mindfulness, such as the body scan or breath awareness.

Your Experience of Taste

Let's try it. You can choose any food for this—anything from three raisins to three bites of a croissant—but it should be simple, natural, and flavorful. Like a raisin, it should not have a one-dimensional taste. For instance, raisins are both sweet and tart. Fruits and nuts are good, but so are grape tomatoes or sweet peas.

The reason MBSR teachers use three raisins, not one or two, is to give students their own experience of rushing from bite to bite. Often students notice they aren't experiencing the taste of the raisin in their mouths because they are thinking about the next raisin. It usually takes about three bites to experience all the nuances of what you notice as you taste mindfully.

Here are the steps:

1. Observe the food. Take it in like you have never seen an almond or chunk of pear or raspberry before. Notice its shape, color, and texture.

2. Touch it. Take the food in your fingers. Notice the surfaces. Notice if it's hard (like an almond), supple (like the buds on a raspberry), or oily (like the surface of a kalamata olive).

3. Notice your thoughts. Do you like this food? What are your usual thoughts about it? How are you labeling it (healthy, harmful, delicious, fresh)?

4. Smell it. Describe the smell. How were you expecting it to smell? Notice what you associate with this smell.

5. Bring it to your lips. Be aware of your arm moving up to your lips. Notice how it feels as it touches your lips. Notice how your mouth responds. Do you salivate as you anticipate tasting this food?

6. Taste it. Let the food touch each part of your tongue, experiencing each taste center. Notice the sensations of sweet, salty, sour, or bitter.

7. Chew it. As you chew your food slowly, notice as new flavors are released. Notice the sensations on your tongue as you roll the food around in your mouth. Notice, for instance, as the liquid and seeds of the grape tomato burst on your tongue. Notice, too, when the impulse comes up to swallow. Don't swallow immediately. Stay with the experience for one more moment.

8. Swallow it. Notice the sensations on the back of your throat as you swallow. Notice your sense of your stomach as it prepares to receive the food. Sense your body being nourished by this food.

As you taste each of the three bites, notice the differences between the first, second, and third bites. Notice when you're rushing yourself through a step because you thought about the next bite. Notice on which bite you were most mindful.

Just Be!

You have about 10,000 taste buds. Certain areas of the tongue heighten certain kinds of tastes. The tip is where we experience sweet tastes. Just behind that, on the front "corners" of the tongue is where we experience salty tastes. Farther back, on each side, is where we experience sour tastes. Near the middle, in the center of the tongue, is where we experience bitter tastes.

Whole-Body Eating

Eating is a whole-body experience involving all of the senses as well as our stream of thoughts and emotions. Nutritionist Marc David teaches a practice he calls "Whole body eating." (For more information, refer to *Ordinary Magic: Everyday Life as a Spiritual Path* (see Resources) and the chapter titled "Conscious Eating," by Marc David.)

Try practicing whole body eating at your next meal. For this exercise, turn off the TV. Set aside the newspaper—even this book!

1. Ask your body whether it wants to eat right now by taking a pause. Placing your attention in the center of your body, take a few breaths and ask yourself if you want to eat. Ask your body what it wants to eat, and allow the answer to come from your body rather than from thinking of an answer.

2. Sit down to eat (yes, you'll sit down for this meal, not stand at the sink!), and take a few minutes to place your attention in your body. Take a few breaths and tune in to the rhythm of your breath.

3. Take a pause, and notice how present you are in this moment. Are your thoughts off in the future—or on your next bite? The comment your boss made earlier at work? The chattering of the TV now?

4. Turn your attention to the food on your plate. Take a minute to see the food, just as you did with the raisins (or whatever food you chose). Notice the colors, shapes, patterns, and textures.

5. Smell the food. Open your awareness to all of the aromas, not just the ones you'd expect to detect because you know what you're about to eat. Allow your awareness of the aromas to come from the food itself, not from your thoughts about the food. What do you notice?

6. Check in with your body. What is your body doing? Are you grabbing for the fork? Are you getting agitated? What's happening in your stomach?

7. Take a bite. Notice how the food tastes, again allowing your experience of taste to come from the food, not from your expectations of what you should taste. Notice the textures of the food in your mouth. Chew the food slowly, and pay attention to the sensations of chewing and swallowing. Notice how the sensations in your stomach change after you've eaten this bite.

8. Ask your body how it feels now. Are you still hungry, or did you feel satisfied by the meal? What messages are you telling yourself about what you've just eaten? Would you eat these foods again, or did they not agree with you?

9. Release your thoughts about food with an expression of gratitude for the food. Move into another activity to transition away from thinking about food.

As in any mindfulness practice, your mind will probably wander off at some point. When you've noticed this has happened, make a soft mental note, *thinking*. Take a breath or two, and then return your awareness to the eating.

It's interesting to watch the stream of thoughts and emotions that pass through the mind as we eat. Without engaging with your thoughts and emotions, simply pay attention to the kinds of stories that are coming up for you—messages you're telling yourself as you eat. Simply notice; don't engage.

Just Be!

Begin your meals with a ritual. It can be a traditional blessing, in which you say a prayer, or a ritual you create with a poem, sharing, or a chime. Adapt it to your belief system. When we say "grace," in the traditional way, we give thanks to the One who gave us life, acknowledge with reverence the earth and the farmers who made this food, and honor those people with whom we share the meal. The word grace implies humbleness, an acknowledgment that this meal is a gift—not something we feel entitled to or deserve but nourishment that is given to us in love. Try developing your own ritual around this.

Serving Up Nourishment

If you regularly prepare food for others, it can be a pleasure ... or a chore. You could prepare food lovingly, with care and reverence for the earth that yielded this food and for the growers who gave their life spirit to grow that food. And as you prepare food for your family, friends, or lover, you could think about the many ways you want to outpour your love to them and the ways they are nourished.

But the fact is, most of us don't have lifestyles that allow us the luxury of slowing down to prepare food this way. Dinnertime is a dash. For too many of us, the definition of a successful dinner is "everybody got fed." Subtle nuances like honoring the origin of our food and experiencing the complexity of flavors get pushed to the side. We don't do this with a lot of grace—there's no time. But when we rush, we lose sight of the fact that food is life.

As Food Editor at the *Albuquerque Journal*, Carolyn is surrounded by foodies. There is the friend who favors vegetarian fare and creates elegant pumpkin soups and earthy vegetarian corn chowder. In her cooking, she emphasizes the relationships she creates through slowing down to prepare food that nourishes those relationships. For her, the food is a bridge between her and the community of filmmaker and writer friends she creates in her life. It's a way of bringing people together.

Then there is the wine columnist who favors California red Zinfandels (7 Deadly Zins is a favorite!) coupled with rosemary-mint lamb, creamy mashed cauliflower, and Belgian-style brussel sprouts. His cooking reminds Carolyn, a former vegetarian, of how good-quality meat can taste. When he organizes the no-turkey post-Thanksgiving potluck, it's a signal to all cooks to rise to the occasion, to cook mindfully rather than throw something together. Anything pumpkin or cranberry or turkey is banished, so you have to think of something else. It's always a pleasure to contribute to the dinner.

Then there is her favorite Emeril (The Food Network's Emeril Lagasse), who has educated her about Thai dry soup and other Asian haute cuisine, and, finally, after all these years of being away from Kentucky, introduced her to a true mint julep. The secret, he says, is soaking the mint in the bourbon for one week before the Kentucky Derby. Tasting a mint julep done right, over finely crushed ice, is to experience taste buds reborn.

Finally, there is one of Carolyn's food writers who organized a full-course wine-tasting dinner featuring only locally produced foods and wines. The wine tasting became secondary to his food creations, which featured the most perfectly ripe tomatoes and sweet bell peppers sautéed in olive oil with fresh basil, the freshest of fresh salmon with a hint of dill, fresh baby greens with roasted beets and, for dessert, raspberries and white chocolate.

And then there's Carolyn, who is more like the rest of us, always a little bit susceptible to slipping into culinary blackout—a syndrome where, for weeks at a time, you simply don't know what to cook. Dinner is just one more thing on the to-do list. Quality goes out the window. "Done" gets top grades.

These five anecdotes illustrate five ways that people join together in being more mindful about preparing the food they share together. They also reveal the richness of experience that we have around food if we can bring our awareness to the present moment, when we're preparing it as well as when we're eating it.

Slow It Down

The Slow Food movement (slowfood.com or slowfoodusa.org), which began in Italy in 1986, is a response to the proliferation of fast-food restaurants across the globe. This nonprofit, which boasts 80,000 members, including 143 chapters in the U.S., promotes awareness of how fast food contributes to the disappearance of local food traditions and people's mindless consumption.

If food is plentiful, even though it's not of good quality, then we lose sight of what it takes to grow and prepare it. After a while, we become desensitized to the care and reverence it takes to prepare a healthy, flavorful meal, when for under $3 a person, we can just get it, and get it now.

The fast-food mentality is so pervasive that it seems unstoppable, but you can start gradually to interrupt its influence in your life. You can commit to one Slow Food meal a month. You can create a community around it, in which you invite people to your home for a potluck with the caveat that every person must bring a dish that he prepared mindfully, with care and reverence for the community of people with which he will share the food. Or, if that seems beyond your reach, know that you can alter the energy of the fast-food moment by, instead of eating in the car, stopping at a park, sitting on a bench, and eating mindfully, savoring every bite.

Notice *why* you're in the time crunch. Why do you need food to be fast today? If it's because you're trying to get to an activity, then give thought to the value of that activity in your life. Remember as you're rushing to prepare or eat food to get to the next activity that eating *is* the activity. You do not have to let the pace of your life govern how you eat.

Taste—the Starring Role

There are no absolutes with food. It comes down to taste. It's how you experience it. Knowing how to pair the right foods together is a way of being mindful of how your family, friends, or guests will experience it.

Remember that their lives are dictated by deadlines, too. They have too many meals that begin with "Remove frozen tray from box." They have unexpected setbacks in their schedules, such as traffic delays (something we promise to delve into in Chapters 14 and 18). As much as possible, stay mindful that when you prepare and serve food to others, it's ultimately about enabling them to do something that they might not get to do often enough—really enjoy the taste. What a gift that is to give to someone else!

The Secret Ingredient

Whether it's mint soaked in bourbon, maple-infused brine to marinate the salmon, or a perfectly ripe peach, knowing just the right technique or ingredient is essential to good cooking. It's a very loving and thoughtful way to come to the experience. When your family or your guests respond with gratitude, it's because of the mindful effort you put into it.

In the movie *Like Water for Chocolate*, Tita pours her heart into whatever she makes. If her heart is filled with sorrow, her concoctions bring tears to the eye. If her heart is filled with love, everyone who tastes a bite is consumed with passionate love. When asked what makes her food so delicious, she always replies, "The secret ingredient is love."

> **Breathe ...**
>
> Preparing a meal using peak-of-flavor ingredients and not relying on preassembled ingredients, such as sauces, is a daunting task if you are time-challenged. While a meal like that can be full of moments to savor, it can be a burden if it feels like an obligation. If it's not your choice, then the gift is not freely given, and you may resent it. If the person receiving the meal does not appreciate the effort, it may not be worth it . Notice if you're preparing a meal out of obligation or if you have undue expectations. Make choices that work for you: don't do it, prepare it for someone else, do it less frequently, or do it on a smaller scale.

Back to the Source

For flavor, it's hard to beat local. It's not just the flavor that brings the food alive; the nutrients are denser in local food because much of the nutritional value gets lost in transit. The experience of buying your food from people whose faces you know adds to the richness of the experience. In Albuquerque, one such character is Kenny the Fish Hugger, who rents a salmon boat in Alaska and sells at growers' markets in Albuquerque and Phoenix. Knowing the story behind your food—and the adventurer who caught it—deepens your connection with the earth. (We'll discuss local food more in Chapter 13.)

As you shop for food, know that selection is everything. You can start with the mindful eating plan you developed in Chapter 11, and let that guide you in seeking out your food sources. But really, it's about inclining your mind a little more toward freshness and ripeness, and that comes through the mindfulness of tasting. When you taste it, you'll know it!

Longtime *Los Angeles Times* food writer Russ Parsons has written a guide to choosing food at its most flavorful peak. In *How to Pick a Peach* (see Resources), he provides a practical guide for identifying food when it's ripe and storing it to preserve flavor. "You can't cheat your way to flavor," he said in an interview with *The Washington Post*. "Flavor only comes from good farming."

According to the Leopold Center for Sustainable Agriculture, which is based at Iowa State University, the food we eat travels on average 1,500 miles. Parsons emphasizes local food because many foods are picked at the time they are most durable for shipping—not when they are at peak flavor—but his attitude is "take flavor where you can find it." For him, flavor is paramount. "Technique is what you use when you have bad ingredients," he says. "If you have good ingredients, you can do the simplest things and look like a genius."

Sutras

> In the beginner's mind there are many possibilities; in the expert's mind there are few.

—Shunryu Suzuki, *Zen Mind, Beginner's Mind*

When we approach our lives with fresh eyes, we see all the possibilities inherent in each moment. Even the most mundane tasks, such as preparing a meal, can be experienced as if for the first time.

Your One Bowl

Emotional eating can cloud our vision of what and how to eat. It can keep us from truly experience eating. Ironically, it can keep us from tending to the wounds of our hearts rather than salve them. We can start to notice when we engage in automatic eating, choose foods that are our "bedevilments," or mindlessly heap huge portions on our plates, as we discussed in Chapter 11. All of these are cues to connect with the emotional experiences we have stored in our bodies and to bring our awareness to our thoughts.

With super-sized restaurant portions, we can lose our sense of what's an appropriate amount to eat. Eating is a visual experience, and when we repeatedly see images in the media, on food boxes, and on menus that are larger than life, we form a definition in our minds of what is the right amount of food. We lose the perspective of what's right for us, as an individual, because we are bombarded with external messages. As we practice cultivating a present-moment internal awareness, we come back to the center, restoring a sense of self.

Buddhist monk Thich Nhat Hanh often refers to his one bowl, saying that he has no need for more or less. The "one bowl" metaphor refers to the Chinese term used by a monk or nun for "the instrument for appropriate measure." Hanh says our eyes are bigger than our stomachs. We don't know what is an appropriate measure. "We have to empower our eyes with the energy of mindfulness so that we know exactly what amount of food we really need." It's from this perspective that we can start to see the portion we put on our plates with new eyes. Becoming more mindful of the serving size on a nutritional label is another way.

Family, Community, and Culture

Foods can call up powerful memories. When we seek them out, we are trying to tap into a happy experience. If you grew up in the Midwest, the taste of roasted corn may epitomize the taste of summer. Tasting it now may remind you of a happy childhood. Or, if you live in the Northwest, summer may be defined as gorging yourself on wild blackberries that grow in thickets along the road. That taste may connect you with the reason you love living there. You love that taste because in that moment you were mindful of appreciating your life. But sometimes we go on automatic, and that becomes a burden.

Live Mindful

During the time she was writing this book, Carolyn's twins started showing an interest in learning how to cook. Her daughter learned how to toast bagels, and her son learned how to make macaroni and cheese. Suddenly what had been routine (and sometimes drudgery) became a fresh experience for Carolyn. To walk the twins through the steps, she had to be fully present for the moment to think through steps so routine that normally she filtered them out, barely noticing they were happening. Try bringing "beginner mind" to your next experience of cooking.

Open these traditions to inquiry. How can you still feel like you have a taste of what you define as "South" or "Christmas Eve"? How can you introduce new tastes that add dimension to the experience? Bring the family to the table with gratitude and appreciation, with empathy and strong bonds, with authenticity and clarity. Perhaps this is what you are truly wanting.

True Nourishment

True nourishment comes in not hurrying through preparing, serving, and eating our meals—or at least, not hurrying through *all* of our meals. It can indicate to us that we are hurrying through life. Ask yourself why. A tendency to overeat often stems from a fear of emotional emptiness. Again, ask why. If you have swung the other direction, into strict dietary rules or following someone else's program, look at what you're feeling about uncertainty and control. Finally, is food a substitute for love? Are you overconsuming or overserving to compensate for something else you haven't yet found?

When you notice these kinds of thoughts, engage in inquiry and connect to the body. Use breath awareness to pause. Use walking meditation, abdominal breathing, full-sensory awareness meditation, or yoga to connect to the body. Use sitting meditation or a mindful write to be with the question of what truly nourishes you. What is missing from the present moment? Mindfulness can bring you to the essence.

The Least You Need to Know

◆ Whole-body eating involves attention to your body and all your senses. Notice your body signals about when it's time to eat and when you're full.

◆ When choosing food to prepare and serve, think of it as the gift of flavor. It's the gift of the present moment.

◆ Be cognizant of portions when you eat. Contemplate what "one bowl" means for you.

Chapter 13

Nurturing Respect, Growing Strong

In This Chapter

◆ Sustaining your body, mind, and soul

◆ Make your voice heard

◆ Local-food movement

◆ Ethical living, simple living

We can build more meaningful lives through our choice to eat mindfully. Because food is a choice we make every day, eating with respect for our bodies, our families, and the earth can build a deeper sense of community and a stronger future.

The movement toward sustainable, organic farming and the attention to local, fresh, and flavorful food are just two ways that mindful choices, at their most basic, can inform the way we fit into the web of life. In this chapter, we'll discuss changes you can make, within and without, that bring you into wholeness.

Building the Connection with Your Food

As you bring mindfulness into your life, your sense of connection to the earth and to the beings who inhabit it grows stronger. Through mindfulness, you develop a more fully engaged way of living from day to day, and the impact of the choices you make, whether it's the food you eat or the way you spend your time, becomes clearer.

In building a connection to your food, you build a connection with others and the earth. Mindful eating, then, becomes mindful community. As we nurture ourselves, we nurture each other, and together, we grow strong. Mindfulness, too, nurtures our ability to be of mindful service, becoming clearer on a more ethical way of living and a more soulful way of contributing to the world.

How *sustainable* are you? A couple in British Columbia decided to go one year only eating food that traveled 100 miles or less. Alisa Smith and James MacKinnon wrote about their experience in *The 100-Mile Diet* and *Plenty* (see Resources). The book struck a chord, quickly gaining media attention and building a community around the website 100milediet.org.

def•i•ni•tion

Sustainability is the commitment to embrace both the needs of the present and the future generations as key decisions are made about environmental, social, and economic factors in a community. Sustainability values replenishing all resources—natural resources, financial capital, and social and cultural networks. Sustainability is about equity between generations. It's a "legacy contract" based on decisions that look to the future.

Farmer, poet, and philosopher Wendell Berry (*The Way of Ignorance*, see Resources) said, "eating is an agricultural act," but we often lose sight of that when we make our food choices in a big store with fluorescent lighting. A new Cornell University study examines locales and determines the most sustainable diet for that area. For instance, for New Yorkers, a diet heavy on vegetarianism with two ounces of meat daily is the wisest use of resources. But sustaining the diet the average American eats uses up to three times more land than the low-meat diet.

Sustainability Movement

What is sustainable? Sustainability is defined in the Brundtland report (1987) as "meeting the needs of present generations without compromising the ability of future generations to meet their needs." That report came from the United Nations-appointed World Commission on the Environment and Development, but it's commonly referred to as the Brundtland report, named after Gro Harlem Brundtland, the prime minister of Norway. The report embraces not just environmental concerns but living conditions, population pressures, international trade, education, and health. It takes a holistic approach to sustainable communities. It sees environmental concerns as being intertwined with the way communities function economically and socially.

Former President Bill Clinton defined sustainability as creating "a life-sustaining Earth, a future in which prosperity and opportunity increase while life flourishes, and pressures on the oceans, Earth, and atmosphere diminish." The movement is growing; it's weaving its way into the public policy and economics. For instance, the state of Oregon says it has a "triple bottom line" with economic development—all businesses and communities must operate with a three-pointed focus on people, places, and profit, factoring in economic, environmental, and social concerns.

One of the gifts of mindfulness practice is that it helps us see more clearly how choices we make in this moment affect our experience in subsequent moments. It's an empowering awareness. When we live in accordance with sustainability, we make choices that lead to a healthier planet, not just for ourselves but for all the earth's inhabitants now and in the future.

Best Food Practices

Two industries—restaurants and home building—are striving to be at the forefront of sustainability, and that's because they are big consumers. According to the U.S. Department of Energy, food service was the commercial activity with the greatest fuel consumption per square foot in 2003, the most recent year for which statistics are available. (A new survey was scheduled to begin in 2007, and an educational website was being planned.) The restaurant and home-building industries form the backbone of our lives—where we eat and where we live—and so they have the ability to usher us into new ways of living with much more mindfulness toward the earth.

The restaurant business, in particular, has come under fire for its energy waste and trash (takeout containers and food waste). Both the National Restaurant Association and the Green Restaurant Association list practices that steer their members toward sustainability, giving tips on everything from eliminating Styrofoam containers, reducing single-use condiment packaging, recycling, conserving water and electricity, and identifying local and sustainable food sources.

Many restaurants have started featuring local filtered water rather than pure spring water that has been shipped thousands of miles and generates tons of clear plastic bottles for the trash heap. Others are featuring sustainable menus, identifying entrées produced only with ingredients that can be found within 100 to 400 miles. Others advertise smart, informed choices on their menus, such as free-range chicken, grass-fed beef, and wild fish that do not come from overfished oceans or chemical-laden ponds.

You can educate yourself about the best food practices, and you can influence local restaurants by asking them questions. If your particular concern is farm-raised salmon or overfished oceans, you can ask them if they follow the Seafood Choices Alliance program, for instance. You can also ask if they use hormone-free dairy products.

Meanwhile, many cities have started programs to recycle restaurant food waste. Many restaurants already donate to local food banks, but the compost programs provide a new use for food waste. In Los Angeles, for instance, restaurants that have signed up with the program have saved about 75 percent on their trash pickup expense because 70 percent of their waste is organic, according to one news report. You can ask local restaurants if they participate in food banks or food compost programs.

Going Green at Home

Here are some simple, easy-to-do sustainable practices:

- ◆ Buy produce, meat, and eggs at local growers' markets.
- ◆ Use solar-heated water for dishwashing, or just use a dishpan so that dishwater can be reused in the garden.

- Install low-output fluorescent lighting.

- Build your own backyard compost tumbler.

- Buy rain barrels. In dry climates, you can make the most of rainwater by capturing all the rain that runs off your roof. You can use the rainwater to water your garden, which can keep a cool green corridor near your house, thereby reducing energy consumption. Then you won't need to run the air conditioning as hard in the summer.

- Plant shade trees along the south and west sides of the house.

- Redirect "gray water" (domestic wastewater) from your washer to the garden.

You can take this to any level you want, putting solar panels on your roof or driving a bio-diesel or hybrid car. In many municipalities, you can make a small contribution each month to your power company for wind power, or you can go all out and install your own. The Green Power Network (eere.energy.gov/greenpower) lists utility companies in each state that provide green power. You can take your roof green; Portland is known for its Green Roof program, which keeps downtown buildings cool in the summer. (A green roof is a rooftop garden that is used for stormwater management and energy savings. For more information, go to the U.S. Environmental Protection Agency website at epa.gov/hiri/strategies/greenroof.html.)

Define your level of participation. You may not want to go as far as the City Bakery in Los Angeles, where the walls are made of wheat, the cups made of corn, the countertops made from recycled paper, and the paper bags have no petroleum-based wax coating. But then again, you might.

For many more useful ideas, consult *The Complete Idiot's Guide to Green Living* by Trish Riley (see Resources).

Let Your Voice Be Heard

We have discussed the sense of uncertainty that permeates our times, particularly since 9/11. Other events of the twenty-first century have reinforced this sense that we have a very small voice in what happens to our planet. The climate crisis has captured our attention. Devastating hurricanes and tsunamis batter countries as we watch islands disappear into the ocean near New Zealand and polar bears drown as the arctic permafrost melts. It is the "age of consequence," as Nobel Peace Prize winner Al Gore says in *An Inconvenient Truth*.

> ## Just Be!
>
> *Footprint* has become a term to describe our impact on the earth. Ideally, we would all be able to live on Earth in an equal flow of giving and taking, and there would be no deficit on either side. Nature is set up this way. We exhale carbon dioxide, which nourishes the plant life. Plants and trees exhale oxygen, which we need to nourish our bodies. After the movie *An Inconvenient Truth* brought attention to the climate crisis, several Internet sites sprang up that enable you to calculate your carbon footprint. Go to climatecrisis.org to find out yours, but also set an intention to notice day to day your impact on the earth in the foods you eat and the trash you generate.

On the local level, we are bearing witness to the disappearance of species as they lose their habitats. Hungry bears who can't find food in the forest walk into health clinics, and coyotes venture into suburban backyards, coming right to the door, snatching cats out of their owners' arms. Bees have lost their bearings because of cell-phone signals (what researchers call Colony Collapse Disorder). We are overpopulating the earth, invading and destroying animal habitats. Knowing all of this, hearing news reports daily about it, can give us the sense that we can't make a difference. It's hard to know how we might have a voice in all of this, but we do.

As a mindful consumer, you have the most powerful voice of all. Know that you are the person who corporations are trying to reach. You decide how you will get electricity and how much you will use. You decide where you will get your water—from a bottle that depleted a spring and will go in a landfill or from a trusted local purifying source. When you hear a corporate leader or politician say we can't change this because consumers demand personal cars, plentiful and cheap electricity, and fresh salad in a convenient plastic bag, you can be the voice that says you want more choices than that.

You also have the ability to influence and nurture good practices, such as local growers' markets and Farm to School programs (more about these in a moment) that get fresh, local produce in the schools (and take the soft-drink vending machines out!). You do this with your personal choices and by voicing your support for them with your time, your words, and your dollars.

A July 2007 survey at the Leopold Center for Sustainable Agriculture showed that 69 percent of U.S. consumers believe that local foods are safer and healthier than foods shipped from afar. The Seattle Sustainable Communities Project estimates that for every dollar spent locally, about 45 cents is reinvested locally, compared to only 15 cents if that same dollar is spent at a corporate chain. The nonprofit also estimates that every dollar that goes back into the economy at least doubles, and in some cases, it can increase tenfold.

Sutras _____

All beings tremble before violence.
All fear death.
All love life.
See yourself in others.
Then whom can you hurt?
What harm can you do?
—The Buddha, *The Dhammapada*
Seeing ourselves in others can have a tremendous impact on the choices we make in our daily lives.

Weaving Yourself into the Web

You can weave yourself into the sustainability web by becoming more educated. You can also become more mindful about overconsumption.

Get closer to the sources of your food. Here is a guide to ways you can take part:

- ❑ Buy food at local growers' markets.

- ❑ Grow your own tomato plants … or peaches … or herbs. Choose a favorite food that you know you'll enjoy, even if it's only a handful and it's only for a week in the summer.

❏ Go to you-pick farms. Many farms advertise in the local paper when it's time to come pick berries or apples. They usually provide a bushel or a basket, and you can spend the afternoon in the field gathering your own food. The tactile experience can be a mindfulness practice that enlivens you to a full-sensory experience of your food.

❏ Participate in community-supported agriculture. Community-supported agriculture programs enable you to directly help local growers by fronting them cash at the start of growing season when they need to plant their fields. At harvest time, you have a guaranteed share of the produce. This takes your support of local farming one step further than frequenting growers' markets.

❏ Sponsor an edible garden at a school, or start one at your workplace. Kidsgardening.org has a directory of schools that use edible gardens, along with data about how the garden enriches the curriculum in a variety of subjects, from math to commerce to science to community service. Some schools have mini-farms with chickens, goats, sheep, and rabbits. A good guide to case-studies at these schools can be found at EcoSchools.com, a San Francisco-based nonprofit that promotes ecological schoolyards as outdoor learning environments. The Edible Schoolyard program was founded by Alice Waters, the chef credited with starting California cuisine and spearheading a local-food revolution (*Chez Panisse Cooking, Slow Food: The Case for Taste*, and *The Art of Simple Food*; see Resources).

❏ Educate yourself about Farm to Table and Farm to School programs, which get local farm-fresh food in the school cafeterias. States that have Farm to School programs include California, Florida, Georgia, Iowa, Kentucky, Massachusetts, North Carolina, New Mexico, Pennsylvania, and Vermont. You can read reports about the pilot program at Cornell University, as well as the ways the USDA supports the program at FoodRoutes.org/FarmtoSchool.jsp.

And just to ease the guilt if you can't do this 100 percent of the time: know, too, that even if you don't shop at local growers' markets, every bite you eat comes from the earth. Even highly processed, packaged foods contain ingredients that came from the earth. The hamburger starter mix has wheat in it, and the wheat came from a field somewhere.

Part of weaving yourself into the web is to create a deeper sense of community in your life. You can deepen your ties with family and extended family; you can create a family of the heart, a core of like-minded compatriots who support common goals. You can get involved in community activities, such as your neighborhood association or your church. Mix it up by rolling up your sleeves and starting a project you believe in. Persuade someone to bring mindfulness meditation to your workplace or school. There is no better way to get to know people than to commit together to accomplish something that improves our world.

Just Be!

In the Buddhist community, a *sangha* is a community of people who share the intention of awakening. Sangha members meditate together and support each other in a variety of ways. Gathering with others who are committed to living in a more engaged and compassionate way supports and strengthens all sangha members.

Ethical Living

The Eightfold Path of Buddhism is not a set of absolute commandments. It's a guideline for ethical living comprised of eight steps that support and are supported by each other. When we practice mindfulness, we begin to connect with our inner wisdom and compassion, which naturally draws us to live in a more engaged way. The Eightfold Path gives us guidelines and direction for bringing wisdom and compassion into our daily lives.

Right Action, one step on the path, is a commitment to refrain from actions that cause harm or increase suffering. Right Action requires discernment. When Anne and her husband were offered the option of using wind power to generate their home's electricity, they first researched the effects of wind power on migratory birds. Some wind farms are placed in migratory bird routes, leading to the killing of the birds. They wanted to support the environment, but they wanted to do it in a way that did not cause unnecessary harm to bird populations.

When they investigated, they learned that the wind farms used by their utility provider are not in a migratory bird path and include extra measures to limit the impact on birds.

We can practice Right Action on the micro-level in the day-to-day, and we can let our mindfulness meditation practices inform those choices. Set the intention that you will wear the lens of Right Action for one day, and see how often you can remember to view the events of your day and the choices you make through these lenses. What constitutes "right" has to come from you—and it comes from your heart.

Simplify and Slow Down Your Life

In Chapter 4, we touched on ways we can simplify our lives, noting ways that our complex lives can sometimes diminish our experience of the present moment. As you practice mindfulness, you begin to see more clearly what's important to you—what you truly need and what you can live without. You begin to see the ways you make life more complicated than it needs to be, and this awareness can guide you to simplify and slow down your life.

Several years ago, Anne and her husband, inspired by friends who had embraced simple living, decided to sell their car and rely instead on public transportation. In some cities this is easy to do, but in Seattle, it's more of a challenge. For two years, they walked or took the bus everywhere—they even took a vacation to British Columbia using only public transportation. And they did this with a young child.

During these car-free years, their world became quite small; their sense of distance changed dramatically. What was once a 15-minute ride to go run errands became a much more involved journey. This was before online shopping, so there was no easy substitute. They learned to plan their errands more carefully, streamlining them into one trip.

It meant they had to be more conscious. They would call stores to be sure they had items in stock rather than running up there to look around. They discovered that the small local hardware store could order anything they wanted. At the grocery store, they could only purchase what they could carry home, so they shopped every day on the way home from work; this meant their food was fresher, and they got to know the people who worked in the store. Their world got smaller and deeper at the same time.

They felt more connected. This was all possible because their son's school was across the street from their home, and their office was only a few miles away. Both had flex hours, so counting on the bus or walking to get back and forth was easy to do. If the bus was late … no problem. On nice days, they would walk to work, stopping for coffee on the way.

They noticed that even though they were doing less and staying closer to home, everything they needed to do somehow got done. Overall, they felt more relaxed and connected to each other and to the community. They got to know the people on the bus and shared the commute with people they might not otherwise encounter.

Anne looks back at her experiences of being without a car as planting the seed of mindfulness long before she began practicing meditation. Waiting at the bus stop was a form of mindfulness practice. Sometimes she would read while waiting, but she soon figured out that it was quite wonderful to simply sit and wait. She could check her watch a thousand times and wish the bus would hurry … or she could notice the tree in her neighbor's yard, feel the breeze on her face, or listen to the softly falling rain. She learned what it is to let go and just be present in the moment.

Anne's simple living was a brief moment in time, and now she treasures that the circumstances converged to allow her to experience it. Her son entered middle school, and that was too far to get to by bus. Her husband got a different job in the suburbs, and she went to graduate school. There they were, back in the car again.

Still, something took hold in those moments of mindfulness and became a practice. Her family has yet to return to the frenetic pace they lived before their car-free days. The lessons they learned from that time have stayed with them, even though it's been several years.

Perhaps your life is more complicated, and giving up the car is impossible. But we encourage you to pay attention to the choices you make about how to spend your time and resources. Are there places where you can simplify? Even small changes can have a ripple effect.

Breathe ...

> But wait a minute! Isn't mindfulness being in the present moment? Then how can we think about creating a better future? When we begin to practice mindfulness, we begin to see how we are interconnected, and we start to make choices for ourselves and the world that lead to the end of suffering. These choices affect the future, but they come from a response to what is happening now. When our hearts are open, we respond to the problems of the world with compassion. When we awaken our inner wisdom and compassion, we can't *not* respond to what's happening around us.

Your Ethical Living Statement

Out of this discussion in these three chapters about mindful eating, sustainability, building a strong future, and making a soulful contribution to the world, you have heard many ideas. It's time to distill this down to what choices and actions resonate with you. Use these prompts to create your own personal Ethical Living Statement:

I vow to cultivate mindful eating by _____

_____.

I can reduce my footprint by _____

_____.

I want to make my voice heard about _____

_____.

I know my power lies in _____

_____.

What I care about most is _____

_____.

Choices I can make now are _____

_____.

Choices I'd like to make are _____

_____ .

Communities I would like to nurture are _____

_____ .

I can live a simpler life by _____

_____ .

The Next Moment

With mindfulness, we stay aware of the present moment, but we also are attuned to how our actions in this moment affect the next moment. It's a paradox, but by staying anchored in a clear and calm present moment, we can see a much broader landscape. We can see where we fit into the web of life and how our actions sustain that web.

The Least You Need to Know

- Sustainability is the ability to meet present-day needs without harming the resources to meet future needs.

- Educate yourself about best sustainable practices at your local restaurants and grocery stores.

- As a mindful consumer, remember that you have the strongest voice in shaping our future.

- Shopping at local growers' markets, participating in community-supported agriculture, and sponsoring an Edible Schoolyard program are three ways to get connected with the sources of your food.

- Let your mindfulness practice ripple out into your life by setting intentions for ethical living and simpler living.

Part 5

Practicing Mindfulness with Love

When we practice mindfulness, through meditation and in our daily lives, we begin to see ourselves and our relationships in new ways. The awareness and compassion these practices cultivate lead us to make more authentic choices. Mindfulness seems to activate and strengthen the function in the brain that attunes us to those around us, making us more emotionally intelligent and compassionate. New research is showing that mindfulness is remarkably effective for people who suffer from depression or anxiety, and it seems to equip people well for facing life's unavoidable setbacks and stresses.

Chapter 14

Mindful Thinking Is Miraculous, Not Magical!

In This Chapter

- The miracle of the present moment
- Mindful waiting, mindful gridlock
- Your media diet
- Right Livelihood, mindless spending
- The miracle of mindful choice

For each of us, mindfulness is an individual journey. Mindfulness sets us on a path that leads us to revelations and opens us to change. It calls us to attention, engaging us in an inquiry about the way we think and decide. It leads us to more mindful consumption of media, more thoughtful speech, and a clearer view of the way we spend and save money. Through the lens of mindfulness, we can see more clearly our relationship with money and work.

The miracles of mindfulness are not in sweeping, dramatic changes in our lives; they are revealed in the small moments of unfolding as we deepen our experience and distill our true selves. We can become more comfortable with uncertainty and change, more at peace with what we are and what we are not. By recognizing what is real, staying in the present moment, and cultivating peace about that, we can experience miracles in multifold ways in our lives. In this chapter, we'll take you deeper.

A Miracle Every Moment

What is the secret to finding the miracles in the real life you are inhabiting right now, in this moment? Fall in love with the present moment. Awareness of the present moment takes you out of wishfulness and into mindfulness and contentment. Wishfulness is mostly about the future—something you want to have and you believe you don't already have in your life. When you wish, you are saying you don't like what is real, and that creates a struggle; you want to leave the real behind and dwell in the wish. But that's not contentment.

Mindfulness doesn't necessarily bring contentment. It can bring on agitation, because coming into awareness of the present moment can reveal to us what we are trying to hide from ourselves. When you experience agitation, take a mindful pause. See if you can just let the feeling of agitation be there. Placing your attention on the physical experience of agitation can help you stay with it. Investigate the experience by asking yourself questions: What's underneath this feeling of agitation? What's happening now that's causing this feeling? What kinds of thoughts am I aware of around this experience?

Breathe ...

Wishfulness is delusion. It's saying: *I want this to be real so much that I will pretend to myself it is so.* The pretending can cause us to suffer by taking us out of reality and away from the truth. We may stay in relationships that aren't healthy because we long to have a home and family. With mindfulness, you can relax into the "what is not so" and meet your longing and hold it with compassion. You can stop trying to construct a pretend life and instead find a way to live with joy in the real world.

Be willing to let yourself feel unhappy. Meet whatever feelings arise. Wishfulness keeps you from being aware that you really don't like what's happening, keeping you in a state of hopefulness that is not based on reality. Wishfulness can lead to magical thinking where you believe that your wishes and thoughts cause or prevent events. Magical thinking is focused on the future, and it may restore hope to think about a brighter future, but it also protects you from feeling what you're feeling. There is a strong tendency—especially in this culture—to misuse mindfulness practice as a way to control the uncontrollable, to take away our pain and distress so we never have to hurt again, to think that if we meditate we'll automatically become something other than who we are, or to think that bad things will no longer happen to us and we won't have to feel sadness.

Our struggle not to feel what we're feeling creates a state of anxiety, because our minds must work very hard to maintain the state of delusion that keeps us from seeing the situation right now as it is. We're in a struggle. We keep trying to force it to be magical, good, positive, rather than simply be what it is. When this happens, we are not letting ourselves have the experience of being calm in the midst of what's happening. We *can* do that. Really. Even though it seems impossible when we first begin to practice. Keep practicing. Let your trust in mindfulness help you to find that calm, balanced place; let it hold your hand and be with you. And you will see. It's not so terrible to say, "Yes, I suffer. Yes, this hurts."

Waiting in Line

We want to fill every minute—with pleasure, of course, not pain. It's our desire to avoid unpleasant situations that keeps us from seeing the present moment. In our go-go-go society, we don't want to be bored—even for a moment. We don't like to wait. We're busy. We don't want a delay, especially an unexpected one.

If we didn't plan for a long wait at the post office or the checkout line, we may feel our time was stolen. We may grouse about how unnecessary it is to wait. We may blame the clerk if we think he's slow, or we may shoot daggered glances at the supervisor if we think she isn't paying attention to the line snaking out the door. We can even feel guilty if we're having angry thoughts and chastise ourselves for not being patient. We may be tempted to grab back the moment for ourselves. We may be surrounded by other people who are filling the moment— listening to tunes on their iPods or talking on their cell phones—to the point that, when it's their turn to be served, they continue their conversation through the entire transaction with the clerk and on out the door, never greeting the clerk. We may even judge these people—we may *be* these people!

Waiting in line is an opportunity to practice mindfulness. The next time you're in line, engage with the present moment without wishing it away. Take a breath; look around you. Resist the temptation to whip out the iPod or the cell phone. If you start to gripe about it, if only in your head, don't judge that; note it. *Here I am, griping,* you say to yourself. Bring your awareness to the man with the Bluetooth earpiece in front of you or the kindergartener behind you. See them as real people, just like you, waiting in line. Resist the temptation to get caught up in daydreams. Stay in the present as much as possible. If your mind does wander, that's okay. Bring yourself back to the present by focusing on your breath for a moment or two.

Mindful Gridlock

"Parking lot" driving is much like waiting in line. When you are in gridlock, and there's no sign of relief in sight, it's a good time to practice mindfulness. Did you know that stop-start driving, where you're crawling along a few feet at a time, is a time when many accidents happen? That's because people get bored and impatient with the gridlock, and their minds wander.

A 2005 report from the Texas Traffic Institute noted that drivers in the United States waste 38 hours per year in traffic. It added up to 4.2 billion hours of wasted time. It's interesting to note that waiting in traffic was defined as wasted time.

When you're driving—or crawling and stopping, crawling and stopping—you can practice body awareness. Bring your awareness back to your breath. Come back into your body, noting how you are holding the steering wheel. Notice your posture. Notice your foot on the brake. Whenever your car is stopped, you can practice coming back to the breath or doing a partial body scan, relaxing each part as you bring your awareness to it. If you are still stopped, you can gradually let your awareness ripple out, noticing the cars around you, noticing the people, noticing your surroundings. When you find your mind wandering, come back to the breath.

When you are in gridlock, your mind is hacked into a million tiny bits. You stop, and your mind wants to wander. It finds traffic boring. You're tempted to micro-multitask—maybe text on your cell phone or read the newspaper. And then you switch; the line of cars crawls ahead a few feet, and you are driving again. It's context-switching on the micro-level.

Practicing mindfulness can help you unify your mind—back to the present moment as it is. You can think, *Stopping now, driving now,* to keep your focus on the present moment. The awareness on breath and on the basic movements of driving can restore wholeness to your chopped-up awareness. This is the miracle of mindfulness; it can bring wholeness to any situation.

Real-Life Decisions

By seeing things as they are, separate from the lenses through which you view them, and by being able to accept this truth, you can make wise decisions that reverberate throughout your life. You can come to view yourself and other people through the lens of compassion. You are able to see more clearly all the choices you are making about where you put your thoughts, energy, and action. Now you can respond differently when making life decisions. You can make more mindful choices about your livelihood and your money.

Mindful Consumption

You construct your sense of yourself and the world with your thoughts. In a sense, you are what you think about most. Have you ever thought about it that way? It's the same principle as the cliché, "You are what you eat." What do you fill your head with? What do you dwell on? What seems "normal" to you? Would you say your thoughts are mostly positive or predominantly negative?

When you practice mindfulness, notice the compelling thoughts, the ones you engage with and don't let go of. These are the thoughts that are like the White Rabbit in *Alice in Wonderland*. When they appear, they can always tease you into chasing them down the rabbit hole. They pique your curiosity like the Cheshire cat. They engage you in a debate like the Mad Hatter. You have a choice in how you respond to these thoughts: do you engage with them or do you let them go? Remember, at the end, Alice says, "Why, you're nothing but a pack of cards!"

> **Just Be!**
>
> Notice when you are being reactive because of something you read or saw in the media. You can notice when you are experiencing anxiety or anger. You can notice when you are experiencing grasping and attachment. Notice: *I want more. I will feel complete if I have this.* Notice how advertising shifts your reference point a bit.

You also have a choice in the thoughts and ideas you expose yourself to. The media you take in influences your frame of reference. Frame of reference is the information on which you draw to form a perspective. This is what you observe and the ideas to which you give meaning. But that's the key phrase here: you give the meaning. You have to be mindful enough to step out of the barrage of information and observe it as it is. You must notice yourself forming the interpretation and notice what you're using to form the idea.

You can be more mindful of the way your media consumption influences the way you think. Pay attention to the ideas and opinions you express; notice where they come from. Before expressing them, take a moment and check inside. Ask yourself, "Is this what I think?" or "Where did this idea come from?" Pay attention to your motives for speaking—is it to take control of the conversation or to get approval? Or is it coming from wanting to share an interesting idea?

No TV

When Anne's son was in kindergarten, she and her husband decided to cancel the cable and stop watching television. The TV had become such a big presence in their home—on all the time, dictating the schedule for the evening. They wondered, "What it would be like to go without it?"

The first few evenings were uncomfortable, but they quickly adapted to their TV-free life. Their son became better able to entertain himself, and they all noticed how much calmer and quieter their home life was. Anne discovered after a few months that she stopped wanting so many things—this was a complete surprise to her, as she'd always seen herself as a critical thinker who was immune to the powers of advertising.

Fifteen years later, Anne and her family still don't watch television and have little desire to go back to it. They do have a TV and use it to watch DVDs on "movie nights"—DVDs that they choose together. Not being ruled by the TV means they have more time for conversation, sharing the newspaper, and enjoying each other's company.

An Open Mind

Studies have shown that mindfulness facilitates learning. Researcher Ellen Langer advocates a mindful learning approach that emphasizes keeping an open mind. Truths are not absolute, and the learner is actively involved in creating the process of education. Students are encouraged to consider how their attitude will shape the direction of the learning. The goal of Langer's conditional learning is to leave the student in a state of uncertainty. When you are still open and you are motivated to inquire, you notice new things. You see with fresh eyes.

Educator Robert J. Sternberg defines mindful learning in this way:

- Openness to novelty
- Alertness to distinction
- Sensitivity to different contexts
- Implicit (if not explicit) awareness of multiple perspectives
- Orientation to the present

The practice of mindfulness attunes us to the present and trains us to tolerate uncertainty and entertain divergent viewpoints. When we are certain, Langer says, "we don't feel the need to pay attention." But the world is in flux. When we stay attuned to the present moment, we can see that, and with practice we can grow more comfortable with uncertainty.

Scientists believe that practicing this creates a physiological change in the brain that tunes it up, making our brains more resilient. It makes us more flexible. The more we make friends with uncertainty, the more we are able to practice present-moment awareness.

Daniel Siegel (author of *The Mindful Brain*, see Resources) says reflection is the fourth "R" in learning, along with reading, writing, and arithmetic. He calls it "mindsight," the capacity to sense the mind in ourselves. It's important to understand the unique way our minds function.

Live Mindful

When Anne was in college, she worked in a grocery store near a beautiful Southern California beach. All day long, people in swimsuits came in to buy treats to take back to the beach. She was stuck indoors in a dorky polyester uniform, listening to piped-in music, insanely jealous of these beautiful people having so much fun. She found the job incredibly boring and hated it. Today, when she thinks what it's like to work in a store, she sees it differently: she sees opportunities for connecting with the customers. She realizes we can find joy in even the most mundane places. Instead of being jealous of others' happiness, we can be happy along with them.

Right Livelihood

Making decisions about *Right Livelihood* comes from a deep heart level, so we recommend sitting with questions about your livelihood and seeing what arises. "Sitting with" can happen in a variety of ways—mindful writing or journaling, just thinking about it at the start of the day, or even writing it on a Post-it note and placing it somewhere you can be reminded of the question periodically during the day. The idea is to plant the seed of the question in the back of your mind and wait patiently for answers to emerge. *Right View* is what you're seeking, the way to view the situation. So, Right Livelihood questions could include the following.

def•i•ni•tion

Right Livelihood is one of the steps on the Eightfold Path, the guidelines for ethical living. Right Livelihood is the pursuit of work that is a meaningful expression of our authentic values. **Right View** is the forerunner of Right Livelihood because with Right View we can see if we are devoting our effort to a profession that honors our Right Intention. The traditional definition of Right Livelihood has been to abstain from work that threatens life and creates struggle, often defined as work that is connected with arms manufacturing, slave trade, meat industry, or alcohol and drug commerce.

◆ Does my way of earning a living cause harm to other beings or to myself?

◆ What stories do I tell myself about my way of making a living? What "shoulds" are involved?

◆ What does my heart call me to be doing?

◆ If I'm not doing what my heart calls me to be doing, what stories do I tell myself about why I'm not doing what my heart calls me to do?

◆ Who benefits from my working?

◆ Are there opportunities during my day to communicate with respect and kindness to others?

◆ What unmet emotional needs am I trying to fill in my workplace?

◆ If I'm unhappy with my work life, who am I blaming for this? Is it really their fault?

◆ What do I need to do to have a work life that feels satisfying to me?

Mindless Spending

The way we manage our money gives us another venue for using mindfulness to make life decisions. Money is a topic many of us like to avoid. We often experience greed, aversion, and delusion around money. These are masks that keep us from seeing our money picture the way it is. People who pile up credit-card debt keep trying to hide the truth from themselves; they push away the truth so they can keep the delusion that they are staying afloat.

Money is a measure of your life spirit—you pour your valuable energy into making it. Let the way you spend and save it honor the way you make it. Money is nothing in and of itself, but it is a vehicle for what you want to attract into your life—joy, abundance, love.

Sit with these questions, much as you did with Right Livelihood:

- Does my way of managing money do harm to others or to myself?
- Do I know my monthly cash flow? My target amount for retirement?
- What stories do I tell myself about my way of managing money? What are the struggles around these stories?
- What weighs on my heart?
- If I'm not reaching my financial goals, what stories do I tell myself?
- Who benefits from my money?
- What unmet emotional needs am I trying to fill with money?
- If I'm unhappy, who am I blaming for this? Is it really their fault?
- What do I need to have a satisfying financial picture?

Where Is the Miracle?

The miracle is in the day-to-day experience of being mindful of your input and how you process it. The miracle lies in the choice you make as the observer of each thought. With each thought, you have a choice about whether you engage with it. You have a choice about the meaning you give to that thought. You also have choices about the people you associate with and the thoughts and ideas you take in from the media.

Insight by insight, instance by instance, we let mindfulness show us what leads us to think, speak, and act the way we do. And the more we look inside, the more we see it's a never-ending process of deepening our awareness and understanding about what it is for each of us to be human.

And with this deeper wisdom, we begin to see how we've constructed our sense of who we are and what's important to us—and in this clearer seeing, we realize that we can *change* our sense of who we are and what's important to us. It's anything but fixed.

Sutras

> I would like to beg you ... to have patience with everything unresolved in your heart and to love the questions themselves as if they were locked rooms or books written in a very foreign language. Don't search for the answers, which could not be given to you now, because you would not be able to live them. And the point is, to live everything. Live the questions now. Perhaps then, someday far in the future, you will gradually, without even noticing it, live your way into the answer.
> —Ranier Maria Rilke, *Letters to a Young Poet* (letter 4, dated July 16, 1903)

It is through sitting with our questions that the answers we seek make themselves known to us. If we try too hard to "find" the answers, we just get caught up in thought, in analytical inquiry. We don't "find" our true nature; it reveals itself to us as we patiently engage in the practice of mindfulness.

Making Choices

As you practice mindfulness and discover all the ways your mind responds to the world and constructs meaning, you learn more about what matters to you. You see more clearly how your stories and reactivity drive the choices you make. You develop a stronger center from which to make decisions about your life.

Here are some of the ways mindfulness practice can affect our decision-making:

◆ **We are more honest with ourselves.** Our stories, which spring from grasping, aversion, and delusion, take us away from the way things are, from what's happening now. The more we practice mindfulness, the more clearly we see how we engage in story-making, and the more we can disengage from the contents of our stories and connect more deeply with the truth of what's happening for us in this moment.

◆ **We are more comfortable with not knowing.** Anne has noticed that since she began practicing, she's not projecting stories onto other people as much as she used to. She no longer assumes she knows why someone is behaving a certain way or saying certain things to her. The truth is, she doesn't know why people do what they do, and she's more comfortable with this not-knowing. She makes up stories about people much less than she used to, and when she does make up stories, she sees them for what they are—just stories. This opens her to seeing the truth about these people, enabling her to listen more carefully and more deeply to what they're saying.

◆ **We personalize less.** Another result of mindfulness is we stop taking things so personally. The more we practice, the less tightly we cling to a sense of "me," and the less tightly we cling, the less we have to defend the "me."

Who Are You?

Our sense of who we are is something we create, and we can become very attached to and protective of our identities. We create stories to reinforce them, and when we have an experience that doesn't fit who we think we are, we can get very reactive.

An interesting exercise is to consider the question, "Who am I?" Sit for a minute with this question. Take a mindful pause. Let your thoughts settle. Now ask yourself, "Who am I?" Write down whatever comes to mind as a reply to this question, whether it's a single word or an entire page. Don't worry if it doesn't make sense. Just write it down. Then, take a pause and then ask yourself again, "Who am I?" Allow the answer to emerge and write it down. Repeat this process several times.

The Least You Need to Know

◆ Mindfulness is not the same thing as contentment. At first, mindfulness may bring up significant agitation.

◆ Seeing things as they are, purified from your interpretations, can aid you in making big life decisions.

◆ You have a choice about the thoughts and ideas to which you expose yourself.

Chapter 15

Healing Relationships

In This Chapter

- ◆ Attuning yourself to others
- ◆ Equanimity practice
- ◆ High participation, low attachment to outcome
- ◆ Authentic boundaries

Our relationships with others mirror our relationships with ourselves. As we see ourselves more clearly, we begin to see others more clearly, and as we cultivate a deeper, more compassionate connection to ourselves, we lay a foundation for connecting with the people in our lives in much richer and deeper ways. Mindfulness as a practice and as a way of living can extend the harmony we experience inside out into the world. Mindfulness lays a solid foundation of humanity, compassion, and authenticity that are the cornerstones of building thriving relationships.

But relationships can easily get off track in our fast-paced lives when our time, dollars, and energy are directed in a million directions. The racing heartbeat of our lives keeps us reactive and blind to taking the long view in a relationship. In this chapter, we'll show you how mindfulness practice can restore grace and transcendence to your relationships.

It Begins Within

Mindfulness isn't a technique for couples counseling or conflict resolution so much as it is a shift in the way you view yourself and the world. This inner shift can change how you function in your relationships. Mindfulness practice reduces reactivity and cultivates authenticity. It *does* appear to work for couples; for instance, at the University of North Carolina, couples participating in a Mindfulness-Based Stress Reduction (MBSR) class called Mindfulness-Based Relationship Enhancement in 2004 reported more acceptance and less distress about the relationship. But it's more than that.

When you practice mindfulness, you practice nonjudgment. You don't judge yourself or others for what they do or who they are. When you have thoughts like, *I would never do that* or *I'm not like that*, you are judging, even if you're not labeling the other person, as in *He has no common sense* or *She's annoying*. These thoughts might seem like the truth, and you might feel clever for your insights about others. You might feel wise because you picked up on these traits in the other person, and you can decide not to be like that person—or decide that you don't want to spend time with that person. Or, you listen to that person a little less, giving no credence to his statements. You in effect dismiss the person; you are pushing him away.

Live Mindful

Meditation teacher Joseph Goldstein once did an experiment in which, for several months, he avoided talking about a person to another person—he stopped gossiping. He was surprised to find that this eliminated about 90 percent of his speech. He realized that much of what he had to say was judgmental. As he stopped gossiping, he became less judgmental of others as well as of himself. Try this yourself. Pay attention to the topics you choose to speak about—your intentions behind your words. Notice if you're doing it for entertainment, venting, or unloading. Notice if it's something you could really talk about directly with the person. And next time, take a pause before you speak, noticing what's happening within.

In your regular mindfulness practice, you can start to notice what you tend to want to push away, and you can gain understanding and insight about why. It is through this that you can see how you create little divides with other people. This is where you fail to join. The term "icebreaker" refers to a simple social technique to make small talk with people to bridge the gap between your worlds. Practicing letting go of judgments—about yourself and others—is the behind-the-scenes work of relationships that builds bridges that span oceans. The more you see the other as different, the more you maintain the illusion of the divide. The more you see the similarities, the more equipped you are to bridge the differences.

Take note: letting go of judgments is not the same as denying they are there. Letting go is recognizing they are there, but not engaging with them. You don't feed them. You don't need to squash them or turn a blind eye. That in fact feeds them. Just notice them.

Attunement

Because mindfulness attunes you to your inner landscape, it also trains you to attune yourself to the internal world of another. This *attunement* lays the foundation for empathy. Research has shown that the ability to do this—to experience empathy or to "feel felt" by another person—promotes resilience and longevity. When you feel understood by another person, you feel at peace. You feel vibrantly alive. You feel connected to the world, to all creation, and to all beings.

When you give this understanding to the person, know that he feels that kind of peace, too. Know that you have just given him the gift of wholeness.

def•i•ni•tion

Attunement describes a state of harmony with another person that occurs when you are attuned to the internal world of the other person. When you are attuned, you experience compassion and loving-kindness for that person.

Attunement is an aspect of emotional intelligence. Mindfulness cultivates emotional intelligence because you explore your inner landscape with friendly compassion; practiced over time, research shows that it induces physiological changes in the brain that increase the capacity for transcendence and empathy. And so you are able to pick up cues from others through their facial expressions, gestures, inflections, and other nonverbal clues. This doesn't mean you know what they are feeling, but rather that you are attuned to know there is something there that merits inquiry.

Breathe ...

If you are attuned to someone, that doesn't mean you can read her mind. You may pick up that something is stirring in her heart or something is amiss, but let that be a signal to you to pay attention and ask her questions about what's happening for her, if that feels like the right thing to do. Don't let it start the stories spinning. Don't make assumptions. Let your sense that something is wrong cue your empathy; meet it with lovingkindness, just as you have practiced doing when your own painful thoughts arise.

For the Good of All

When we practice mindfulness, we practice for the benefit of all beings, not just ourselves. As we practice, we begin to see more and more the ways we are connected to each other. We see the humanity of each other. As we become less reactive and less caught up in our stories and projections about each other, we see more clearly that the other person is somebody just like us, trying to get along in life and doing the best she can.

Equanimity practice can help us pull ourselves out of reactivity. Equanimity belongs to a set of concentration practices that cultivate certain qualities of heart. *Equanimity* means staying rooted and balanced and nonreactive, regardless of what's happening around us. It isn't apathy or indifference; it's a solid, grounded stance in the midst of the vicissitudes of life. We can practice equanimity whenever we feel ourselves becoming reactive when we're with others.

Equanimity practice works with two ends of a spectrum—seeing the other person as human, just like you, but also not getting caught up in that person's pain, merging with him or her and losing a sense of who you are. Equanimity practice keeps you centered and balanced.

The traditional equanimity phrases are "I am the owner of my karma. My happiness or unhappiness depends on my own actions, not on the wishes of others." Karma is the law of cause and effect—thoughts and actions taken in this moment affect your experience in subsequent moments.

To engage in equanimity practice, repeat these phrases silently to yourself, similar to the *metta* practice we introduced in Chapter 7. When you feel yourself becoming reactive to another, try taking a pause before you speak, and focus on yourself. Notice any feelings of reactivity or anger that are arising, and notice if you're holding any tension in your body or mind. Repeat the phrases to yourself a couple of times, alternating between yourself and the other:

"My happiness or unhappiness depends on my own actions, not on your wishes for me. Your happiness or unhappiness depends on your actions, not on my wishes for you."

You can alter the language of the phrases if you wish:

"May I meet this moment with balance and care."

"May I be open to this experience."

"This is what's happening for you right now. This is what's happening for me right now."

Mindfulness cultivates empathy and compassion for others by connecting us to the qualities of the heart that are clouded by our reactivity. Staying with our thoughts in the present moment can reveal to us how grasping, aversion, and delusion distance us from other people. These keep us in our stories, and not in the authentic present moment. In mindfulness practice, we can see the distance the story creates (*He's not that into me* or *She's always mad at me*); the moment reveals the choice to join. We can change that. We can choose to join. We can start to see that our stories about others' emotions and actions are not about them; they are about us. Attending to our feelings, to how their actions make us feel, can bring clarity. *I'm noticing I feel rejected when he focuses on his work* or *I'm noticing I think she's angry when she's quiet* is information that takes us to a wound—a wound we can heal through compassionate inquiry.

Sutras

Meditation teacher Aura Glaser has a lovely practice for seeing ourselves in each other. She encourages us to consider the other person, and then say these words to ourselves:

Just like me, this person wants happiness and doesn't want suffering.

Just like me, this person doesn't want stress and illness and misery.

Just like me, this person wants comfort and safety and ease.

We all want to be happy and safe and live with ease, although this truth gets so easily lost. It's good to remind ourselves of this!

Reactivity vs. Authenticity

Equanimity practice helps us find a solid, middle place to stand—a balanced place that is less caught up in greed, aversion, delusion. When we operate from a place of greed, aversion, or delusion, we become caught up in reactivity. When we're reactive, our stories drive our words and actions. To heal our relationships, we need to return to our true selves, to the inner wisdom and compassion we all possess. This is our authentic place—a place of healing and connection.

We don't always notice when reactivity kicks in. Sometimes we can get swept up in it before we realize that we're there. Here are some signs of reactivity:

- ◆ Your mind starts racing. It's difficult to listen to the other person.

- ◆ You feel angry and want to take over the conversation.

- ◆ You get an excited rush and strong desire to have something that you want *right away*.

- ◆ You lose patience with rational thought and don't want to take the time to think something through.

With relationships that have become highly reactive, the place of healing is authenticity. We can orient our intentions to returning to this place each time we notice we are not there. In mindfulness, we return to the present moment again and again. In the present moment, we discover authenticity.

Reactivity Bullets

Another sign of reactivity is the kinds of thoughts we have when we're reactive. They often are "you" thoughts that contain the words "always" or "never": *You never listen to me.* Another sign of reactive thought is when you're taking things personally: *You're doing this just to make things more difficult for me.* You can tell you're having a reactive thought when the focus of the thought is not on what *you're* experiencing now. Remember, you cannot possibly know what a person is thinking or why she's acting a certain way unless you ask.

When you find yourself having reactive thoughts, take a moment to return to a more balanced place; then choose a nonreactive way to respond. Nonreactive speech takes the form of "I" statements in which you speak of your own experience: *When you did not help me solve this problem, I felt frustrated.* Or, *When you pick up the newspaper while I'm talking to you, I feel hurt and angry.*

When we're reactive, we're not in touch with what we are feeling in the moment. Here are four steps that will help you:

1. Notice your thought.

2. Notice your interpretation.

3. Notice your emotion around it.

4. Choose a response.

Notice Your Thought	Notice Your Interpretation	Notice Your Emotion Around It	Choose a Response
He's just being stubborn. He refuses to get a new job because he doesn't care enough about himself.	*Thinking he's stubborn. Thinking he doesn't care about himself.*	*I feel worried about him.*	"When I see you staying in a job that makes you miserable, I feel sad and worried for your well-being."

continues

continued

Notice Your Thought	Notice Your Interpretation	Notice Your Emotion Around It	Choose a Response
She doesn't want to go to the party because she doesn't want me to have a social life.	*Thinking that the reason she doesn't want to go to the party must be about me.*	*I'm disappointed. I wanted to go to the party.*	"When you don't want to go to parties, I'm disappointed because it's important to me to enjoy an active social life."
She always does that to me. She will never understand me.	*Thinking this has happened too many times before.*	*I feel hurt.*	"When you do that, I feel hurt."

Not Being Attached to Outcome

When we practice mindfulness, we cultivate the ability to observe our thoughts rather than automatically engage with them. We recognize that we have a choice in the way we respond to each thought that comes along: maybe you engage in a pleasant fantasy because it's fun and entertaining, or maybe you choose not to engage with it because it's interfering with your ability to listen to a someone you care about. With mindfulness, you notice that the fantasy is happening and have curiosity about it. Maybe you even decide to investigate it a little, noticing the emotions that are coming up or the feeling in your body as the fantasy plays out.

Nonattachment is openness to whatever arises. Nonattachment with high participation means noticing the thought, acknowledging it, but not trying to control the stream of thought.

Detachment is one notch on the spectrum from denial; it's a form of aversion. Apathy and indifference are the far and near enemies of equanimity. In order to detach—to pretend we don't care—we must avoid seeing what we truly care about. We hide it from ourselves. We say,

"It doesn't really matter that he didn't call to tell me about the change in the schedule," or "It's not that big a deal that she flirted with my friend." When we detach, we willfully remove ourselves from caring about something we do in fact care a lot about. When we detach, we withdraw. We don't participate in the relationship by sharing how what is happening affects us and what we think about it.

Nonattachment with high participation is different. Let's work with the scenario of the unreturned phone call:

> Initial thought: *It doesn't really matter that he didn't call to tell me about the change in the schedule.*
>
> Noticing thought: *I'm noticing that I want to pretend it doesn't matter.*
>
> Truth thought: *It does matter, though, and that's uncomfortable.*
>
> Sitting with it: *I am uncomfortable in this moment because I'm feeling disregarded.*

Let's take this through another loop:

> Initial thought: *I can just decide that he's not someone I want in my social life. It won't do any good to speak to him about it. I'll just not return his phone calls.*
>
> Noticing thought: *I'm noticing I want to wall myself off.*
>
> Truth thought: *I don't like it when people affect me.*
>
> Sitting with it: *I am agitated in this moment because I am not in control.*

High participation is the commitment to stay with a troubling thought, to watch it work its way through, to let it go deep enough that you can get to the pain beneath the thought rather than detach from the experience.

Be a Journalist

When we become reactive in relationships, the other person becomes a screen onto which we project our hurts, our longings, and our unmet needs. This screen clouds us from seeing who the other person truly is—a unique human being who has thoughts, feelings, and a desire for happiness just like we do. And this is truly tragic because it takes us away from attunement and from feeling felt.

But mindfulness practice and equanimity practice can clear away these reactivity clouds and return the clarity we need to experience the other with fresh, open eyes. Look at the other honestly without turning away or manipulating the situation. Let yourself regain a sense of wonder for this situation, for the other person.

As the People/Film Editor for the *Albuquerque Journal*, Carolyn brings a sense of wonder to assigning and editing profiles of remarkable people—remember, everyone is remarkable! When a journalist interviews a remarkable person, he wants to capture the essence of a person. The journalist asks questions about every facet of that person's life, touching on the significant turning points that shaped the person's vision. The journalist's intention is to render that person's life story. *What is the story you tell about your life, and how does that reveal who you are?* the journalist wants to know. Ideally, a good, objective journalist approaches questions with an open mind, allowing whatever arises to shape the story. The journalist knows that's where the freshness lies. That's the exclusive! A good journalist does this, even if thousands of other publications have written profiles of Bill Gates, Bono, or Tiger Woods. A journalist seeks to capture a snapshot of this person *at this moment in time* as this person is now.

Try approaching your relationships with longtime friends and loved ones with this freshness. Don't pretend you know the stories. A friend tells a story of a woman who was in marriage counseling with her husband and heard him tell a story about a turning point in his life that, to her mind, she had heard a million times. But because of the setting, she was committed to fully listening, and her husband was encouraged to give the story in narrative form, which he did with more color and feeling. He brought the story to life. This time, upon hearing the story, she truly understood how this experience had shaped her husband. She saw his motivations in a new light. She had empathy for his experience.

In any relationship, you can make a commitment with each other that you will honor a certain set of values in the way you interact with each other:

- **Be a journalist.** Be open. Don't make assumptions. Be curious about the other person.

- **Be authentic.** Pledge to each other that you will do the behind-the-scenes work. Say that you will explore your inner landscape so that you are not self-silencing. You will not abandon yourself. You will be true. You will always do your best.

- **Be human.** Using mindfulness to drop beneath your own stories helps you dwell with the pain that drives them. Instead of being reactive to your stories, allow yourself to be vulnerable. Also understand that the other person has pain, too, beneath the stories, and allow the other person to be human. Know that all people are doing the best they can at that moment.

- **Be generous.** Equanimity practice can help you stay balanced when you feel upset because of the emotions of others. Know that others have the same desire for compassion and lovingkindness that you do.

Getting Off Track

Long-term relationships can get off track if we fall into a pattern of reactivity. This can happen all too easily in our world, which runs at a frenetic pace. It's easy to chase after other pursuits, focusing on career, money, hobbies, kids … lots of things are easier to control than other people (okay, not kids!). We start to focus on the differences and lose sight of the bonds we have built. It's a cliché, but we often take each other for granted. When we are not mindful, we may avoid seeing the relationship clearly. We may live for years in a pattern of magical thinking about the relationship, or we may live in denial about aspects of the relationship that need tending. We can go "unconscious" in our relationships.

Just Be!

In Kahlil Gibran's poem "The Prophet," the prophet says "let there be spaces in your togetherness and let the winds of heaven dance between you." He encourages the young lovers to see love as a moving sea, something that is always changing. It can be difficult when a relationship hits a crisis point to allow the relationship to have its own movement like the wind or the sea. In your mindfulness practice, allow yourself to look at the changes in your relationship in an open and non-reactive way. This is honoring the nonpermanence of a relationship—that just like us, relationships are always changing.

Taking the Long View

Mindfulness takes us out of the fix-it-now mentality with relationships that keeps us in a cycle of reactivity. With mindfulness, we can train ourselves to sit with a relationship for a while. We can let ourselves be with it, accept it as it is, give it time. In any relationship, one person may be ready for more engagement than the other at any given time. Intimacy is a dance between solitude and togetherness. Because we are always growing, one person may grow in new directions that the other feels uncertain about. Because we are complex human beings, we have a full range of emotions. Mindfulness practice can help us be comfortable with exploring a wider range of those emotions. We can allow ourselves to be at the ends of our own spectrums and to tolerate those mood fluctuations in another person.

Practicing mindfulness increases our emotional resilience. As we practice, we become acquainted with the ebb and flow of emotions through our minds. This enables us to relax around the ebb and flow of emotions in those we share our lives with. We open up to the awareness that the person we love experiences the same flux that we do, but his or her essence does not change. We allow ourselves to be open to more than one response, to let things be uncertain between us for a while. We let the bad moods pass. We open to allow complexity in our relationships. We take the long view.

The Least You Need to Know

◆ Notice when you turn away from the opportunity to "join" with others because of judging thoughts.

◆ When you practice mindfulness, you practice attuning to yourself, and this helps you attune to others.

◆ Equanimity is a technique you can practice to cultivate empathy and compassion and to see that another person is like us.

◆ In relationships, you can get out of reactivity. You do this through mindfulness, returning to your authentic present-moment experience.

Chapter 16

Lessening Disappointment and Frustration

In This Chapter

- ◆ Thinking is not the way out
- ◆ Dropping to the heart level
- ◆ Finding peace and contentment
- ◆ See your desire, meet your longing

Disappointments and frustrations stem from unmet desires. Mindfulness practice can strengthen us to weather setbacks and experience the sadness that is simply part of life. It even seems to have the power to interrupt the downward spiral of depression.

Mindfulness restores balance to our experience, guiding us to find liberation in the present moment. It redirects us to experience life directly, freeing us to stop resisting the truth and see it. Using mindfulness to clearly see this truth brings a sense of inner peace that does not depend on our circumstances or on getting what we want.

Taking It to Heart

When we experience setbacks, we become sharply aware of what we wanted and didn't get. We can become so caught up in the object of our desire that we think of little else. We internalize the loss. We take it to heart. And then we create stories around the loss, sometimes even wrapping our identity in the setback. We can begin to see ourselves as always on the losing end of life, and our self-esteem can suffer. Mindfulness practice guides us to turn toward the pain of our loss, so that we can attend to it directly. Yes, disappointment hurts. But what turns that hurt into suffering is the way we grasp at what we wanted and didn't get.

Mindfulness practice gives us a way to attend to the pain of our losses by releasing the mind's grip on the object of our desire and turning our attention to ourselves, to our broken hearts. This is where the healing happens.

When we turn away from pain and disappointment, we contract our awareness and our body around the difficult feelings that accompany these experiences. We unconsciously train ourselves not to feel the emotional pain in an attempt to protect ourselves. Over time, these unexpressed, unresolved emotional experiences build up, becoming more and more difficult to ignore, and we have to contract even further to keep ourselves from feeling.

Anne has worked with clients who were so completely shut down that they reported feeling nothing, or almost nothing. Many of these people used alcohol either to access their feelings or to numb them. What brought them to therapy was a desire to feel joy and happiness again—they only wanted to feel the joy and happiness, not pain and sorrow. To heal, they needed to welcome back in not just the joy, but also the sorrow.

Don't Think It Through

Another way we turn away from our broken hearts is to get caught up in thinking and problem-solving. We try to "find a way" to make the pain go away, often strategizing how to get what we wanted after all.

There's nothing wrong with problem-solving; it works great when we're trying to balance the family budget or figure out what's wrong with the car. But there is no prescription for sadness and despair. You cannot think your way out of emotions.

Often it's our search for a reason for the pain of a setback that leads to the self-recriminations. We can feel like there's something wrong with us because we can't stop the pain or "get over it." Self-recriminating thoughts like these can swirl around us like dust devils, adding to our shame and clouding our vision of who we truly are.

Back to the Heart

Mindfulness could also be called heartfulness, say the authors of *The Mindful Way Through Depression* (see Resources), because it is really about a compassionate awareness. Meet your disappointment and frustration with lovingkindness—without judgment. You don't have to figure it out. You do want to accept that it is happening—because it is. To accept it, you have to let yourself see it. To see it, you have to notice that you are turning away. Let yourself feel whatever you're feeling; let yourself grieve the unmet desire.

As Anne works with clients who are at a point where they no longer feel, she guides them to notice whatever they're feeling, even if what they're feeling is "nothing." Feeling nothing *is* feeling something. Her clients start to see what nothing feels like. They begin to hear more clearly the messages they tell themselves about the futility of feeling their disappointment and despair, and they see how these messages keep them frozen and shut down. The more they open to their feelings, whatever those feelings are, the more they begin to notice what they're feeling. At first, the feelings are so subtle that they're barely noticeable, but over time, they become stronger and easier to see.

A word about *depression:* in this book, when we talk about depression, we are referring to the deep sadness that is part of the ebb and flow of life. When depressed feelings become severe enough

def•i•ni•tion

Depression is the shutting down of the heart. It's a sadness that has been chronically internalized to the point that we see life through the lens of hopelessness. It is the experience of numbness caused by turning away from pain.

to interrupt our ability to function in our daily lives or lead us to have serious thoughts of harming ourselves or others, it's a sign that we may be experiencing clinical depression. Clinical depression is a serious disorder that requires therapeutic intervention. Mindfulness practices are helpful for clinical depression, but it's important to also seek help from a therapist or medical professional if you suspect you may have clinical depression.

Sadness has a hold on us because it's deeper than the thought level; it's at the heart level. Mindfulness practice teaches us to stay with our thoughts with compassion. We can drop into the heart level, where we don't have to look for objective facts, and we can see that in truth our thoughts are not factual. They are not the truth. In this way, we can start to trust our hearts.

Despair, sorrow, and depression are calls to turn inward, attend to our hearts. People often have a strong reaction to this idea—*Isn't that just wallowing in it? Shouldn't you be putting your sadness behind you?* The answer to both of these questions is no. It isn't wallowing in sadness to pay attention to it and watch it unfold. To wallow in sadness is to hold on to it, feed it, and milk it for all you can. That's not mindfulness—that's reactivity. And putting it behind you is a way of pushing the sadness away rather than allowing it to pass on its own.

Another objection to the idea of turning within and feeling whatever you're feeling is that you have too many responsibilities. There's no time for breaking down and falling apart, you may say. This is a completely understandable concern. Fortunately, we humans have this amazing ability to set our feelings aside when we need to. This is not the same as denying or suppressing feeling. To set a difficult emotion aside, fully acknowledge that it's there, naming it if that's helpful. Intentionally set it aside for later, even saying to yourself, "I'm setting this aside," or imagine yourself putting the feeling in a box or up on a shelf, if you like.

Please note: when you set a feeling aside, you eventually have to come back to it. It will wait patiently for a while, but it will want to be recognized. Set the intention that you will make space for this feeling to emerge later at a better time.

Live Mindful _____

Anne's brother died suddenly and tragically one week before Christmas in 2003. In the weeks that followed, she experienced a crash-course in grief, watching how her mind, soul, and body reacted to having her little brother wrenched from her life. The pain was too much to hold inside; even if she wanted to, there was no way she could have put it behind her and act as if she felt fine. During those days, her mindfulness practice helped her open to her experience with acceptance and love. Her practice sustained her as she rode the waves of her heart-rending grief, and as she stayed with the grief, she discovered the sweetness buried within it.

Liberation in the Truth

It's a paradox, but you can find liberation in facing the most unpleasant events in your life. The most challenging and trying experiences can be the best teachers. We're not putting the sheen of optimism over this. Truly, if we can use mindfulness to approach difficulty this way, we can train ourselves to be more open to problems when they arise.

We have the power of choice in every moment because we have the power of choosing how we will respond to what we're experiencing from moment to moment. We can choose how we create meaning around each experience.

We also can choose what we will see. We can choose not to turn away from the pain that our setbacks and disappointments bring us. Through mindfulness, we can become more at ease with the way our lives unfold. We can loosen our attachment to certain outcomes. We can bring our inner resources of wisdom and compassion to the difficult experiences.

Mindfulness can bring us to the true essence of the pain: our longing to have things be the way we want them to be. When our desires are unmet, we feel disappointment, frustration, even despair. We can ache with longing for these unmet desires. We can open our awareness to the longing, allowing ourselves to see it with clarity and kindness.

The Nature of Life

Happiness and contentment are not one and the same. We can be content amid the most ambiguous of circumstances or the most challenging of times. We run into trouble when we expect that we should always be happy, because we become attached to a form of happiness that's conditional—it depends on things being a certain way. Contentment is a current that runs deeper than conditional happiness and does not depend on circumstances. Contentment is something that can flow through our lives, and it can be discovered in the present moment, even when that moment is trying or difficult.

Contentment can be found in the present moment when we understand that the very nature of life is that we will experience the ebb and flow of gain and loss. Author Sharon Salzberg explains that, "When we open to this truth, we discover there is no need to hold on or push away." We can stop trying to control things so we will feel safe—because we can know that we will feel safe in meeting whatever is actually happening. When we accept the mystery of life and cultivate an ability to receive and meet it *without judging what it is*, we experience the source of lasting contentment. "Acceptance is the source of our safety and confidence," Salzberg says. Instead of struggling to control what comes in, we can simply engage with what is.

As Anne's clients practice turning inward and noting what they're feeling, at first they mostly see sadness, anger, and other forms of aversion. "Keep looking inside," she tells them. As they open to their painful emotions, the haze of their attachment and delusion begins to clear. And they begin to notice something else contained within their pain— the solidity of truth. They begin to have little moments of connection with what's happening in the moment, and as painful as it may be, it resonates deeply with them.

Chronic unhappiness can set in because we believe we must keep sadness at bay. We believe we can be happy all the time, and we believe we must control our reality. When we fail—when sadness pierces through the veil—we can feel like a failure. Suddenly, it all seems hollow. The identity we created for ourselves—Happy us! Great job! Loving partner!—was circumstantial.

With mindfulness, we devote the time to explore our true essence. We know ourselves as vulnerable because we have taken the time to drop down to the heart level. We have practiced dwelling with our uncertainties, our sorrow, our anger, our fears, our helplessness. We know our stories, and we know they are not us. We know our essential nature. We've gotten used to being around ourselves.

Turning Back

When we avoid sadness and disappointment, we turn away from our longing. With mindfulness, we can greet this longing again with friendliness. We can say, "I want love" or "I want to feel safe." We can let ourselves feel the pain when we perceive we don't have those things. With mindfulness, we can see clearly when our thoughts send us into the past: *I'm worthless* may come from *I could never please my father.* So when we experience a setback, we don't see it as part of the learning curve; we go right back to the pain of childhood. But when we do this—assign a childhood story to the task, and explain it away—we fail to notice the desire. We miss the opportunity to see the desire and learn from the loss.

Breathe ...

There is nothing incompatible between mindfulness practice and taking medication. If you are taking medication for depression symptoms or to help you sleep, there's no reason to discontinue it. Living mindfully means practicing kindness to yourself and to all beings, and this means taking care of yourself.

The pain of loss can affect our sleeping and eating patterns. We may eat differently when we are in emotional pain—eating too much or too little. We may not get enough sleep, or we may start to sleep more than we usually do. At night, as we attempt to fall asleep, the demons can come up. Our desires haunt us, and our minds can start to churn away at reversing the setback. Or maybe we fall asleep with no problem, but are wide awake a couple of hours later spending the rest of the night tossing and turning.

According to the authors of *The Mindful Way Through Depression*, 80 percent of people who suffer from depression call their doctor because they are suffering from aches and pains that they cannot explain. Much of that is linked to fatigue. Our bodies tense up when we experience a stream of negative thoughts, and it keeps looping more input into the fight-or-flight response. So we stay that way. We churn away at our negative thoughts about the experience. No wonder we're exhausted!

The body scan we introduced in Chapter 5 is an excellent technique for dealing with the insomnia that so often accompanies painful emotions and depression. By intentionally and systematically placing your attention in the body, you not only disengage from the thoughts racing in your mind, but you also relax the body. This is a wonderful combination for inducing sleep. In Resouces, we've listed body-scan recordings you can purchase to help you practice. Or, you can read the body-scan instructions we gave you in Chapter 5 into a tape recorder. Either way, try using recorded instructions to do a body scan at bedtime, and make a commitment to practice the body scan every night for several days.

Just Be!

When our sleep patterns get disrupted, we tend to fight them. We try to stick to our usual routine and patterns. We try harder to fall asleep or to get up early, and these responses rarely bring us the restful sleep we need. If you need more sleep, allow yourself to sleep—take a nap, go to bed earlier, or sleep in, if you can. If you have insomnia, pay attention to things like caffeine intake and your activity level in the evening, but if sleep just isn't coming, don't fight it. Use the time you're lying there awake to practice meditating lying down or doing a body scan. And if your change in sleep patterns is severe or persistent, see a doctor or therapist.

Placing Your Trust in Body Awareness

You can place your trust in coming back to the body. Massage can move the energy in the body, and so can yoga. Breath awareness brings you back into awareness of the emotions stored in the body. Breath and body awareness cue you in to the body's output of information about your emotional state and can reveal a constant state of tension or exhaustion.

When you notice self-recriminating thoughts because of a setback, you can pause, place your attention on the body, take a few breaths, and notice what it's like to breathe. If it's helpful, make soft mental notes to yourself, gently labeling first the thought (*scolding* or *berating*) without judgment, and then the feeling in your body (*tensing* or *hurting*).

You may find that when you place your attention into the body, either through bodywork or through taking a pause, a feeling of sadness will well up. Maybe tears will start to come. Let the tears come, if they can. The wave of sadness may feel enormous and you may find yourself thinking that if you begin to cry, you'll never stop. Chances are, you will stop crying, probably sooner than you think. Let those tears fall.

And if your body wants to do something else, maybe curl up in a blanket or rock back and forth, that's okay, too. Let your body guide you as you stay with the waves of emotion that want to emerge.

A Vehicle for Change

If there is one thing to take away from this book, it's the power of the present moment. Coming back to the present moment can shift the colors of your life from dull gray to vivid. Notice we didn't say happy; we said vivid. Real. We can rest in the real. Yes, we may have failed. Things may not have turned out the way we desired. Yes, we may feel despair and not see the way out. Yes, we may feel profound sadness.

But we don't say yes to *I'm inadequate.* We don't say yes to *I can never get a break* or *There must be something wrong with me that I can't get what I want.* We don't say yes to thoughts that strike deep at our self-esteem. We step outside of the interpretation. We notice that we're having these thoughts about self-esteem. But we don't have to engage with them. We don't have to believe them.

The present moment enables us to experience life directly with beginner's mind. If we know that our suffering comes from the stories we create about the events of our lives—and not from the events themselves—we can let ourselves be there for the freshness of the experience as it is. Let yourself be there for the uniqueness of your experience. You can start to notice the flavor of your thoughts and your way of responding to disappointments and sorrows.

Sidestep the relentless commentary of your thoughts. It's a little bit like being at a party and stepping outside for a breath of fresh air while the party goes on. (And you can literally do this, too, if you experience a setback or hurt at a party—you can take a pause!)

Conditional Happiness

Our pain around setbacks and losses lingers when we believe our happiness depends on ideal conditions. In *The Sun My Heart* (see Resources), Thich Nhat Hanh says peace can exist only in the present moment. He says it is ridiculous to think, "Wait until I finish this, then I will be free to live in peace."

Let's think about what *this* is: it's an unmet desire. What is that desire, and how will it bring us happiness? Hanh cautions that if we think that way, peace will never come. Chasing after our unmet desires keeps us focused on the future. We don't want to mortgage the present moment for future happiness. Didn't we do that a moment ago? Think back on your desires of the past—some of them met, some of them yet unmet. At some point, a "now-met desire" was unmet. Now, are you happy, or have you moved your thoughts to the next unmet desire? Hanh says, "If you want to be at peace, you must be at peace right now."

We are not here to talk you out of having desires. Rather we are here to help you bring mindfulness to your experience of longing and to release your attachment and grasping toward the objects of your desire.

The present moment brings fresh air to our experience, putting a spaciousness around it. The desires that are unmet and the disappointments around them have more space to be. And they don't seem so overwhelming or profound. They aren't who we are. They are small aspects of our experience as humans in a world in which things don't always happen the way we want them to. In this way, we no longer contract around the experience.

Sutras _____

> *Don't surrender your loneliness*
> *So quickly.*
> *Let it cut more deeply.*
>
> *Let it ferment and season you*
> *As few human*
> *Or even divine ingredients can.*
>
> —Hafiz, *The Subject Tonight Is Love—60 Wild and Sweet Poems of Hafiz*, translated by Daniel Ladinski

When we feel disappointment and despair, it's an invitation to care for ourselves in a tender, openhearted way. It's a call to turn inward and attend to our feelings of longing. Allow the sadness you feel to be there and to unfold within you. Know that within that sadness, there's also sweetness and the deeply resonating truth that comes when you see the present moment with clarity and kindness.

Intention, Not Force

You cannot will yourself out of despair and disappointment. You know this if you have ever tried to talk a friend out of a bad mood. Remember, this is not something on the thought level; it's a matter of the heart.

You can notice the thoughts you have that keep you in despair. You can instead set an intention that you will stop trying to force your will on the circumstances, expecting life to have a certain outcome. The intention instead can be that you will allow experiences to emerge on their own.

You can set the intention that you will see your painful feelings as an opportunity to turn inward and care for the pain and longing that comes when your desires are not met. You can see your sadness as a teacher and a friend.

Our Dragons

The poet Rainer Maria Rilke exhorts us to trust the difficult and to arrange our life in accordance with that. He encourages us to meet our challenges with friendliness—they are not against us. If the world has terrors, "they are *our* terrors; if it has abysses, these abysses belong to us; if there are dangers, we must try to love them." They are dragons, but we must remember that in ancient myths, the dragons are always transformed into princesses. We make them dragons when we magnify the sadness and disappointment with our stories. We see the frustration and despair, and we don't want to see it. We see the gap between our desire and our reality, and we fill it in with a story about our worth. Rilke says, "If a sadness rises in front of you larger than any you have ever seen … you must realize that something has happened to you, that life has not forgotten you, that it holds you in its hand and will not let you fall." Remember, it will not let you fall.

The Least You Need to Know

◆ We contract around the experience of setbacks and disappointments, limiting our view; mindfulness expands it.

◆ Thinking and problem-solving can exacerbate pain because they feed our interpretations.

◆ Depression happens at the heart level when we shut down and go numb.

◆ Chronic unhappiness becomes conditioned when we believe we must keep sadness at bay and we turn away from the present moment.

◆ Open your heart to your longing and see the learning offered in the moment.

◆ Coming back into the body with mindfulness gives us a safe place and way to move the energy.

Part 6

Living Mindful in a Mindless World

It's difficult to perpetuate anger when you are living mindfully because mindfulness practice brings you to a compassionate place of understanding what is out of balance for you. Mindfulness also cultivates deep listening. The combination of healing anger and old wounds with the skill of listening is a powerful tool for personal and global transformation. As you practice, little transformations take hold that bring lasting changes in your life. And then you become more mindfully engaged in the world. Imagine the possibilities for being the change you want to see in the world.

Chapter 17

When Anxiety Attacks

In This Chapter

- A new way to look at anxiety
- Tolerance for the experience
- Living with uncertainty
- Finding a safe place

"If we are honest with ourselves, most of us will have to admit that we live our lives on an ocean of fear," says Jon Kabat-Zinn. That ocean of fear is anxiety, which in its more severe forms can seriously impact our ability to function in our daily lives. At its worst, it can lead to panic attacks or lure us into traps such as substance abuse.

Mindfulness helps us build a tolerance for staying with anxiety so that we can face it directly rather than trying to run away from it. Practicing mindfulness with anxiety helps us channel the energy, allowing it to pass so that a sense of calm, focused energy can return. In this chapter, we'll show you how to dwell with uncertainty.

A New Relationship with Anxiety

Terrorist alerts. Food scares. A climate crisis. Category 5 hurricanes. Collapsing World Trade Center Towers. Threats to our security are all around us. It's not just the twenty-first century—we're wired to respond to threats and have been since the beginning of humankind. The fight-or-flight response is programmed into us for our survival. But anxiety is a fight-or-flight response to something that is happening in the mind.

Anxiety is a feeling of mental agitation or turmoil in response to a perceived threat. Unlike fear, which is a reaction to something specific and actually happening, anxiety is a feeling of excessive worry or fear in anticipation of something that may or may not happen. Anxiety can be triggered by something specific, such as fear of public speaking or being in open places, or can be experienced randomly and not connected to anything. This feeling of excessive worry can be accompanied by sensations such as heart palpitations, restlessness, muscle tension, irritability, and difficulty falling or staying asleep.

def•i•ni•tion

> **Anxiety** is a signal to pay attention to ourselves and what's happening inside. When we feel anxious, it's as if a part of our inner world is crying for attention. The more we ignore these cries, the louder they scream. An **anxiety disorder** is an extreme pattern of anxiety that can be so severe it interferes with a person's ability to function in daily life. Anxiety disorders include phobias, such as agoraphobia (fear of crowds in expansive places), panic disorder, obsessive-compulsive disorder, generalized anxiety, and post-traumatic stress disorder.

Anxiety may be triggered by a present event, and it may be heightened by a past event, but it is almost always focused on the future. Past events can amplify anxiety; for instance, when we think, *This always happens. I'm trapped in a pattern* or *I remember how traumatic that was. Oh no, it's happening again.*

We experience anxiety because, as humans, we have the ability to think, plan ahead, and adapt to our circumstances. These cognitive skills set us apart from other animals, and these skills are what make it possible for us to build civilizations and create works of art, among other things. The downside is that we can also imagine terrible things happening to us, and this causes a physiological fight-or-flight response. For humans in primitive societies, the threat was real—a tiger in the jungle—and that threat has entered our collective mythology. For modern humans, new myths emerge for each generation, it seems. For those who were schoolchildren in the 1950s, the threat was a nuclear attack. The alarms would blare, and the schoolchildren would "rehearse" fight-or-flight response, crawling under their desks. In the twenty-first century, the 9/11 attack on the World Trade Center Towers and the Pentagon have become the new myth, and the orange terrorist alerts warn of danger.

Every day, we receive little alarms, our own personal version of an orange alert. Our bodies react to these perceived threats as though tigers are about to pounce, bombs are about to fall, or towers are about to collapse. However, nothing like that is happening. There is no tiger, and there's nowhere to run.

Stop Running

It's important to understand that anxiety is not bad or toxic. Nor is it something we get rid of. We can't stop anxiety. It's unpleasant, and if we don't attend to it properly, it can harm our health. But it's not anxiety that's the problem; it's how we respond to it that can cause us harm.

Our first instinct with anxiety is to run away—that's natural. But running away or pushing it away only makes the problem worse. Mindfulness teaches us to stay with it. It interrupts the automatic response. It gives us a way to greet the rush of anxiety in a grounded and accepting way. Then we can make it more tolerable and reduce our turning away.

We can become anxious about being anxious and can get caught up in a spiral of increasing anxiety. But the only way to make it go away is to face it. To face anxiety is to say, "Anxiety is there, and I'm going to allow myself to experience it and feel its unpleasant sensations as much as I can tolerate, because the only way to heal anxiety is to go through it." By not resisting the anxiety, we make room for it to pass away and for a sense of calm to return. Accept it and allow it to be there.

Defining the New Relationship

To heal anxiety, we create a new relationship with it. We need to see that anxiety is a signal that something inside ourselves needs our attention. Mindfulness can help us cultivate the ability to tolerate the alarms; if we can stay with the experience, we can begin to see what's setting off the alarm.

When an aspect of our lives isn't working, anxiety often signals it. If we have a way of operating in the world or undue expectations on ourselves, anxiety can arise when we see that. Maybe we have stories we tell ourselves that are unrealistic or demanding, such as *I have to be perfect* or *I can't ask for help*. Mindfulness slows us down so we can see the freeze-frame: thought, interpretation, reaction. Many times we miss the interpretation. The situation is unpleasant because we believe we must be perfect or self-sufficient. In the mindful relationship with anxiety, we slow down to ask, "Why must this always be so?"

Intense anxiety may be calling us to attend to old psychic wounds. These wounds are so deep and so desperate that they increasingly call for our attention. So no matter how much we turn away, they call again. This is how a tendency toward anxiety can spiral downward. Everything we do to try to stop it, like pushing it away, just brings it back.

You can start to create a new relationship with your experience of anxiety. Set the intention that you will practice facing your anxiety more directly. When anxiety arises, name what's happening as a way of turning toward the experience rather than away from it. Say to yourself, or even out loud if that's helpful, "This is anxiety," or "Anxiety is happening." Accept what's happening—the pounding heart, the rush of adrenaline, and the racing thoughts. As you'll see later in this chapter, these are only the body's response to a perceived threat, nothing more.

Remember the three characteristics of existence—suffering, impermanence, and nonself:

◆ **Suffering happens.** You can't prevent pain, suffering, or anxiety. It's part of being human.

◆ **Everything changes.** The universe is in a constant state of flux. Anxiety will pass. The more you release your resistance to it and allow it to be there, the sooner it will shift and pass away.

◆ **It's not you.** You don't have to identify with the anxiety. It's just a phenomenon that you're experiencing, but it doesn't define you. It's not a sign that you're crazy or that there's something wrong with you.

Building a Tolerance

Practicing mindfulness with anxiety builds a tolerance for the experience. The tolerance enables you to sit with the anxiety without trying to change it.

Building tolerance works for the small, fleeting experiences of anxiety as well as full-blown panic attacks. Anxiety is very much an in-the-body experience because anxiety triggers the fight-or-flight response. Our hearts beat faster, our digestion shuts down, adrenaline floods the bloodstream. Our reflexes are poised to spring away from the wild animals, the nuclear bombs, the terrorists.

Anxiety typically includes some very unpleasant physical sensations. When a person is having a panic attack, the pressure around the heart can be so strong that it feels like they're going to have a heart attack. The thought *I'm having a heart attack!* increases the adrenaline running through the system, increases the fear and dread, and this usually increases the constriction around the heart.

While the goal of using mindfulness to work with your anxiety is not to make it go away, you can use a variety of techniques to release energy and calm yourself when anxiety strikes. This helps you stay present with the anxiety, and it keeps the anxiety workable. You will still feel anxious, but these five techniques can help you avoid intensifying or prolonging your anxiety:

◆ **Come back into the body.** Bring your attention to the physical sensations in your body. Breathe as deeply as you can. Framing anxiety as a physical experience helps you avoid getting caught up in thoughts and stories that exacerbate it.

◆ **Sing.** Singing and other physical activities redirect the energy of anxiety. Singing uses the breath and activates the voice box, giving the energy a channel for release.

◆ **Go outside.** Spaciousness softens anxiety. Go outside. Look up at the blue sky. The physical energy of anxiety can feel confining. By going into a more open space, it's as if you're creating a bigger container for the anxiety. The energy feels big, so you need a big place for it.

◆ **Narrate it.** Step back and name what you're experiencing as it's happening, sort of a play-by-play: *racing thoughts, heart pounding, wanting to run, anxiety is happening.*

◆ **Engage in concentration practice.** Focusing on the breath and equanimity practice are two forms of concentration meditation that can calm you and help you stay present with the anxiety.

Other physical activities also help, such as brisk walking, running, bicycling, and team sports. Deep abdominal breathing can calm the roiling sea inside.

You can channel body energy through outlets such as exercise and physical activity. These activities allow your experience of anxiety to pass through, rather than blocking it and/or feeding it. Your anxiety will eventually pass if you get out of the way.

Over time, you'll find as you practice not engaging in a struggle against your anxiety that your episodes of anxiety don't last as long or feel as strong.

Breathe ...

When you start meditating, you may feel more anxious when you practice. No longer are you relying on the stories to distract you and take you out of the experience of anxiety. It's nothing to be alarmed about. If you feel too anxious to sit in meditation, try a walking meditation instead, or meditating with your eyes open. If even that's intolerable, try taking a walk outside, singing, or exercising—whatever it takes to enable you to be with the experience, if only for a few minutes at a time.

An Uncertain World

We live in an uncertain world. We always have. With a constant stream of news about security alerts, pet-food contamination, lead paint on children's toys, climatological catastrophes such as hurricanes or tsunamis, and global warming, it's easy to let our fears about the future pile up. We can turn away from them—to a point—but this creates a low-level state of fear that is easily heightened. We can go from 0 to 60 mph on the fear scale in seconds. Know that this constant clamorous state around our psyches has an effect. We can live in a collective state of being stuck in a fight-or-flight response.

Practicing mindfulness can change this collective reactivity one individual at a time. By practicing mindfulness and working with the anxiety you feel, you come to know what it is to know something different from the state of anxiety that dominates the culture. The more intimately you know your inner world, the more you are capable of being the observer of the uncertain world surrounding you. You can say, "This is just anxiety. This, too, will pass."

From that place, you can make more mindful choices about how you participate in the culture and how you take action, something we'll delve into more in Chapter 20.

With the equanimity practice we introduced in Chapter 15, you can cultivate an inner peace that is unshakeable in the face of a barrage of news. Equanimity cultivates a sense of balance and acceptance that comes from within, no matter what is happening in the outside world. So you can have equanimity no matter your emotional state or the circumstances of your life.

Anne's Seeds

Since Anne was a teenager, she's experienced anxiety. Now she believes that the seeds of her anxiety were sown when she was a child—a sensitive, shy girl who was often overwhelmed by the activities and personalities of the people around her. Anne learned to cope by shutting herself off from her awareness of the physical sensations of her emotional responses to the world. By the time she hit adolescence, she was pretty much cut off from her awareness of her body, and she stayed that way until she was in her mid-40s. Basically, she was asleep for 30 years!

> **Just Be!**
>
> Take a news fast! Some people—even a journalist like Carolyn—don't access media for one day on the weekend. Others take a news fast during the aftermath of a tragedy—after the shooting, the hurricane, or the plane crash, they take a break for a few days. For the constant, low-level stressful news, such as the climate crisis or the subprime mortgage meltdown, it can be helpful to take a few days or a full week away from the news. A hike in the woods or a camping trip can take you far away from the impact of the news and get you in touch with a world far more calming and constant.

But it wasn't a peaceful slumber: her mind and body continued to send her signals that she was disconnected, and she experienced these signals as anxiety, primarily in the form of uncontrollable—and extremely distressing—thoughts. The more she tried to make these thoughts go away, the louder they became. And each time she got stuck in this loop, her body-mind would react in the physiological ways we described above—the adrenaline would surge, and she would feel a strong urge to flee. But there was no way to run away from her mind and its frightening thinking patterns.

In graduate school, she began learning about anxiety: what it is and how staying present with it reduces it. She started working with her own therapist. She discovered vipassana meditation and began practicing it regularly. Her practice taught her to focus on the physical experience of anxiety, noticing the ways her mind would react with story making and resistance. She saw how she was increasing the anxiety by trying to engage with her distressing thoughts.

Through regular practice, Anne continues to cultivate a grounded center from which she can observe what's actually happening when she experiences anxiety. In this process, she learned a lot about herself and how she is in the world. She began to welcome the frightening thoughts in, realizing that they were coming from a part of herself that was trying to reintegrate. In the process, the thoughts became less frightening, and she became less reactive to them. Her anxiety levels decreased. She found compassion for herself and her mind, which was just doing what minds do when they want us to pay attention.

Anne still experiences anxiety from time to time, but now she can see it coming. She checks in with herself when she notices her heart or thoughts racing, and she stays with the experience. She takes care of herself, much in the way she takes care of her son when he's not feeling well. She's given up always trying to know *why* she's anxious; she knows now that if there's something in her life she needs to attend to that it will become clear to her if she's patient enough. She doesn't need to start analyzing her experience; doing so only increases the anxiety. The obsessive thoughts have pretty much stopped, and they stopped because she attended to them, not because she pushed them away.

Anne's life is calmer now. She makes choices based on what feels right and true. She stands up for herself more now than she ever has in the past. Anne is grateful for her body and all the signals it sends her about what's happening in the world around her. As an adult, she can remove herself from situations that feel overwhelming, which is something she couldn't do as a child. Her life feels more purposeful, and she feels much more at ease.

Live Mindful _____

Big events are part and parcel of daily journalism—watching journalists pull them off is a study in anticipatory anxiety. Anticipatory anxiety is a particular strain of anxiety that focuses on the outcome of a big event. It might be a challenge we're facing such as surgery or a court hearing. It could even be an event we are looking forward to—a family celebration or an awards banquet (and we're the honored guest). Whatever the event, it's important to remember: 1. You don't know for certain what's going to happen, and worrying about it only increases your anxiety. 2. It's not happening in the present moment. 3. Make plans, but also trust in your ability to respond in the moment to what's happening around you.

Masking Anxiety

Turning away from anxiety and the stress that triggers it can send us into the lure of disguises. It's easy in this world to be tempted into submerging our feelings by overindulging in food, abusing alcohol and drugs, or spending money we don't have.

Recent statistics from the Substance Abuse and Mental Health Services Administration showed a 49 percent increase in youths going into rehabilitation treatment from 1992 to 2001. Marijuana was responsible for much of that increase, rising from 23 percent to 62 percent of admissions, but opiate abuse (heroin or narcotic pain medications) spiked from 12 percent to 18 percent, and methamphetamine abuse crept up from 2 percent to 6 percent.

Turning away from anxiety only increases it. Yet it's what we instinctively do. For many people, the anxiety and fear they experience become so severe that they self-medicate with recreational drugs or alcohol. This works while the substance is in effect, giving some temporary sedation and relief from the distress. The problem with this strategy is that because it gives only temporary relief, it supports a reactive stance toward anxiety. In addition, anxiety can be a side effect when coming down from a substance.

Weathering the Storm

In the moment of anxiety, you can almost only think about weathering the storm. The five techniques we mentioned earlier in the chapter—coming into the body, physical activity, spaciousness, narration, and concentration meditation—can help you with the intense energy of the moment.

Please note, though, that if you are experiencing anxiety that is severely interfering with your ability to function or if you have experienced trauma, we advise you to seek a trained therapist who can temper the experience and guide you through it. It's important to keep your practice workable. If you have experienced trauma, the physical sensations or the severity of the anxiety may be more than you should face alone.

Allow It to Pass: Narration

When you experience anxiety, you can narrate to yourself what's happening as it unfolds. By narrating it, you are the observer, and you pull yourself back from engaging with the anxiety. A narrator gives an account of events or a running commentary to what's happening. You can see more clearly what's happening moment to moment.

Christopher K. Germer (*Mindfulness and Psychotherapy*, see Resources) compares this process to cutting up a scary movie into individual frames and laying out the frames on the kitchen table to examine them. We lay bare the raw facts of the experience minus the interpretations we give to them.

As you engage in narrating, notice what's happening in your body. Notice your breath. If it's too hard to sit still, move. Get up and walk, run, or do jumping jacks.

As you narrate, you can also use reassuring self-talk to help yourself stay with the anxiety. Try saying the following to yourself:

> This is just anxiety.
>
> I can allow it to pass.
>
> I can tolerate this experience.
>
> My racing heart is just a physical reaction.
>
> I will decide what to do later after the anxiety passes.

Any phrase that provides reassurance you can get through this experience and stay present with it is helpful. Be careful not to use the self-talk as a way to force yourself to feel calm. The anxiety will pass, and the calm will happen. The more you allow and accept the anxiety, the easier it is for it to pass.

Sutras

Breathing in, calming the body, breathing out, calming the body.
—Thich Nhat Hanh, Vietnamese Buddhist monk

Thich Nhat Hanh suggests connecting phrases with the breath to help us focus and calm ourselves. When we breathe in, we say to ourselves, "Calming the body." When we breathe out, we say, "Calming the body." The rhythm of these phrases and the breath are soothing and help us take deep full breaths—concentration and breathing at the same time.

Stories You Tell Yourself

Do you have trouble letting things go? Do you have a tendency to analyze events and examine everyone's motives? Do you like to look at all facets of a situation in the name of fairness? Is your favorite question "why"?

Analyzing a situation to death can be a mild form of anxiety that paralyzes us from acting. We hold back, preferring to delve deeply into the situation rather than confront someone or face a terrible truth.

Making choices can be an anxiety-filled experience, because when we choose option A, we "un-choose" all the others. Worrying about making the wrong choice is a form of anticipatory anxiety that can stop us in our tracks. Because making choices can cause anxiety, we find a variety of ways to avoid making up our minds. We can defer to another—choose based on what we think we *should* want, or choose as a rebellion against what we think others want us to do. We can obsessively run through all the options, changing our minds daily about what we want to do.

Solid authentic choice is based on your inner wisdom; that is, it comes from a sense of what you *want*. Anxiety makes it difficult to connect with this inner knowing. By practicing mindfulness, you cultivate the ability to drop below the experience of anxiety and reconnect with the inner resources you need to make a choice.

Triggering Inquiry: Going Within

As you continue using the five techniques—coming into the body, physical activity, spaciousness, narration, and concentration meditation—you'll find you develop a tolerance for the experience of anxiety. From that place, you can start mindfully investigating your experience of anxiety.

Over time, you may come to see how certain situations trigger anxiety for you. Your external triggers may launch the anxiety episode, but often these events are projections of your inner suffering. You thought you turned away from those painful experiences only to see them embedded in the little events and day-to-day encounters in your life. Or you catch a reflection of a painful thought or experience, like refracted light, in a news story that activates the worry inside, and the anxiety loop starts again.

When you start practicing mindfulness, you begin to discover that there are many layers to your experience. The more you practice, the more layers you uncover. You discover the increasingly subtler ways that you create suffering for yourself. Maybe you make things harder than they need to be. We can hide these aspects of ourselves and not question them for years. Our way of adapting to situations can feel "normal" to us, and we may not be aware that there is another way of functioning. We may function fairly well, so we don't notice how maladaptive our way of operating is. Mindfulness may reveal this to us many layers deeper, enabling us to open up and adapt in new ways.

The Least You Need to Know

◆ Anxiety is a signal to pay attention to the emotions and the interpretations that fuel the emotions.

◆ Mindfulness cultivates the ability to tolerate the alarm bells.

◆ The goal is not peace, but rather to calmly stay with the experience so you can get to the truth.

◆ Anxiety is a high-energy experience. Channeling the energy through activity can give you a release.

◆ Narration is a mindfulness technique of using play-by-play commentary—not story making—to decrease the intensity of anxiety so that it may pass.

◆ Concentration meditation can soothe you. You can use sutras this way.

Chapter **18**

The Flames of Anger

In This Chapter

- ◆ The secondary emotion
- ◆ Know your anger
- ◆ Venting, pausing, and "anger babies"
- ◆ Road test: anger and driving

Learning how to stay present with the high-energy experience of anger and to do this with compassion is one of the kindest, most challenging practices we can integrate into our lives. The rewards are many, because in today's world we may meet anger at every turn, in many disguises.

Mindfulness practice teaches us how to sit with our anger so that we can see what's out of balance. With this insight, we can see how to restore harmony.

Meeting Your Anger

Anger isn't just the combative words of two fed-up people. It isn't just the rage that explodes on the road when traffic snarls into our day, throwing off our plans. Anger is embedded in the daily irritations, the annoying quirks of our loved one. It's fueled by discontent, and it creeps around our armored hearts masked as cynicism. It's submerged beneath alcohol and substance abuse, a mask for low self-esteem and feelings of unworthiness and powerlessness.

We often disguise anger because it's an unpleasant, highly charged emotion, and it's socially undesirable. But anger is a signal that something is out of balance for us. It's a call to pay attention, to drop deeper. Anger is often accompanied by agitation and a strong urge to do something *now*. It is high energy that wants an immediate outlet. The energy can feel bigger than our bodies.

Anger is often termed a secondary emotion because it's a cover for another—sadness, sorrow, fear, or pain. With mindfulness, we can acknowledge the experience of anger. It's a very real emotional experience. And we can get to the root of the anger, to the secondary emotion that is driving the anger.

In this chapter, we'll give tips and tools for using mindfulness to recognize and manage your anger. Here are simple steps of mindfulness and anger:

1. Stay present with your anger.

2. Allow it to be there, and allow it to pass away.

3. See your experience of anger with compassion.

A regular practice of mindfulness builds the skills that can help you stay present with your anger, allowing the energy to pass. The practice trains you to be the observer of your thoughts and emotions, not the puppet of them. So you can choose how you will respond to your anger rather than become reactive and out of control.

In her psychotherapy practice, Anne works with people who come to therapy to "get rid of" their anger. They know they're angry but can't find a reason why. They believe that they shouldn't be angry or that they should just "get over it," but the anger keeps coming up in a variety of ways. They may find themselves losing their temper over minor annoyances or being sarcastic, critical, or passive-aggressive. As Anne works with these people, she guides them to see how they're resisting their experience of anger and helps them learn how to use mindfulness and anger-management techniques to keep their experience of anger workable. Over time, these people begin to discover the pain and fear underneath the anger and learn how to channel their anger energy in more productive ways rather than have it "leak out" inappropriately.

Getting to Know Your Anger

Mindfulness of your moment-to-moment experiences can help you see when anger is arising. Many of us have difficulty recognizing anger because of family or cultural messages about anger; we may have witnessed frightening episodes of anger in our family of origin, for instance, or anger may be the big taboo in our family. In this section, we'll describe the hallmarks of anger.

Mindfulness practice cultivates your inner wisdom. When you are angry, you are not operating from wise mind; you don't think rationally or clearly. But you can rest assured that if you stay present with the experience of anger, you can let it pass, and clarity will follow.

Because we resist our experience of anger, we don't always recognize how angry we are even though it may obvious to those around us. And blinding ourselves to our own experience of anger can cause us to be highly reactive to anger in others—we can't tolerate anyone around us being angry. Returning to wise mind helps us see more clearly when we're angry, and helps us stay present when people around us are angry. Author Alice Walker calls this "honoring the difficult." When we honor the difficult in ourselves by recognizing our anger, we can more easily honor it in others as well.

Just Be! _____

Being angry seems to be synonymous with yelling or losing our temper. But there's a difference between the experience of anger and what we do in reaction to it. We feel angry, and we may react to it by yelling or crying. Mindfulness can help us work more skillfully with anger by helping us stay present with the experience of anger and allowing it to pass; then in the calm that follows, we can choose how to respond to it.

Anger is a big taboo in our culture, so it can be hard to unmask it. In our culture, many women get the message that "anger is not lady-like." It's not nice to be angry, they are told, and that keeps their anger frozen in place. On the other hand, many men in our culture get the message that their anger is dangerous. It can come from witnessing a raging father and being on the receiving end of that rage, or it can come from cultural currents about misuse of power. It doesn't matter whether it's women who cry tears of frustration that mask the anger deep down, men who rant at the TV during a football game, or those who take two-martini lunches to submerge anger that's scary because of their childhood experiences. These are our stories about anger. And we each must explore what's underneath these stories by staying present with the anger that drives them.

Where Did We Put That?

Anger is palpable. It's challenging to let that highly charged energy be there. Like a caged animal, the energy of anger demands to go somewhere—anywhere—out, in, up, down, sideways, or deep down. It's a raging spring-melt river, cutting a whitewater path down the mountain. In the moment, the angry person doesn't care where all that energy goes. He only wants it to go.

Anger demands that we give it a quick, on-the-spot answer. It wants to go somewhere. So most of us, by the time we grow to adulthood, have had years of practicing where to put our anger. We take our cues in how to respond through instructions from our parents or influences of family, culture, and society.

Over time, each of us develops our unique way of expressing anger (or not expressing it). In your regular mindfulness practice, you can start to notice what you do with anger. You can see the direction your anger energy wants to take, and you can see the ways you react to it by stuffing it, directing it toward yourself or others, or numbing yourself to the experience.

Inward anger takes the form of self-criticism and judgment, and we can be very cruel in the ways we talk to ourselves. Reasons we turn our anger inward include a belief that anger is wrong, toxic, or dangerous, or that our needs and feelings aren't important.

Outward anger is just the opposite—we direct our anger outward when we blame or criticize others for their words and actions. We think people are stupid, don't care, or just don't get it, and we can get caught in a loop of angry thoughts about them.

Stuffed anger happens when we tell ourselves we can't be angry. We suppress our angry thoughts. We turn away from our experience of anger. We can have all kinds of stories we tell ourselves to convince ourselves we aren't angry. We may rationalize the behavior of the person who made us angry or convince ourselves that if we feel angry, then we're angry people. We do this because we believe it's not nice to be angry. We don't want to scare or upset people if we let them know how we truly feel.

Sideways anger takes the form of sarcasm, cynicism, or passive-aggressive behavior. We form a worldview that focuses on unhappiness; at the root of it is anger we don't want to feel. We can feel "grumpy" or dissatisfied and find ourselves making sarcastic comments that can be cutting and hurtful at times.

Submerged anger is numbness. It's a more extreme form of stuffing our anger. When the energy of the anger we're stuffing is high, it's difficult to ignore it because it wants to be expressed. When this happens, people will shut themselves off from their awareness of anger by disconnecting from their physical experience or by numbing themselves with drugs, alcohol, or other addictive behaviors.

Hitchhiker anger is suppressed anger that attaches onto a feeling of irritation or frustration about something that is happening in the moment. We can tell this is happening when we blow up over something relatively minor, like someone cutting us off on the freeway or someone going through the grocery express checkout with 16, not 15, items. We may have an appropriate response of anger to the event, but suppressed anger "hitchhikes" to this experience, and it becomes rage. You can notice this free-floating, unattached anger when it hooks up with something deeper, and it comes up in intense ways that are out of proportion to the experience.

The following table shows ways that different forms of anger manifest in behaviors and thoughts.

Places We Put Anger	Type of Anger	How It Manifests
Inside	Inward anger	Judgment, self-criticism, beating yourself up
Outside	Outward anger	Combative behavior, picking fights, blaming others
Down	Stuffed anger	Pushing anger away, denying that something bothers you
To the side	Sideways anger	Sarcasm, passive-aggressive behavior, discontent, cynicism
Attached to something else	Hitchhiker anger	Rage in response to feelings of irritation, minor annoyances (such as slow drivers or noisy leaf blowers)
Way down	Submerged anger	Addictive behaviors such as alcohol or substance abuse, self-destructive behaviors such as overeating, "feeling nothing"

Working with Anger

Whether you turn your anger inward or outward, stuff it, or numb it, mindfulness can give you a way to respond more skillfully to your experience of anger. When you notice anger arising, watch how you react to it and what direction you send it. When you notice anger arising, say to yourself, "I feel angry right now," or "Anger is happening," or whatever phrase helps you notice your anger.

When you notice that you're feeling angry, drop your attention into the body and focus on the physical sensations of anger. Just as you learned to do with anxiety, you can narrate to yourself what's happening as you feel anger—for example, *heart pounding, want to scream or run, stomach churning.* Remember to keep returning to the physical sensations; when your mind gets caught up in story, name it *story making* and return to the body.

Because anger is so highly charged and we can become reactive and even destructive in the ways we react to it, it's helpful to use anger-management techniques to keep the experience of anger workable. Try these various techniques to help you stay present with the anger:

- **Distraction.** It may seem like a paradox to use distraction as you practice mindfulness, but just as sending boxers to their corners introduces a break in a boxing match, using distraction introduces a break in that it takes you away from the energy of anger so that you can reconnect with your wise mind. Distract yourself by placing your attention on something completely neutral and outside yourself, such as counting the cars in the parking lot or looking at the trees outside your window. Do this with the intention of calming the body and taking a break.

- **Concentration.** Activate a calming effect through concentration meditation, focusing on the breath or another object of concentration and meditate. Equanimity practice can be very helpful with anger, as it is with anxiety.

- **Self-soothe.** Self-soothing can be especially helpful if you tend to turn your anger inward or suppress it. Engage in an activity that feels good to you—it doesn't matter what you do as long as it's not harmful to yourself or others. You may decide that going for a walk or listening to music would feel good, or you may decide to have a bowl of ice cream. Just be clear with yourself what you're doing and that you're doing it to soothe yourself. Stay present with the experience.

- **Physical activity.** With more energetically charged forms of anger, physical exercise is an excellent way to get some of the energy out of the body. Any form of vigorous exercise will do; just be sure you use mindfulness to stay present with the experience of anger and don't use the energy of the exercise to fuel more angry thoughts and stories.

Venting, Pausing, and Soothing "Angry Babies"

Buddhist monk Thich Nhat Hanh encourages us to think of anger as if it were a crying baby guiding us to hold and soothe it. He discourages venting anger by doing such things as punching pillows, believing that it's acting out our anger and feeding it. But we believe you can be intentional in your pillow punching. If you feel like punching a pillow or going to the gym for some kickboxing, go ahead and do so. You can avoid feeding your anger by using mindfulness to stay present with the physical experience of anger and naming what you experience from moment to moment. When you catch yourself imagining your boss's face on the pillow or punching bag (why is it that our bosses are often the target of our anger?), name it "boss thoughts," and return to the physical experience of punching.

And if the energy of your anger is not so strong, then holding it like a crying baby is a lovely way to soothe yourself and stay present with the experience. If this practice resonates with you, allow yourself to talk to yourself as you would a crying child. If it feels helpful, you can even imagine yourself as a child and notice all the feelings you have about the younger you.

When you notice anger arising and if the energy isn't too high, you can take a mindful pause—breathe deeply, and place your attention in the center of the body. Notice the physical sensations you're experiencing and name them. Continue to breathe for a few minutes more. Notice the anger, but also notice what else you're feeling. Assure yourself that whatever you're feeling in this moment will pass, that it's okay to feel what you're experiencing.

Just Be!

When you feel angry energy building, pause and notice what is happening in the body. Notice how connected you feel to your wise mind and decide whether to say anything in response in the moment. Know that unless the building is on fire, you don't have to do or say anything right now. Know that even if it was the "right time" to say something, you can still come back later and talk about what happened; the right time is when you are ready to speak. You can always ask for a clarification or apologize. You can wait until you see the situation more clearly before taking action.

Rage and Other Tales of the Road

These days, if you live in a city or drive on a highway, you have to be a road warrior. Navigating your way to work—or anywhere—is a high-wire proposition. Remember we mentioned in Chapter 14 that Americans lost 4.2 billion hours in 2005 in traffic? That same study estimated that Americans waste 2.9 billion gallons of fuel annually while stuck in traffic. The Texas Traffic Institute study put a dollar figure on the cost of lost time and spent fuel: $78.2 billion a year.

It's no wonder that rage can rule the road these days. Road rage, congested highways, and mindlessness have conspired to make driving a horror.

Mindful Driving in Traffic

Driving is a ripe environment for hitchhiker anger. Add to that the apparent privacy of being alone in a car, and you have a recipe for road rage.

For many of us, traffic brings up the sense of loss of control. If someone crashes into another car, and wreckers have to come out and extricate their crashed cars from the freeway, we have to wait until we can inch around that. When there's an accident, though, it's very clear: *Ain't going to get there.* At least not when you thought you were going to get there.

We may view the growing congestion in cities as evidence of the lack of control we have in our lives. It may be that the city has grown up around the place you work to the degree that a traffic-free corridor is now the busiest intersection in the city—instead of "My city is gone," it's "My city has landed on top of me."

Other external forces can shape our commute. Maybe you have moved farther out but kept the same job, or maybe you married someone who lives farther from your job. It's easy to feel helpless and forget that no matter what's happening to us and around us, we always have a choice in the way we respond.

Mindfulness of Driving

You can stay present with the highly charged energy of road rage by being mindful of your anger and bringing your awareness to driving itself. When you feel your temper rising behind the wheel, try doing the following:

◆ Take a few deep breaths, and notice the feeling of the breath in the nostrils as you breathe in and out.

◆ Narrate out loud what you're experiencing. Notice we said what *you're* experiencing. Don't say, "That guy is a jerk who doesn't know how to drive." Instead say, "Feeling really angry at him for cutting in front of me." Name the physical sensations and emotions that you're experiencing, as you continue to breathe.

◆ Notice any places where you're clenching or tensing—for example, white knuckles on the steering wheel. Release the clenching.

◆ Without taking your eyes off the road, pay attention to something neutral such as the feeling of air coming in through the window or the sound of your tires on the road.

◆ Notice the noise level in the car. Do you have the radio on? Are you listening to something that annoys you, like a commercial or talk radio? Turn it off, or switch to audio that's more soothing.

◆ If it feels appropriate, use *metta* phrases from Chapter 7 to cultivate compassion for your fellow drivers. Remind yourself that you're all in this together—that it doesn't have to be a rat race or you against them.

Breathe ...

It's important to monitor your emotional state when you practice *metta* while driving. Because *metta* practice can stir up aversion, it may actually fuel feelings of anger and frustration, which can lead to road rage. If you find your anger increasing when you use *metta*, use anger management techniques instead to calm and focus yourself.

Creating Choices

We can help ourselves out by becoming a new kind of road warrior—
one who doesn't just prepare for the road conditions but also prepares by
creating conditions that help keep us from boiling over into road rage
when the traffic gets thick. We can leave a little early each morning or,
if it's an option, consider working different hours. We can choose music
or recorded books that are interesting and soothing to listen to rather
than fueling our anger with talk-radio debates.

When you only allow a small window for threading the needle—when
it absolutely, positively must happen now—you're setting yourself up for
reactivity. Anger happens when we have an attachment to something
that's being taken away. We have the expectation (and the dire need!)
to get to work on time, and then traffic happens and we're either late or
we spend the entire drive worrying we'll be late.

We have choices. Understanding that can be liberating. They may not
be easy choices—we may have to move, change jobs, or find other ways
to commute. It may require difficult conversations with your boss about
telecommuting one day a week.

These external forces can be a reference point in our lives for our feelings of powerlessness. It can be a real reactivity point. But we do have
power in our responses. We do have a choice, but it means getting
involved in being a voice in city development and voting.

While we can't control what happens to us and around us, we can
affect our experience in each moment in the way we respond to what's
happening. This is the Buddhist concept of karma: our experience in
each moment is the product of a set of conditions, many of which are
outside our control. Many, but not all. Our response to our experience
in this moment creates seeds that become some of the conditions that
create our experience in subsequent moments. In this way, our present
thoughts influence the future. We can respond to our frustration with
compassion for ourselves by naming our experience of anger and talking ourselves through it instead of riding the bumper of the car ahead
of us. We can regain our focus through breath and body awareness. We

can look at what's beneath the surface—feelings of powerlessness, anger at the spouse who wanted to live in the suburbs, dissatisfaction with our job, lifelong patterns of not feeling seen and heard ....

Time Stress

A close cousin of road rage is time stress. For a good chunk of society, there is simply not enough time. This is going to sound like we're crazy, but the antidote to the time crunch is downtime—intentional nondoing.

The moments you devote to mindfulness practice enable you to sidestep the flow of time. You can let go of your need to mold time to the constraints of your life. Time spent in inner stillness shifts your perception of time. You emerge with a sense of calmness and a centeredness that changes your experience of time outside of your meditation sessions. Mindfulness practice trains you to flow along with time rather than struggle with it or feel driven by it. This is the power of the present moment. There is a saying that Carolyn loves: "The moment when I started having enough time for everything was when I started doing only what was most important."

Be mindful of these concepts with time:

◆ Time is a product of your thoughts. How you think of time is how you will choose to respond to time.

◆ Live in the present moment. You can waste a lot of time dwelling on the past, and it's usually quite unsatisfying. Or you can spend a lot of time worrying about the future, and it causes distress.

◆ Take time intentionally to meditate.

◆ Simplify your life. It's when you're spread too thin that you feel stressed. Get to the heart of what's really important for you.

Sutras _____

> *All composed things are like a dream,*
>   *a phantom, a drop of dew, a flash of lightning.*
> *That is how to meditate on them.*
> *That is how to observe them.*
> —The Diamond Sutra

Our experience, our sense of the world around us, is composed of a series of constantly shifting, changing moments, like the frames of a film. Each discrete moment has its roots in the previous moment and is a seed for the subsequent moment. The way we respond to a feeling of anger affects how the anger unfolds: holding on to it paints a view of life that increases our rage; working skillfully with it helps it pass so we can reconnect with our inner wisdom, which can guide us to respond appropriately to what's happening around us.

Moment-by-Moment Mindfulness

For each of us, anger is a unique experience. There is no one technique that will work for everybody. Nor is there one technique that will work for you in every instance of anger.

It's only through the practice of moment-by-moment mindfulness that you can see what technique will carry you through the feeling—that is, will enable you to stay with the experience of anger.

Live Mindful _____

Anne has found that listening to music helps her stay present with her anger. Energetic music with affirming lyrics gives her an outlet for all that energy and frames her experience in healing ways. For example, reggae music helps her connect to her outrage about suffering in the world. Alanis Morrisette expresses the pain of relationships in a way that resonates with her. And if it's a quieter anger about loneliness and disconnection, songs by Joni Mitchell and the Indigo Girls remind her she's not alone. She knows that it's a tricky business to find music that helps heal rather than fuel her anger, and she's careful to stay aware of her emotional state as she listens and sings along.

Right View, Wise Mind

Our inner wisdom is with us even when we're raging and when anger has apparently taken over. Mindfulness can get us in touch with our inner wisdom. By exploring our inner landscape, we become intimate with it. This creates a place of tranquility from which we can know our anger and cool the flames.

The Least You Need to Know

- Anger is a sign that something is out of balance.

- Anger is a secondary emotion that masks other feelings, such as sadness, hurt, rejection, fear, pain, jealousy, and frustration.

- We hide our anger from ourselves when we send it out, down, in, or sideways. Mindfulness can reveal the ways we push away or hide our anger.

- Mindfulness can help us unmask cultural and family messages we have gotten about anger.

- We can manage our feelings of powerlessness while in congested traffic by using breath and body awareness and by sending compassion to ourselves.

- When anger is highly charged, use moment-by-moment mindfulness to decide on the technique that best manages it.

Chapter 19

Deep Listening

In This Chapter

- ◆ Beyond "either-or"
- ◆ Insight dialogue
- ◆ Nonviolent communication
- ◆ Sabbath: creating a space

Deep listening is a profound mindfulness practice that begins by listening deep within. When we cultivate acceptance of ourselves, we can expand our acceptance for others.

Insight dialogue and nonviolent communication are two ways to practice deep listening. In this chapter, we'll show you how to bring deep listening into your daily life, transforming your relationships and creating a new way to see the world around you.

Mindfulness gives you the tools for exploring your inner landscape; deep listening is a way to explore your outer landscape. Let your mindfulness practice give you a new lens for seeing what you find there.

Listening with Your Entire Being

When we practice deep listening, we are listening with our entire being, not just listening to words and thinking about them. When anything arises to distract us as we're listening, we notice it and set it aside, returning to the experience of listening. We set the intention of understanding what it's like for the other rather than pushing our own agenda, knowing that we'll have our turn to speak and be heard. When we practice deep listening, we recognize that each of us has our own truth and that it doesn't have to be "either/or."

When we're listening, we have to allow our minds to do what they're doing. Trying not to get distracted or caught up in story is not helpful. We have to accept that we'll do that and allow it to happen, noting it, and returning to the listening. It can be there in the background, and we can still listen to the other.

The Deep in Deep Listening

The depth in deep listening comes when we pay attention not just to what's happening with the other person, but in how we're affected by what the other is saying. What do you feel as you listen? What do you notice?

Practicing mindfulness cultivates the ability to notice all the threads and layers of our experience and hold them in our awareness simultaneously. So you could be listening to someone, and feel distracted. You might feel sad that you missed what she just said. You might hear her words and wonder what she's feeling, notice the expression on her face, realize that you've looked at your watch three times in the past 10 minutes, then remember something she told you the other day about her father, or remember something similar that happened to you. And then you realize how difficult it is for you to listen to her describe how she's hurting and realize that you're clenching your shoulders, and so on.

These experiences can all be there in the mind at the same time. They *are* there, but we have a tendency to get caught up in one thread or try to silence all the others. Mindfulness helps us recognize the multiple threads, creating enough space around them so that we can accept that they're there and not try to control them. We can have all that going on in the mind, *and* we can listen deeply to the other at the same time. Really! We fail to listen deeply when we devote so much energy to fighting and controlling the activity of the mind. But if we just notice the struggle and stay there with it, we have more energy for listening.

The next time you're in a face-to-face conversation with someone, practice listening more deeply:

◆ As the conversation begins, take a deep breath or two. Pay attention to your posture or stance. Are you facing the person or turning away? Turn toward the person. Set aside your magazine, or turn away from your computer screen and face the person fully. Make eye contact.

◆ As you listen, use the other person's words and expressions as an object of attention just as you use the breath as an object of attention when you meditate.

◆ If you notice any tendency to interrupt or get caught up in thinking about what you want to say, release it, and return to listening.

◆ As you listen, notice the facial expressions of the other person. Notice what feelings come up for you as you listen, what feelings the other is expressing to you. See if you can get a sense for the words between the words.

Releasing Your Grip

Through mindfulness practice, we learn to loosen our grip on these lenses we create, and in so doing, we develop a sense of reality that's much more fluid, changing, and responsive to our day-to-day experience. It's much closer to the truth. We transcend that reality into a deeper meaning of our experience. For example, you can become very angry one day at a friend who you perceive is shaking up her marriage, but realize the next day that your agitation was more about your fears that your own marriage is stale.

When we loosen our grip, we can allow ourselves to see things more clearly. We don't need to be "right" or have it all figured out. As our grip on our stories loosens and as we see our projections for what they are, we begin to see the other in a new way, as someone more like us than we were willing to see before. Our sense of the other becomes fuller and more complex, and we diminish our need for the other to be a certain way to compensate for what we feel is lacking in ourselves. In this process, empathy, compassion, and a feeling of deeper connection naturally begin to grow.

> **Just Be!**
>
> It's important for us to be respectful and honest with each other about whether we're in a place where we can listen deeply; and if we're not, to speak up and say so and agree on a later time to have that conversation. Deep listening isn't something that gets foisted on us. It's an invitation to engage in an intentional way.

This is why, for instance, Buddhist monk Thich Nhat Hanh suggested after 9/11 that what the world needed to do was assemble all the great thinkers from all different backgrounds and fields of expertise. The group would explore the problems of the day using deep listening. It sounds quaint—many people thought so—but the story demonstrates the power of mindfulness to transcend our engrained patterns. Through deep listening, we can release our tenacious grip on our thoughts, our stories, and our projections. And we can do this collectively, or one on one.

Group Listening

We can practice deep listening in conversation with one person, and we can practice it in groups. When deep listening is practiced in a group, the tone of the conversation changes; rather than competing to have their views heard, group members extend to each other the attention and respect that they want for themselves. Rather than "taking" time, there's a giving and receiving that happens.

Anne facilitates a support group for adult children of people who have Alzheimer's. Each month the group gathers to share what's happening with their parents and how each person is dealing with it. The meeting begins with deep listening. Each person takes as much time as he or she needs to share his or her experience, and everyone else listens without interrupting. People in the group share their feelings of sadness, help-lessness, and fear, and in this way, they all feel heard, understood, and connected to each other.

It is much the same in mindful writing practice, another form of group listening. As each person reads from his writing practice, the others say, "Thanks for sharing." All is received with warmth, compassion, and gratitude. This takes the listener out of the natural inclination to critique. (This is something that writers do a lot of!) "Recall" takes deep listening one layer deeper. As you listen to the person reading, you are attuned to her inner world. You can do whole body listening, attuning your breath and your body awareness to the words. You can feel it in your body when a detail or snatch of dialogue from the other person's inner world resonates with you. Some people feel it as a tingling on the spine, a bond between speaker and listener, the heart in the throat, or the stomach flipping. It can be tension, or it can feel like a connection. These little resonances are the ways our minds attune to another. They are your body's call to attention.

Putting Deep Listening into Practice

Insight dialogue and nonviolent communication are two practices that provide a structure for deep listening. We'd like to introduce them to you here, and encourage you to explore these practices further as a way to bring deep listening into your life in an intentional way.

Insight Dialogue

Insight dialogue is a form of interpersonal meditation practice that brings the practice of mindfulness into our experience with other people. One of the foundational ideas of insight dialogue is mutuality, the idea that we are interconnected. These are the steps of insight dialogue:

1. Pause.

2. Relax.

3. Open.

4. Let trust emerge.

5. Listen deeply.

6. Speak the truth.

When you pause, you stop the grasping and clinging that color your *interpretations* of what another is saying. When you pause, you might be right in the middle of an emotional reaction—an emotional spike or a rush of thought—so you need to relax. You can bring awareness to places in your body where you are tense. Then comes step three, to open: let your awareness expand to accept all that is around you. This is the mutuality, the acknowledgment of the other without trying to change, persuade, or push away.

def•i•ni•tion

An **interpretation** is more than a rendering or a translation. An interpretation gives meaning to the words or actions of another person or an event. An observation or documentation is about what happened, but an interpretation is about what it means.

From these three steps, trust emerges, and deep listening can happen. From that place, you speak your truth.

Nonviolent Communication

Nonviolent communication is a method developed by American psychologist Marshall Rosenberg. It's often referred to as compassionate communication, and its goal is to create a flow between us and others based on mutuality, the honoring of all the people participating. The method teaches people to inspire compassion from others as they respond compassionately to others and themselves. The focus of nonviolent communication is on observation, feeling, needs, and requests. The two parts are empathic listening and honestly expressing.

Here's what nonviolent communication means:

◆ Make observations free of judgment.

◆ Hear your own deeper needs.

◆ Hear the deep needs of others.

◆ Identify what you want.

◆ Articulate it.

In more practical terms, ways you can contribute to peaceful, compassionate communication are to notice what's happening inside:

◆ Focus on saying what you want—not what you don't want.

◆ Reinforce actions that will help a person be what you would like—instead of telling that person what you want her to do.

◆ Tune in to the other person's feelings first. Then decide if you agree or disagree.

◆ Notice if you say "no" more often than you say "yes," and if you do, notice the unmet needs that keep you from saying "yes."

Insight dialogue and nonviolent communication are powerful ways to practice deep listening and communicating. In Resources, we've listed books about these practices as well as links to websites that list classes and workshops you can take to learn these practices in depth.

Sutras

The point is that our true nature is not some ideal that we have to live up to. It's who we are right now, and that's what we can make friends with and celebrate.

—Pema Chödrön, *Awakening Lovingkindness*

Mindfulness practice helps us see our true nature more clearly. When we practice deep listening, we begin to see more clearly the true nature in others. Making friends with ourselves in this way paves the way for making friends with the people in our lives.

Holding a Space

We can't always tell in the moment what's in our own hearts. It can take time for the truth to emerge. It's vital to honor that and to hold a space for ourselves and for the other. With mindfulness practice, we do it for ourselves, and so we do it for all beings.

There will always be things going on inside that aren't clear. We can share that. We can say what we are aware of: "I'm feeling unsettled about this but it isn't clear why ..."; "I'm finding myself wanting to argue, but I don't know where it's coming from ..."; "I feel sad/bad ..."; "I'm angry right now and need to take a break, but I want to talk to you after I've calmed down ..."; and so on. This is authentic communication.

So, holding a space for ourselves means being patient with ourselves. When we are listening deeply and speaking authentically, we don't need to have all the answers or win the argument or have our way. We share our experience as best we can. We hold open the possibility that our thoughts and feelings are likely to change and shift, that what we felt to be absolutely true yesterday looks different today. One way of thinking about it is to take a new measurement each time. And this is the nature of things; it's the way things are.

> **Breathe ...**
>
> "I really understand you, but ..." can be a sign of many things. It can be a sign that you don't feel heard. How much clearer it would be to say, "I don't feel heard" than to keep saying the same thing over and over. It can be a sign that you want your point or idea to be the correct or right one, and that you want to "win." It can be a sign of thinking there can only be one truth—yours or theirs. Turn inward and see what you're experiencing as you find yourself saying things like, "I understand you, but ...." What's really happening? What do you want to say?

Sabbaths and Retreats

We need to create space in our lives for deep listening. If we pack our days full and are always rushing, then there's little room for opening ourselves to deeply listening to one another. There are many ways to create space. Make a commitment to keep the TV off during dinner or to say no to some activities and commitments in order to have a simpler life. You can create space by knowing what's important to you and how you want to be spending your time. You then make choices based on that. Take a pause and ask yourself, "What do I really want to do in this moment?"

Creating space is a way to practice sabbath. Sabbath is the practice of taking an intentional pause, whether it's for a few hours, an entire day, or an even longer period of time. When we practice sabbath, we are creating conditions that encourage the practice of deep listening.

The famous poet and environmentalist Wendell Berry spent seven years writing a book inspired by his "sabbaths" with nature in the form of meditation poems in *Sabbaths* (see Resources). Watching a flock of cedar waxwings eating wild grapes on a November afternoon, he notes, "Though they have no Sundays, they are full of sabbaths."

Like Spring Cleaning

When we begin to practice mindfulness, we set off on a journey inward, seeing our inner landscapes with fresh eyes. We learn about ourselves and how it is for us to live in this world. We face our demons directly and begin to recognize them as parts of ourselves we had cast aside long ago, and see that they aren't our enemies after all. We begin to welcome them back in, so to speak.

Going on retreat is a way to deepen our practice even further. At the beginning of a retreat, the participants enter into silence—there is no speaking except in interviews with the teachers. It may seem daunting to think about keeping silent, but many people discover that it's a huge relief! In the space of the silence, we can take the time to explore our inner worlds much more deeply. It's often compared to spring-cleaning: while meditation is like taking out the trash, a retreat is like cleaning your whole house.

Live Mindful _____

Anne and her husband sometimes have one-day silent retreats at home in which they practice sitting and walking meditation and listen to recorded talks by meditation teachers. It's a wonderful break from their busy lives, and it deepens their meditation practice and connection to each other. It also provides them with some lightness and humor—when their teenage son sees his parents doing walking meditation in the living room, he's pretty convinced they are truly weird!

A Guide to Retreats

A retreat can strengthen and inspire your regular mindfulness practice. Meditation centers offer retreats as short as one day and as long as three months. A list of retreat centers appears in Resources.

When choosing a retreat, consider the length. While many people do a seven-day retreat as their first experience, it isn't necessary to start out that way. Consider doing a one- or two-day retreat if an entire week of silence feels like too much or if you don't have a lot of time to spare.

Also consider the meditation tradition of the retreat. Anne practices meditation in the vipassana tradition, which has a gentle, welcoming approach. At vipassana retreats, participants are encouraged to treat themselves with kindness and compassion and to practice mindfulness in all activities, not just during the meditation periods. She finds this a safe, welcoming environment for practice.

You can find retreats in a variety of traditions, including Zen Buddhism and combined meditation/yoga retreats. Lay teachers, as well as monastics, lead retreats. Some retreats are geared toward men, women, or youths as well as people of various backgrounds and ethnicities.

Many people experience a deep sense of calm and stillness on retreat, and it's wonderful and soothing when this happens. But you can also experience a lot of unpleasant sensations and emotions—Anne has spent entire retreats engulfed in anxiety, for example. On retreat, it isn't what you experience that's so important; it's how you meet that experience. And each retreat is different—just because this retreat was pleasant or unpleasant doesn't mean they will all be that way.

The Least You Need to Know

- Deep listening is more than hearing the words of another or noticing your thoughts about those words. Deep listening is something you do with your entire being.

- Our minds are capable of holding multiple threads. Our struggle comes when we fight that.

- Loosen your hold on controlling your reality; instead, open to meet what it is.

- Insight dialogue teaches deep listening in one's interpersonal relationships.

Chapter 20

Like Gandhi Said: We Must Be the Change

In This Chapter

- Careful, alert, engaged
- Seeing your power
- Cause for hope
- You in the web of life

Can mindfulness change the world? Imagine a world where each of us is actively engaged and vibrantly alive. Imagine each of us seeing our path and passionately making a contribution. Imagine what we can do together.

No more stories, only truth. No more grasping, only liberation. No more greed, simply generosity. No more "aversion," only compassion and lovingkindness. That's potent. That's the landscape of mindfulness.

Viewing the world through the lens of truth and tranquility, we can see how the choices we make together in the present moment are the choices that have the power to change … everything.

Engaging the Mind

When we practice mindfulness, we are engaging with the world and inclining ourselves to seeing things as they are. The more we practice, the more we see. It's not always pleasant—in fact it's very unpleasant at times—but it connects us with what's solid and real, which is our experience from moment to moment. As we practice by watching our own experience, we begin to see the truth of the three characteristics of existence—impermanence, suffering, and nonself. These three characteristics are solid, true, and enduring—qualities you can trust.

As we practice, we begin to see how flimsy our stories are and how easily they fall apart. The more we see this, the less we cling to them, and the less we "need" them. We become more comfortable with a state of flux.

We can also begin to see what our stories are trying to tell us. What stirs our compassion? Often, if we are agitated about an issue or have an aversion to a political leader, that tells us there is something inside ourselves that merits inquiry. If we're furious about traffic, maybe it goes deeper than the delay and frustration. Perhaps it reveals our impatience with outdated systems of transportation, lack of confidence in our leaders, our own disenchantment and self-disenfranchisement, or judgments about the greed of SUV makers. And if so, then what's that about? Okay, that's a barrel-full, but hopefully you get the idea. We must tap into our hearts and see what we really care about. We project our stories onto political leaders, corporate executives, or whomever. But we must get to the heart of the matter.

You Have the Power

We can see our power in a situation when we see the traps we create for ourselves through our reactivity and story making. This helps us see the only thing we can really change—how we respond to our experience.

If we as individuals can see the power in our moment-to-moment responses, then we can see that each of us, in every moment, has a choice. We can see our way out of the traps, past the layers of belief that we create with story making—beliefs that we cling to so tightly that they appear to be the only truth, the only way. Through mindfulness practice, we can see the power of the open and capacious moment.

There are more, bigger, better solutions than we know to the world's problems, if only we can let ourselves see them. We see the power in small revelations at first, and then our sense of power grows.

We must also tap into our own compassion for the situation to see how we might be a voice. To make our voice heard, we must know why it matters to us to speak or vote on this issue. And, to believe that we can persuade an influential person to change the situation, we must believe that that person is just like us: *Just like me, this person wants a safe world for his or her family. Just like me, this person wants wholesome food, good health, and a long, happy life. Just like me, this person wants peace for our planet.*

Karma is the law of cause and effect: our actions in one moment affect what happens in the next. We would add, too, that the actions we *don't* do take affect the next moment, too. When we don't notice the thoughts we push away, we wall ourselves off from our power to see what we care about and how we might play a role in changing it.

So knowing that, we can commit to being open to receive the information. We can see when we get agitated, push away, or numb ourselves to the issues we care about. We can notice when we tell ourselves that one voice doesn't make a difference, and we can also be attentive to others who see what we see and care about what we care about. Then we can see we aren't the only voice. We can join the dialogue—or start it!

Breathe ...

Is mindfulness self-absorbed? If you sit off alone by yourself with your thoughts, aren't you being selfish? The intention of mindfulness practice is to purify your heart, liberating you from greed, hostility, insensitivity, judgments, and anger ... whatever arises. These thoughts obstruct your awareness and compassion, but if you don't know they are there, you can't see how you can transcend them. And transcending your suffering benefits all beings, not just yourself.

The Power to Change Yourself

Carolyn is a lifelong optimist. She comes by it honestly, from a father who described himself as a "cock-eyed optimist," echoing a Rodgers and Hammerstein show tune.

Yet during the writing of this book, Carolyn found herself saying to a brand-new friend in a café, "I'm thinking I don't like the twenty-first century very much." The writing of this book triggered Carolyn to go deeper into mindfulness, and along with that call to attention came the call to heed her discontent about the forces at work in the world rather than mask it with magical thinking.

Normally, she would have pushed these thoughts away, focusing on something positive and remaining blind to the news reports (something that's hard to do if you're in daily journalism!). But this time, she heeded the call to sit with her discouragement and discontent. She did not feed it (well, only a little!).

Instead, when she noticed it, she greeted it. This enabled her to work through it, to give voice to it, to breathe her way through it, to name it, and stay with it calmly. It enabled her to find deep within a constancy—a contentment that doesn't shift and flux with the passing thoughts. And through this experience, staying in the present moment, even when it was unpleasant and painful, she experienced little openings—people she met, things they said—that showed her the power she did have.

The Power in Deep Listening

We can take our deep listening skills from the interpersonal level to the family level, to the community level, or for that matter, to the world-summit level. Deep listening has a ripple effect. Listening within ripples to our interpersonal relationships, which ripples to family, which ripples to community, and so on.

We can know our stories and cultivate the ability to notice all threads of our experience. Through mindfulness practice, we can open ourselves more to all the layers of what's happening for others. When we are willing to examine those layers, we can see the common ground.

Through deep listening, we can come to clarity about wise speech. We can know that we are coming from the right place—the place of a clear, compassionate heart.

Wise speech leads to right action. Even if we don't persuade someone to our way of thinking, we have taken right action when we state our views with mindfulness and compassion. We must have compassion for all threads of the experience, and at the same time we must stay true to what is right for us.

Live Mindful

Anne's meditation practice has shifted the way she lives her life. She is more in touch with what really matters to her, and this affects her choices about how she spends her time and who she spends her time with. She has seen how often she will "go along to get along" rather than speak up about what she wants or thinks is right. Seeing this makes it increasingly difficult to keep silent or to say "yes" when she really wants to say "no." As her compassion grows, it becomes harder and harder to see herself as flawed and deserving of the unkind words or rude behavior of others. She sees more clearly how to speak up in these situations using kindness and empathy.

Building Hope

Mindfulness fosters faith—not faith in a deity or set of beliefs, but faith in the way things are in this life. The practice builds faith in the deep truth that things change, yet we have an unshakable inner wisdom that can guide us no matter what happens to us. (A faith in a deity or set of beliefs may illumine this inner wisdom.)

Practicing mindfulness teaches us to stop struggling so much. We use mindfulness to interrupt the fight-or-flight response, the conditioned state of stress we live in when we aren't aware of the struggle against our perceived threats. Mindfulness changes how our bodies feel. It changes the conditioned response. And so the cloud of anxiety, despair, and hopelessness lifts. It may be a low-level, chronic state of hopelessness—a numb brand of apathy—but the intensity of our response to the situation in the world leaves us depleted, exhausted, and not very hopeful. We must first notice what disenchants us so that we can begin to build hope.

Contentment: Happiness That Lasts

Mindfulness practice puts us on a path toward waking up, toward being free. As we practice, we lessen our need for the conditions of our lives to be a certain way before we can be happy. We move from striving for conditioned happiness to finding the deeper sense of peace and happiness within. We can transcend the circumstances.

In doing this, we loosen our grip on the future—the future we're trying to create to rid ourselves of unpleasant circumstances. We come back into the present moment, and we see that that is where the power lies. In the fully realized present moment, we are liberated from the need to control the future; the present moment is perfect as it is. We can then make choices—the right choices—for Right Action that create a stronger future.

In this liberation lies contentment. Contentment is different from happiness, which is fleeting and depends on circumstances. Contentment is a deep happiness that you carry around with you wherever you go no matter what is happening. Contentment lasts. It's an inner peace built on the foundation of mindfulness. Built into contentment is trust in the present moment. We can trust that the present moment is exactly as it was meant to be.

Creating Wholeness

Mindfulness practice restores our sense of wholeness and enables us to see where we fit into the web of life. This is the lens that mindfulness gives us, and it's through this lens we can see how we can be of service to the world.

We find wholeness when we connect with the body through the breath and the body scan. We can find wholeness in nature. We can find wholeness in ending the struggle against our stories, trying to make them true (if we're grasping) or not true (if we're pushing away). We can find wholeness with each other when we step out of reactivity and into deep listening.

Wholeness comes in the body from recognizing the conditioned state of the fight-or-flight response. It comes in the mind from integrating all thoughts, good, bad, and ugly, and from ending the resistance to the three characteristics of existence: impermanence, suffering, and nonself.

We can see now how we have divided our worlds: body separate from mind and emotions; happy thoughts separate from unpleasant thoughts; good people separate from bad people; what lasts separate from what fades away; what is part of us separate from what is not. These divisions create agitation—and suffering. They keep us from seeing what we most need to see: there is no division in our world other than what we create in our minds. Seeing this, we can ease our suffering. We can ease the suffering of others.

See Your Contribution

One of the most direct ways in which we change the world is through our livelihood. Through mindfulness practice, we can come to see more clearly our skills, our purpose, our unique contribution, and how they fit into the world.

Many times we let our stories dictate what we take on or what we push aside. We may tell ourselves we are lacking in time or talent—maybe we want to help but don't want to get sucked into anything that involves public speaking. Or maybe we have a few hours a week to volunteer but we don't because we don't want to end up running the board—we believe that's what always happens when people see our leadership skills. Whatever the story is, it's about limitation. The limitations may seem very real, and it may not be the time to join up. Or, with mindfulness, we can investigate if there is something else we can drop from the schedule so the limitation is no longer there. We can see if our hearts are calling us to act and it's only our fear that holds us back.

That said, the true contribution to the world is in the moment, right where you are. Each moment presents an opportunity for healing. The stressful thought comes. You notice it. You relinquish your judgments of yourself or another person, and you join with that person. You accept yourself. You see the whole spectrum of your talents and skills. You see them and you nurture them, and when the moment comes—in the neighborhood association meeting, the corporate training, or wherever you find yourself—the words come.

Building a strong future depends on being in the right place at the right time—and seeing that every place is the right place and every time is the right time. We can see that with mindfulness. Sometimes our livelihood places us right where we need to be. We tend to think of service to the world as an extracurricular activity, but it can be integrated into our daily lives through our livelihood and our family and community interactions.

Mindfulness teacher Jack Kornfield says spiritual service comes not from giving in the ego-sense in which we draw attention to our accomplishments. It's true that we may find motivations in the mix when we set about to live with Right Action and contribute to the world. The spirit of service asks much more of us, he says. It asks us to touch and act from "a deeper place, a chord of the heart that responds to life out of connectedness and compassion, independent of results."

Trappist monk Thomas Merton, in a letter to Jim Forest, echoes this idea of service in response to suffering that's happening in this moment. When you are doing the right work, you have to remove it from the hope of results. "You may have to face the fact that your work will be apparently worthless and even achieve no result at all, if not perhaps results opposite to what you expect. As you get used to this idea, you start more and more to concentrate not on the results but on the value, the rightness, the truth of the work itself." Merton reminds Forest that the big results are not in your hands or mine. Contributing is not about personal satisfaction; it's about doing the right thing.

What brings us the most peace is being clear on this point: the truth and rightness of the work itself. Be clear on your talents and skills. Be clear on how you are already in the right place. Be clear on how you can contribute. Use wise speech; take right action. This is how you can be of service.

Sutras

Tell me, what is it you plan to do
with your one wild and precious life?

—Mary Oliver, *The Summer Day*

Think of how rare it is to be born into this life and survive to adulthood. We take it for granted, but many people on this planet struggle against disease and poverty and spend their days working hard just to survive. This isn't a guilt trip; it's a reality check. Living under conditions in which you can even consider engaging in mindfulness practice is a gift. Your life is short, and it's precious. Whether you're 15 or 95, you can still make changes; you can still deepen your experience on this earth. It is never, ever too late.

Form Your Belief System

Many religion traditions have a commitment to mindful, compassionate service. We have discussed Right Action in the context of Buddhism, but in Christianity, the basis for service is found in the Gospels, the first four books of the New Testament. Jesus emphasized the need to take care of those on the margins of society. The way many believers take this to heart is to reach out to the poor and the marginalized, offering help and care without expecting anything in return, without attempting to convert them to their way of thinking. Creation care is one movement taking hold in Christian circles that resonates with mindfulness. It stems from the conviction that God has charged us with living mindfully and in harmony with nature, and that we have a responsibility to care for the earth.

> **Just Be!**
>
> No matter your belief system, you can come into clarity about your contribution to the world. The key is to go inward and engage in deep listening with an open heart. Paying attention to your inner landscape can tap into what you have the most compassion for and guide you to where to pour your energies.

Changing How You Are in the World

Mindfulness practice changes how we operate in the world. As we disengage from fixed notions of who we are, we are free to make choices more in accordance with our inner wisdom. When we are open, we can see more possibilities than we ever realized. There are others who have resources to help us with what we care about most. There are those who are just as compassionate as we are, if only we can see past the differences that separate us.

Socially Engaged Buddhism

It's a popular stereotype that people who meditate are escapist or disengaged. Socially Engaged Buddhism is a *sangha* that seeks to take the ideals of wisdom and compassion out into the world. The central thought behind the movement is that "genuine wisdom is manifested in compassionate action."

def•i•ni•tion

Sangha literally means group or assembly, and it refers to a community of "noble ones," other Buddhist practitioners who have committed to the path of opening and awakening. The word connotes a harmonious, supportive community.

Buddhist teachers Joseph Goldstein and Jack Kornfield say in *Seeking the Heart of Wisdom* (see Resources) that inner practice and social service are vital steps on the spiritual path. You have to take the first steps by turning to your inner landscape and opening yourself to personal transformation. The rest of the story is that you have opened your heart to a whole other dimension of heart-centered action.

Both teach that embracing personal ethics such as Right Speech or mindful consumption and cultivating generosity are the foundation of spiritually aware and engaged service.

Whether you are Buddhist or not—remember, we told you that you don't have to be Buddhist to practice mindfulness!—understand that this approach is about being clear on what you value and developing a personal ethic in order to be spiritually aware and to make a contribution to the world.

Caring for Creation

"It's all nature!" mindfulness meditation teacher Sayadaw Tejaniya said, grinning, on a retreat Anne attended last summer.

Perhaps your heart is with nature, and you see the way all of life is interwoven, as the Bioneers (bioneers.org) say: "It's all alive. It's all intelligent. It's all connected. It's all relatives." (Bioneers founder Kenny Ausubel, by the way, was a central adviser to Leonardo DiCaprio's environmental documentary, *The 11th Hour*, released in 2007.) It may be that the climate crisis stirs your soul and calls you to action. Maybe you have always known of your love for nature—you're a gardener, a hiker, or an all-around nature lover. Perhaps if you were practicing a form of contemplation or reflection before you started this book, it was always centered on nature, either the human nature of your inner landscape or the natural world of your outer landscape.

Whether it's an issue that has resonated with you most of your life or whether it has been activated in recent years with the fears about global warming, this is the time to listen to it. When a message or an idea resonates with you, hear that. Heed the call.

For All Beings: Compassion in Action

Poverty, war, or children may be the issues that weigh on your heart. These are difficult challenges that can sometimes feel insurmountable. It can seem that one person won't make a difference. These are issues about which we can go numb.

But as you know, the change starts within. It starts when we cultivate a balanced, compassionate heart through *metta* and equanimity practices. When our hearts become open, we find tenderness and acceptance for ourselves while the divisions we've created between ourselves and others fade away. We see the humanity in each other, and we can't *not* act when our hearts call us to respond to suffering in the world. The Christian Golden Rule reflects this awareness of an ethic of reciprocity: *Do unto others as you would have them do unto you.*

Healing our divisions—conservative or liberal, upper class or working class, Caucasian or person of color, gay or straight, North American or Middle Eastern—we see that we're all in this life together, and that just as we want to be happy and have a good life, so do the other members of our human family.

Time for Reflection

We invite you to reflect on the practices you have tried during the course of reading this book. Interestingly enough, the process of writing this book was profound for Anne and Carolyn. Both felt turbulence as they went deeper and deeper into the concepts. At each crucial juncture in the writing, they were called to attention to see the whole of their inner landscape. It was painful at times, and they each shared that the process of staying mindful while writing a book about mindfulness was ushering them into new inner territory. Chapters they thought would be easy because they believed they already knew a lot about those topics turned out to be the most challenging. Eating, for instance, was one that Carolyn thought would fall together nicely, given the knowledge she's acquired as Food Editor of the *Albuquerque Journal*. Anxiety, for instance, was one that Anne thought would roll right out of her. But in both instances, they found out more about what they *didn't* know and received the call to go deeper.

Practicing mindfulness can be frustrating. Both authors realized they had to come to the experience of writing these chapters with beginner's mind—and when they became open to meeting the experience as it was, they discovered new insights. Opening to this with compassion was key in soothing the agitation they felt around recognizing their "not knowing." At some point, Carolyn said, "I don't know, really, and I'm here to listen and see." And then she saw. It is like that with mindfulness.

The fruits of mindfulness practice can be subtle and take a long time. No matter what you have tried and no matter how small the steps, that is the practice. If this book helped you take a pause here and there, if it has helped you see more of your inner landscape, if it has given you a glimmer of how stressed, anxious, and agitated you are at times, then you have begun the journey.

If you have had 100 questions and still felt confused about 99 of them, that's a great start. If you have sat for 30 minutes and at minute 29 realized you spent the whole time daydreaming, that's mindfulness.

When Anne first started meditating, it was pretty miserable much of the time. (There! Do you feel better?) She didn't feel like she was really doing anything other than noticing how darn busy her mind was. She would spend entire sittings caught up in thought, trying to extricate herself and come back to the breath, and a second later going back to planning her day or whatever else her mind thought it had to do. (A lot of the time her mind played perky pop songs from the '70s—*very annoying!*) But she kept doing it because she had talked to people who meditated and heard them share their experiences. She read books that helped her understand why she was doing this in the first place. She meditated in the safety and support of a sangha (at Seattle Insight Meditation Society) and had a dharma buddy at home to meditate with.

She kept at it, and after a while she began to notice very subtle changes in the way she looked at the world and saw herself.

A regular meditation practice gives a good foundation and support for practicing mindfulness in daily life. Finding a group of practitioners—a sangha—is an excellent way to build support and find resources for continuing to deepen your practice. You'll also find a list of books, websites, and other resources in Resources. Seattle Insight Meditation Society (www.seattleinsight.org), in particular, has a wealth of resources including recorded talks and online meditation courses.

We started out this book telling you that you don't have to be a Buddhist to practice mindfulness. And then we've talked about Buddhism throughout the book! What's up with that? Buddhism is not strictly a religion. The Buddha was a man who found a way to wake up and end suffering, and he began teaching what he discovered to others. These teachings have survived more than 2,500 years because they resonate so deeply with those who take them to heart. Buddhism gives us a set of practices and a way of understanding the mind that are separate from any religious belief system.

People in some religious traditions would have you see this book and Buddhist teachings as a cult or as a turning away from God and Jesus. But this comes from a fundamental misunderstanding of the practices of mindfulness and meditation. You do not worship the Buddha when you practice mindfulness; you explore your inner landscape, which includes your mind and your soul. Your mind and your soul are gifts from God or Allah or Spirit—why wouldn't you want to explore them and open your heart to them as fully as you can?

There are many ways to connect with others around these practices. You may choose to access mindfulness through Mindfulness-Based Stress Reduction (MBSR) and other mindfulness techniques that are secularized from Buddhism and focused on health. You may want to find a trained psychotherapist who uses mindfulness in his or her practice and holds group sessions and classes. Or you may find an MBSR group through private-practice psychologists or university medical clinics.

Whatever you have tried since starting this book—from mindful driving to mindful eating—it is a gift to yourself. It's the beginning of a new way of living. We hope you continue to deepen the practice as you travel along the path.

The Least You Need to Know

◆ Notice your stories about the world. Let them inform you about what matters to you. Notice what you have compassion for.

◆ Deep listening cultivates the ability to do wise speech; wise speech furthers Right Action.

◆ To build hope, you must first see what disenchants you.

◆ Your contribution is possibly right where you are, in your livelihood or in your community. Use mindfulness to gain clarity about your talents and skills.

◆ Take time to reflect on your experience of mindfulness in the course of reading this book. Take heart, even if it's been challenging; the rewards are many.

◆ A regular mindfulness meditation class builds foundation for change. Find a meditation community in your part of the world.

Resources

Further Reading

Here's a guide to books that we have found to be good for deepening your understanding of mindfulness and the practices we have covered in this book.

Mindfulness and Buddhism

Brach, Tara. *Radical Acceptance: Embracing Your Life with the Heart of a Buddha.* New York: Bantam, 2004.

Chödrön, Pema. *The Places That Scare You: A Guide to Fearlessness in Difficult Times.* Boston: Shambhala Publications, 2001.

———. *When Things Fall Apart.* Boston: Shambhala Publications, 1997.

———. *Wisdom of No Escape.* Boston: Shambhala Publications, 1991.

Epstein, Mark. *Going to Pieces Without Falling Apart.* New York: Broadway Books, 1998.

———. *Thoughts Without a Thinker: Psychotherapy from a Buddhist Perspective.* New York: Basic Books, 1996.

Gach, Gary. *The Complete Idiot's Guide to Understanding Buddhism.* Indianapolis: Alpha Books, 2004.

Germer, Christopher K., editor, Ronald D. Siegel, and Paul R. Fulton. *Mindfulness and Psychotherapy.* New York: Guilford Press, 2005.

Glaser, Aura. *A Call to Compassion: Bringing Buddhist Practices of the Heart into the Soul of Psychology.* York Beach, ME: Nicholas-Hays, 2006.

Goldstein, Joseph. *Transforming the Mind, Healing the World.* Maywah, NJ: Paulist Press, 1994.

Goldstein, Joseph, and Jack Kornfield. *Seeking the Heart of Wisdom: The Path of Insight Meditation.* Boston: Shambhala Publications, 1987.

Greenspan, Miriam. *Healing Through the Dark Emotions: The Wisdom of Grief, Fear, and Despair.* Boston: Shambhala Publications, 2003.

Gunaratana, Bhante Henepola. *Mindfulness in Plain English.* Somerville, MA: Wisdom Publications, 2002.

Hanh, Thich Nhat. *Anger: Wisdom for Cooling the Flames.* New York: Riverhead Books, 2001.

———. *The Miracle of Mindfulness.* Boston: Beacon Press, 1999.

———. *Peace Is Every Step: The Path of Mindfulness in Everyday Life.* New York: Bantam, 1991.

——— *The Sun My Heart.* Berkeley, CA: Parallax Press, 1988.

Kabat-Zinn, Jon. *Coming to Our Senses: Healing Ourselves and the World Through Mindfulness.* New York: Hyperion, 2006.

———. *Full Catastrophe Living: Using the Wisdom of Your Body and Mind to Face Stress, Pain, and Illness.* New York: Delta, 1990.

———. *Wherever You Go, There You Are: Mindfulness Meditation in Everyday Life.* New York: Hyperion, 2005.

Kornfield, Jack. *A Path with Heart: A Guide Through the Perils and Promises of Spiritual Life.* New York: Bantam, 1993.

———. *After the Ecstasy, the Laundry: How the Heart Grows Wise on the Spiritual Path.* New York: Bantam, 2000.

McElroy, Susan Chernak. *All My Relations: Living with Animals as Teachers and Healers.* Novato, CA: New World Library, 2004.

Piver, Susan. *Joyful Mind: A Practical Guide to Buddhist Meditation.* New York: Rodale, 2002.

Salzberg, Sharon. *Faith: Trusting Your Own Deepest Experience.* New York: Riverhead Books, 2002.

———. *Lovingkindness: The Revolutionary Art of Happiness.* Boston: Shambhala Publications, 1995.

Santorelli, Saki. *Heal Thy Self: Lessons on Mindfulness in Medicine.* New York: Bell Tower, 1999.

Siegel, Daniel L. *The Mindful Brain: Reflection and Attunement in the Cultivation of Well-Being.* New York: W. W. Norton, 2007.

Suzuki, Shunryu. *Zen Mind, Beginner's Mind.* Boston: Shambhala Publications, 2006.

Welwood, John, editor. *Ordinary Magic: Everyday Life as a Spiritual Path.* Boston: Shambhala Publications, 1992.

Welwood, John. *Toward a Psychology of Awakening: Buddhism, Psychotherapy, and the Path of Personal and Spiritual Transformation.* Boston: Shambhala Publications, 2000.

Williams, J. Mark G., John D. Teasdale, Zindel V. Segal, and Jon Kabat-Zinn. *The Mindful Way Through Depression: Freeing Yourself from Chronic Unhappiness.* New York: Guilford Press, 2007.

Spirituality

Artress, Lauren. *Walking a Sacred Path: Rediscovering the Labyrinth as a Spiritual Practice.* 2nd ed. New York: Berkley Publishing Group, 2006.

Berry, Wendell. *Sabbaths.* New York: North Point Press, 1987.

Flynn, Carolyn, and Shari Just, Ph.D. *The Complete Idiot's Guide to Creative Visualization.* Indianapolis: Alpha Books, 2005.

Flynn, Carolyn, and Gary R. McClain, Ph.D. *The Complete Idiot's Guide to Oracles.* Indianapolis: Alpha Books, 2006.

Flynn, Carolyn, and Erica Tismer. *Empowering Your Life with Massage.* Indianapolis: Alpha Books, 2006.

Hafiz. Translated by Daniel Ladinsky. *The Subject Tonight Is Love: 60 Wild and Sweet Poems.* 2nd ed. New York: Penguin Compass, 2003.

Kushner, Rabbi Lawrence. *Kabbalah: A Love Story.* New York: Broadway Doubleday, 2007.

Oliver, Mary. *New and Selected Poems, Volume One.* Boston: Beacon Press, 1992.

Rumi, Jelaluddin. Translated by Coleman Barks. *The Essential Rumi.* New York: Penguin, 1995.

———. Translated by Coleman Barks. *The Soul of Rumi.* New York: HarperOne, 2002.

St. Theresa de Avila. Translated by Mirabai Starr. *The Interior Castle.* New York: Riverhead Books, 2003.

Tolle, Eckhart. *Stillness Speaks.* Novato, CA: New World Library, 2003.

———. *The Power of Now: A Guide to Spiritual Enlightenment.* Novato, CA: New World Library, 2004.

Yogananda, Paramahansa. *Autobiography of a Yogi.* Los Angeles, CA: Self-Realization Fellowship, 1998.

Food and Sustainability

Albers, Susan. *Eating Mindfully: How to End Mindless Eating and Enjoy a Balanced Relationship with Food.* Oakland, CA: New Harbinger, 2003.

Berry, Wendell. *The Way of Ignorance.* New York: Shoemaker & Hoard, 2005.

David, Marc. *Nourishing Wisdom: A Mind-Body Approach to Nutrition and Well-Being.* New York: Harmony, 1994.

———. *The Slow-Down Diet.* Rochester, VT: Healing Arts Press, 2005.

Gerrard, Don. *One Bowl: A Guide to Eating for Body and Spirit.* New York: Marlowe & Company, 2001.

Madison, Deborah. *Local Flavors: Cooking and Eating from America's Farmers' Markets.* New York: Broadway Books, 2002.

Kingsolver, Barbara. *Animal, Vegetable, Miracle: A Year of Food Life.* New York: HarperColllins, 2007.

Parsons, Russ. *How to Pick a Peach: The Search for Flavor from Farm to Table.* New York: Houghton Mifflin, 2007.

Petrini, Carlos. *Slow Food: The Case for Taste.* New York: Columbia University Press, 2001.

Pollan, Michael. *The Omnivore's Dilemma: A Natural History of Four Meals.* New York: Penguin, 2006.

Riley, Trish. *The Complete Idiot's Guide to Green Living.* Indianapolis: Alpha Books, 2007.

Smith, Alisa, and J.B. Mackinnon. *The 100-Mile Diet: A Year of Eating Locally.* Toronto: Random House Canada, 2007.

———. *Plenty: One Man, One Woman, and a Raucous Year of Eating Locally.* New York: Harmony, 2007.

Waters, Alice. *The Art of Simple Food: Notes, Lessons, and Recipes from a Delicious Revolution.* New York: Clarkson Potter, 2007.

Waters, Alice, and Paul Bertolli. *Chez Panisse Cooking.* New York: Random House, 2001.

Wills, Judith. *The Food Bible.* 2nd ed. New York: Fireside Books, 2001.

About Mindful Writing

Cameron, Julia. *The Artist's Way.* New York: Jeremy P. Tarcher/ Putnam, 1992.

Goldberg, Natalie. *Writing Down the Bones: Freeing the Writer Within.* Boston: Shambhala Publications, 1986.

Miscellaneous

Breathnach, Sarah Ban. *Simple Abundance: A Daybook of Comfort and Joy.* New York: Warner Books, 1995.

Diamant, Anita. *The Red Tent.* 10th anniversary ed. New York: Picador, 2007.

Dominguez, Joe, and Vicki Robin. *Your Money or Your Life: Transforming Your Relationship with Money and Achieving Financial Independence.* New York: Penguin, 1999.

Goldberg, Myla. *Bee Season.* New York: Anchor Books, 2000.

Websites

Here's a guide to websites and other resources mentioned in this book.

Food

cfsan.fda.gov/~dms/opa-bckg.html   This website, published by the U.S. Food and Drug Administration, lists the latest research about food ingredients and packaging.

slowfood.com and **slowfoodusa.org**   These websites give information about the Slow Food movement.

tcme.org   Official website for the Center for Mindful Eating with recent news reports and research.

whfoods.com/foodstoc.php   A list of the World's Healthiest Foods at a website run by the nonprofit George Mateljan Foundation.

Health and Mindfulness

healthfinder.gov   This website, published by the U.S. Department of Health and Human Services, offers the latest research about mindfulness and health.

livingmindfully.org/benefits/mindfulness_research.php   This page at Mindful Living, by therapist Micki Fine, lists many recent medical studies applying mindfulness in various ways, from smoking cessation to psoriasis, chronic pain, anxiety, and more.

womensmindbodyhealth.info/mmresearch11.htm   The Women's Center for Mind-Body Health lists numerous medical studies applying mindfulness-based stress reduction.

Mindfulness Programs

Innerkids.org   This organization teaches mindful awareness to children in pre-kindergarten and middle school.

marc.ucla.edu   The Mindfulness Awareness Research Center, at the University of California at Los Angeles, includes latest press reports and research.

MindandLife.org   Mind & Life Institute is dedicated to creating working collaborations between scientists and Buddhism. The Institute held a summit on the applications of mindfulness for depression in 2007. A DVD is available from the site. The Dalai Lama is the honorary chair of the institute.

MindSightInstitute.com   The MindSight Institute is an educational organization that focuses on developing insight and empathy in relationships.

umassmed.edu/cfm/index.aspx   Center for Mindfulness at the University of Massachusetts includes research, guided meditation tapes, information about MBSR programs across the country, and information about Jon Kabat-Zinn retreats.

Buddhism

bpf.org/html/turning_wheel.html   Turning Wheel: The Journal of Socially Engaged Buddhism, founded by Susan Moon.

www.dharma.org   Insight Meditation Society and Barre Center for Buddhist Studies.

www.dharmaocean.org   Dharma Ocean Foundation.

www.dharmaseed.org   Dharma Seed online library of recorded talks by meditation teachers.

www.lifebalance.org   Life Balance Institute.

www.metta.org   The Metta Foundation includes information about Insight Dialogue and a schedule of workshops.

www.plumvillage.org   Plum Village is the community in France headed by Vietnamese monk Thich Nhat Hanh.

www.seattleinsight.org   Seattle Insight Meditation Society.

www.spiritrock.org   Spirit Rock Meditation Center.

Miscellaneous

cnvc.org   The Center for Nonviolent Communication site includes basic concepts, teaching tools, and articles.

Audio Meditations

Many people find that audio CDs and tapes strengthen their practice. Here are a few to try:

The Center for Mindfulness (www.mindfulnesstapes.com) offers many guided meditation tapes and CDs by Jon Kabat-Zinn. Additionally, a guided meditation CD is included with the purchase of the book *The Mindful Way Through Depression: Freeing Yourself from Chronic Unhappiness.* (See earlier listing.)

Chödrön, Pema. *Getting Unstuck: Breaking Your Habitual Patterns and Encountering Naked Reality.* (Audio CD). Sounds True, 2004.

————. *The Pema Chödrön Audio Collection: Pure Meditation: Good Medicine: From Fear to Fearlessness.* (Audio CD). Sounds True, 2005.

McManus, Carolyn. CDs for Health and Healing. See www.carolynmcmanus.com for more information.

Ray, Reginald. Meditating with the Body: Six Tibetan Buddhist Meditations for Touching Enlightenment with the Body. (Audio CD). Sounds True, 2003.

Index

R

S

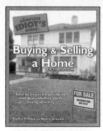